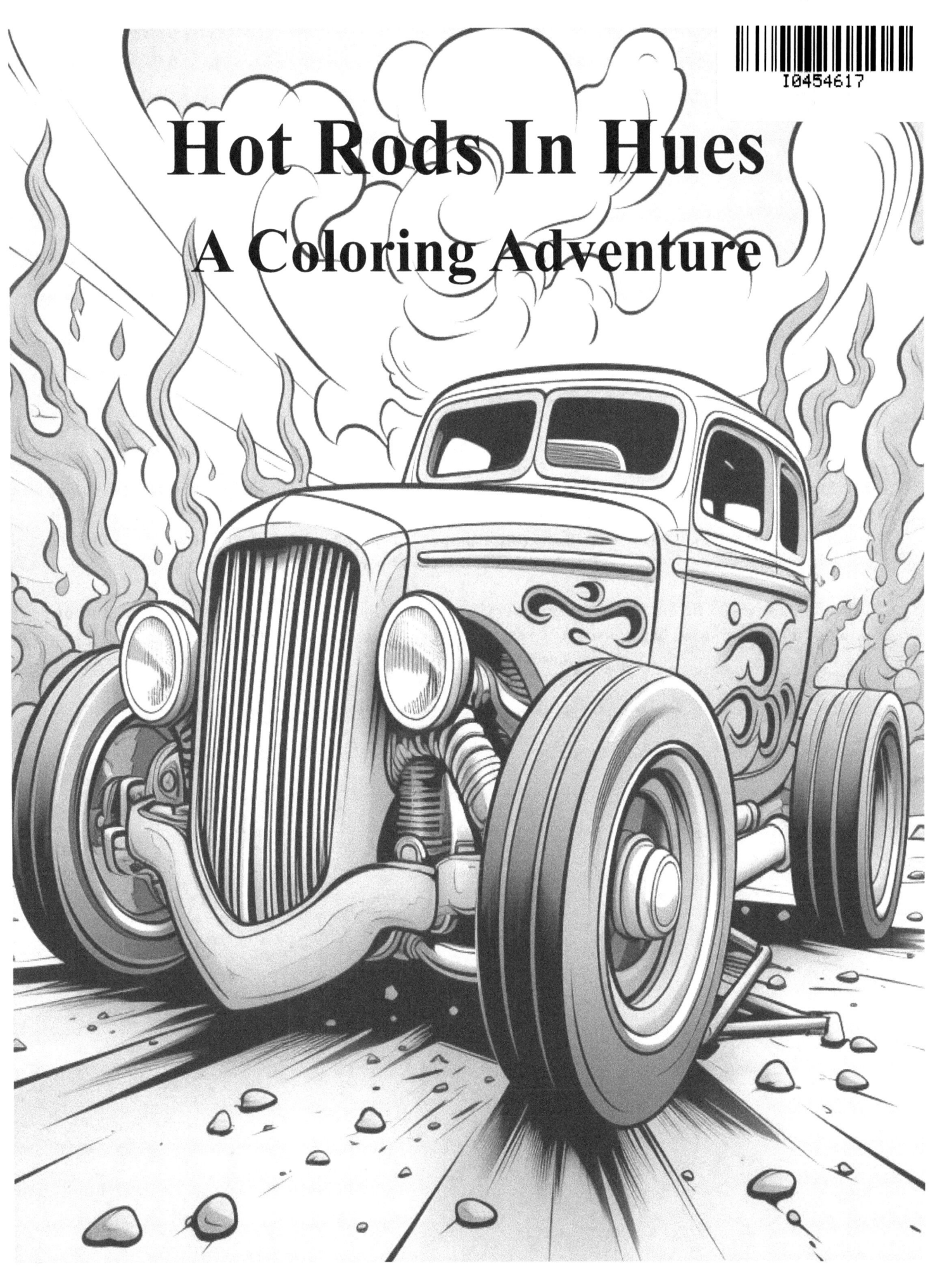

Hot Rods In Hues
A Coloring Adventure

"Dedicated to all the tireless souls who fuel their dreams with the roar of engines, the scent of burning rubber, and the never-ending pursuit of horsepower. May your love for hot rods ignite a lifelong journey filled with thunderous joys and endless horizons."

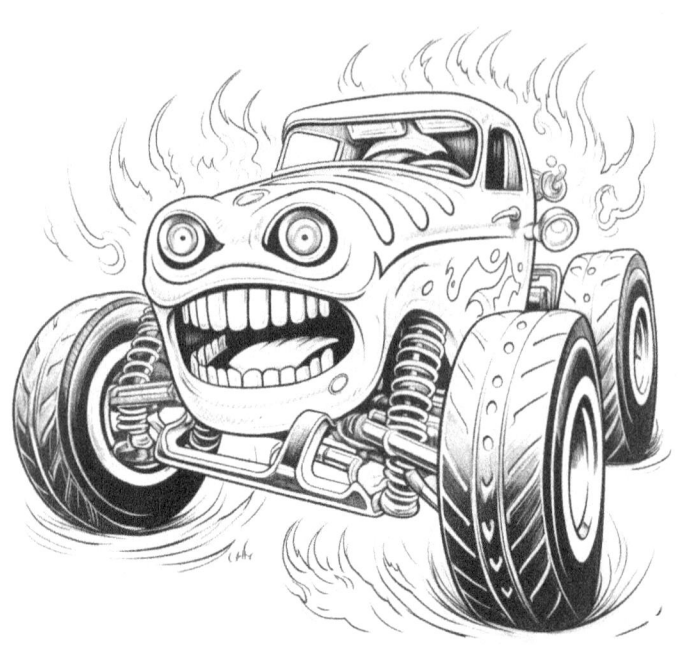

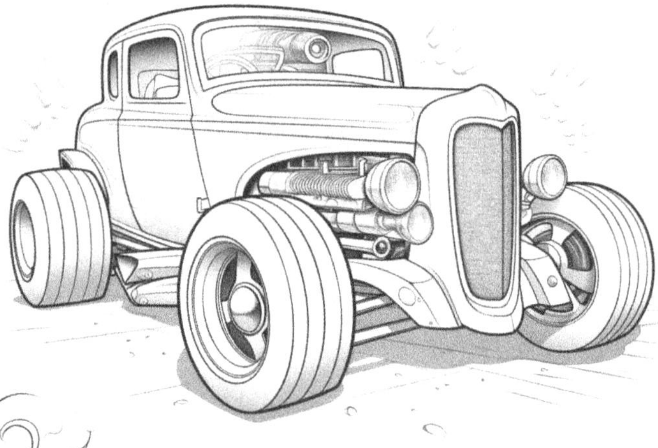

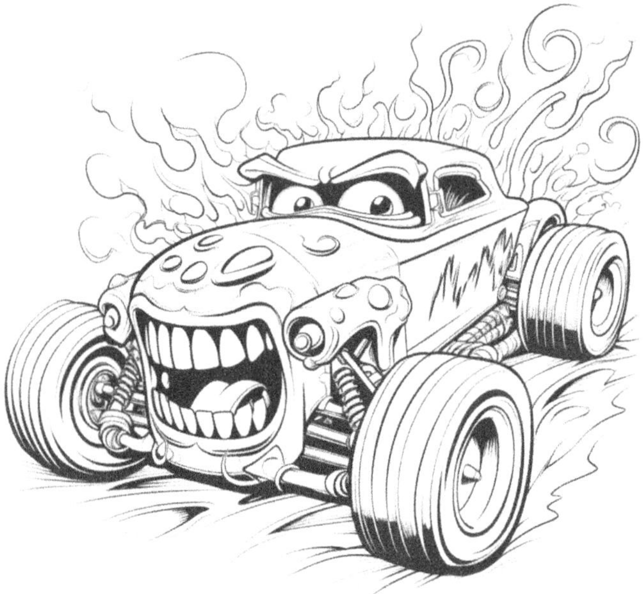

"Hot rods aren't just machines; they're roaring symphonies of passion, craftsmanship, and the relentless pursuit of speed."

Bryan Johnson

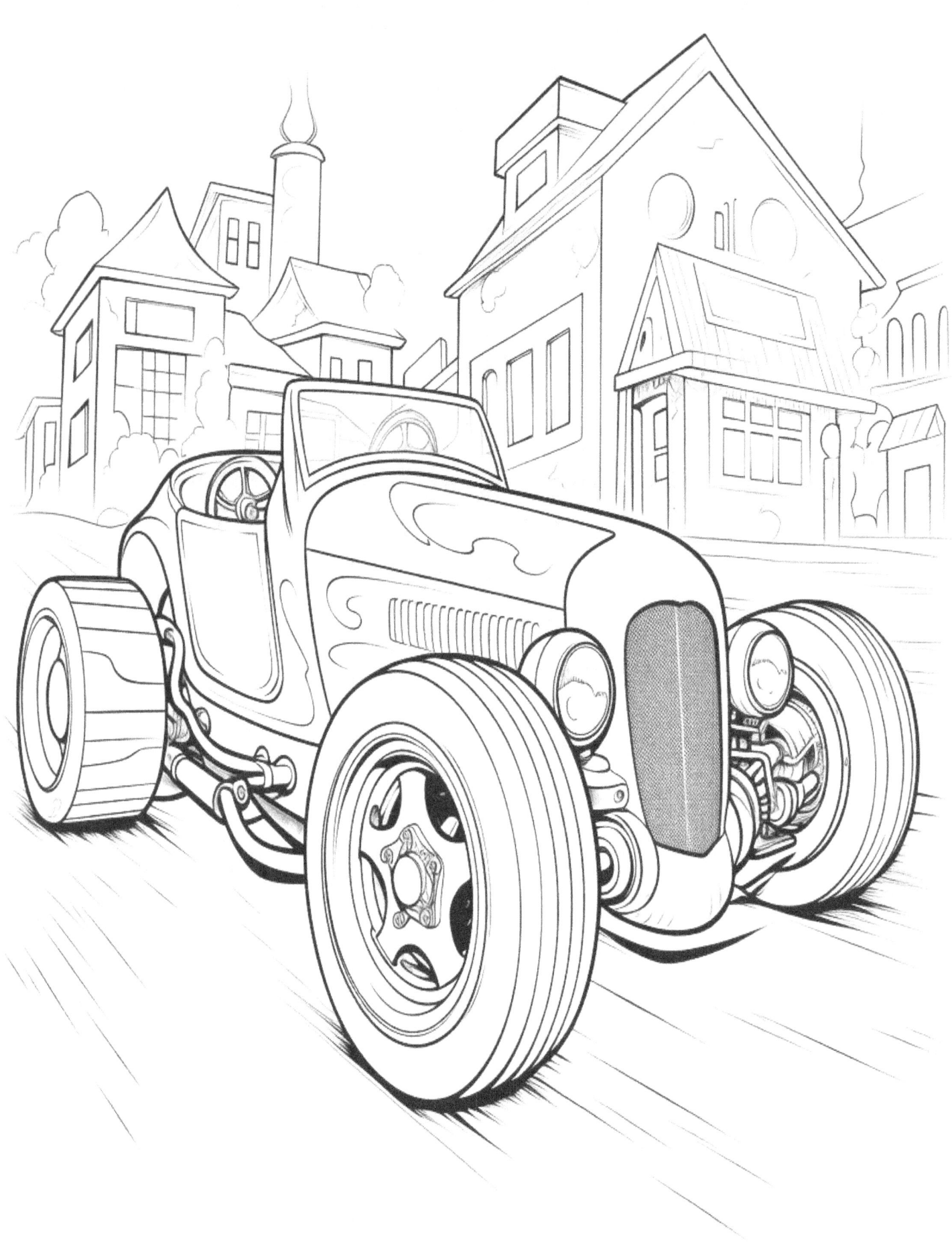

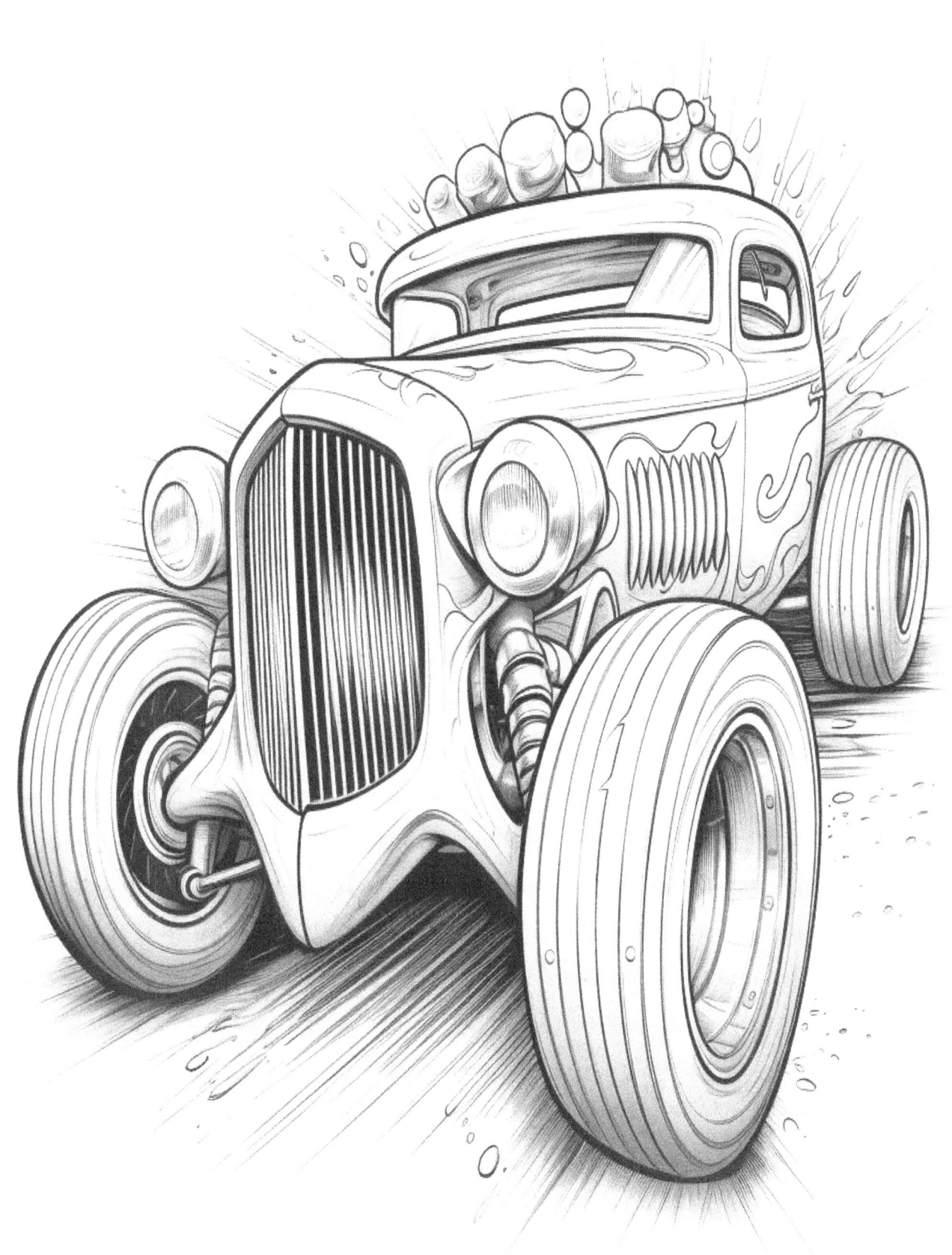

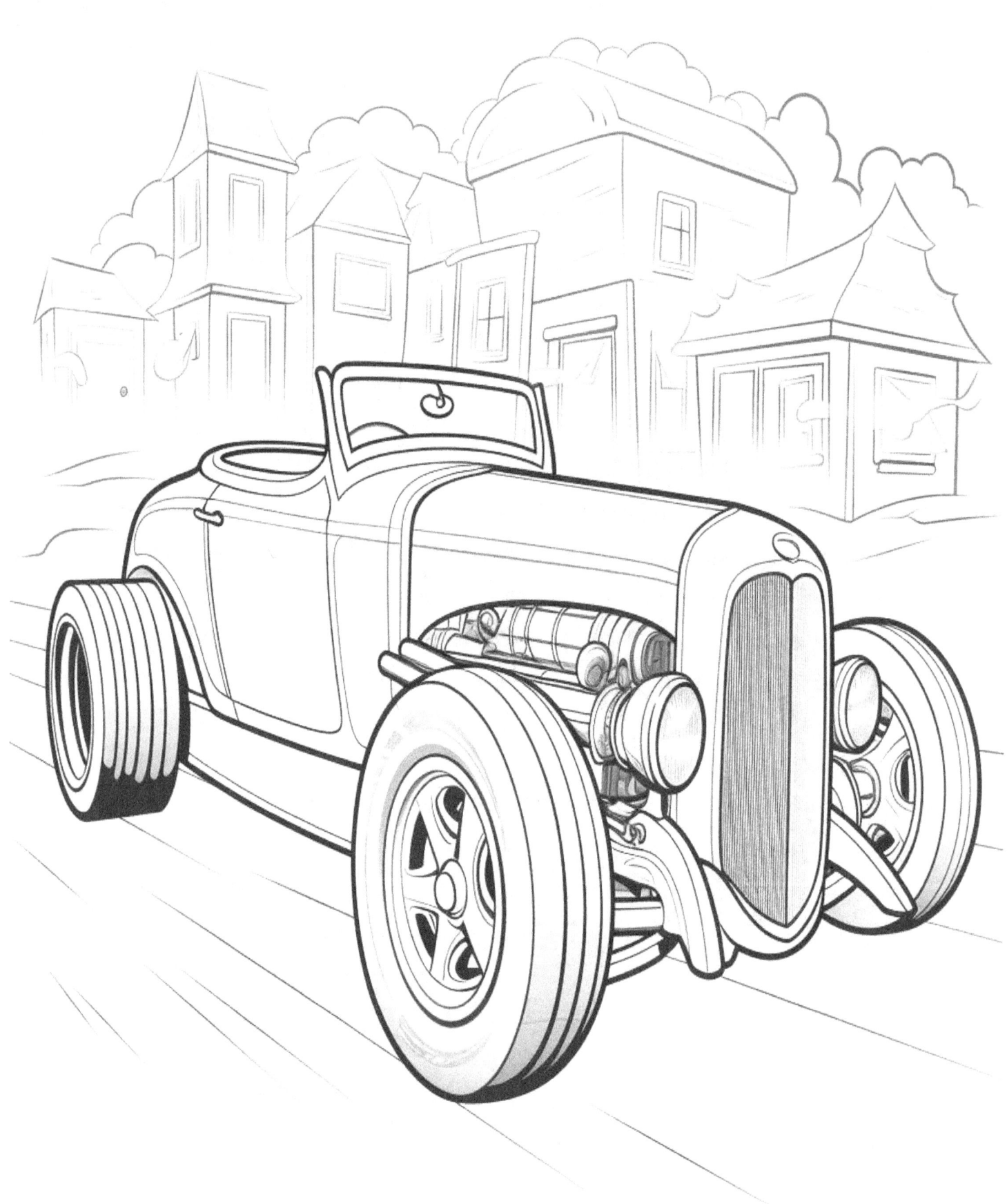

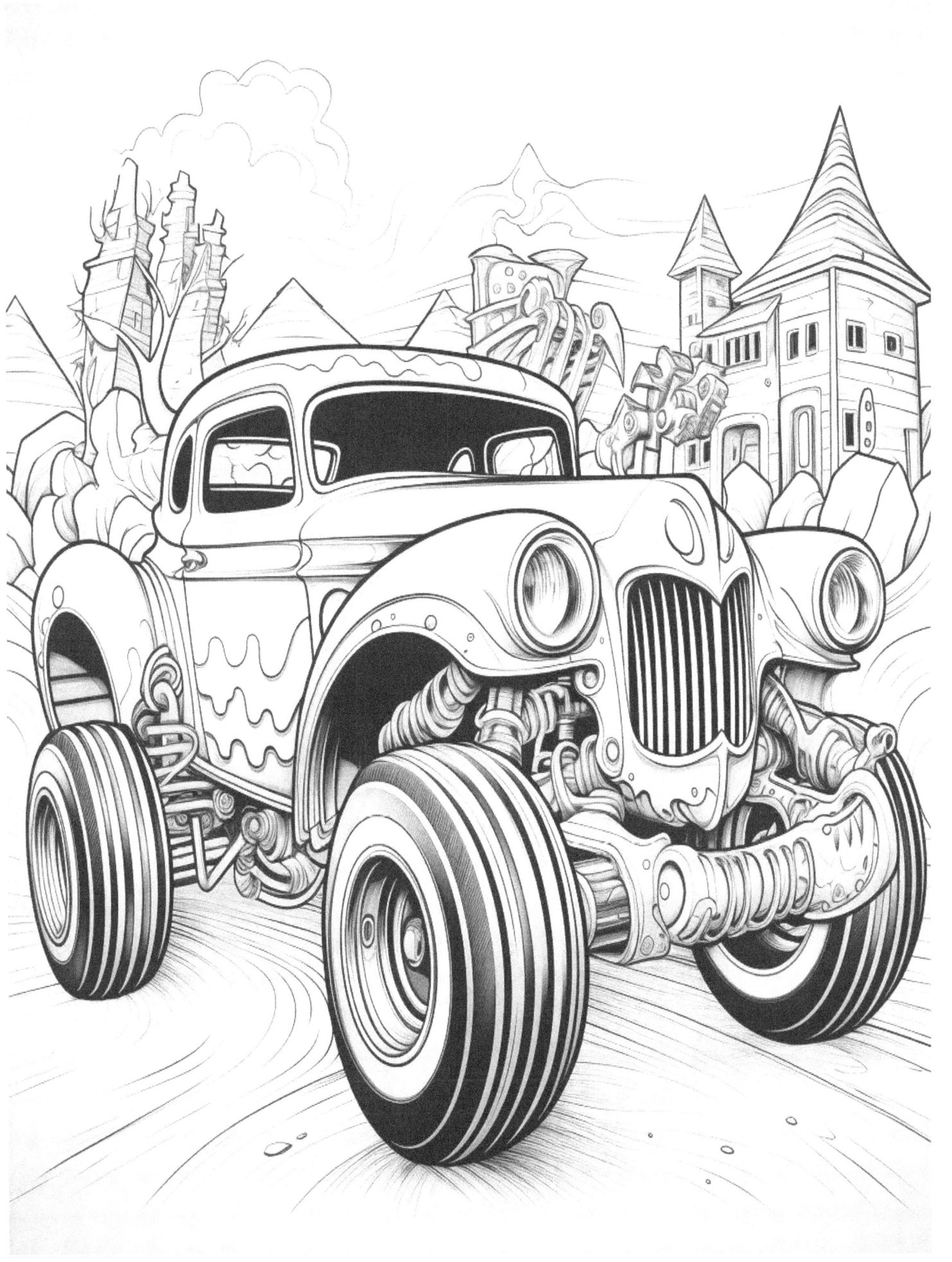

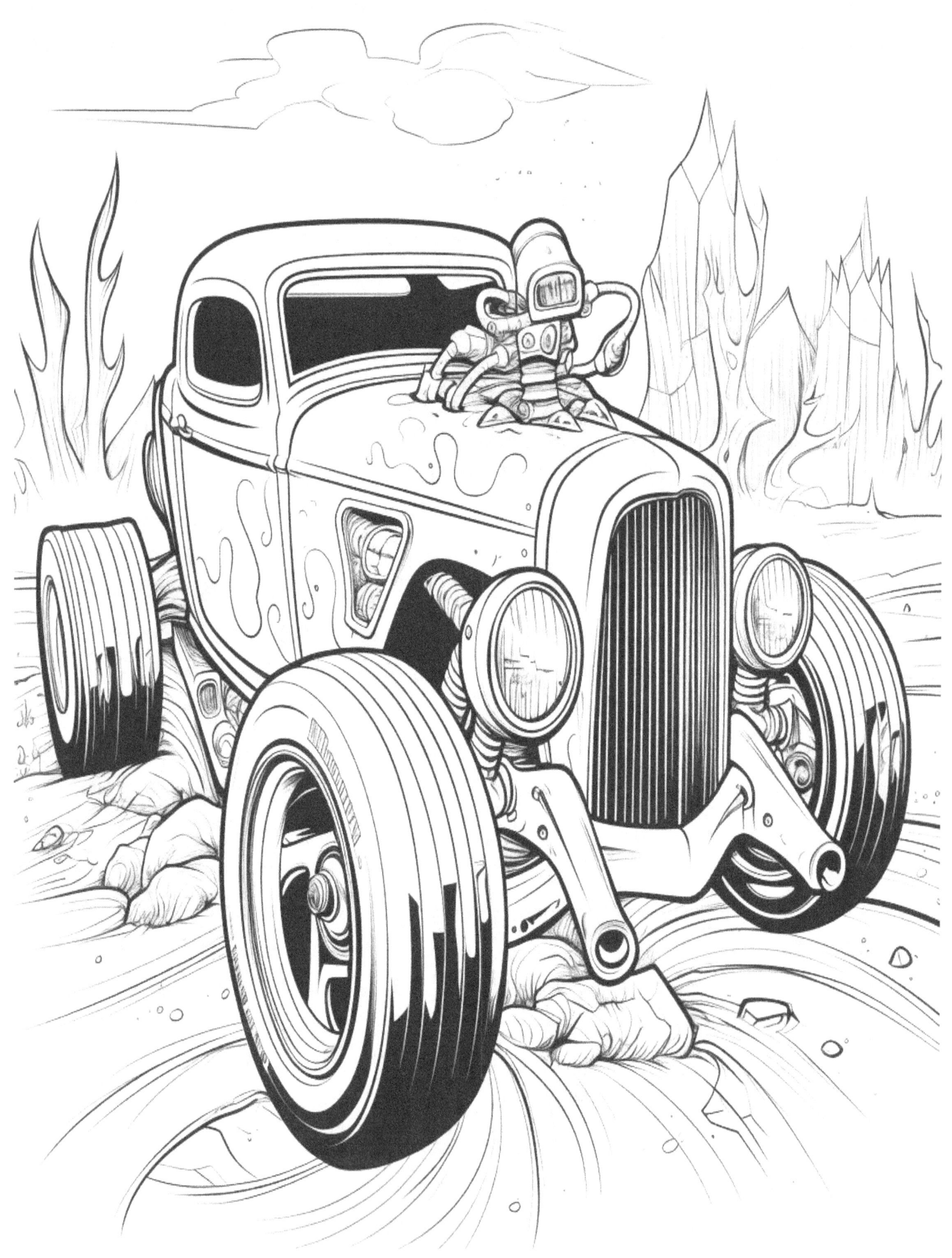

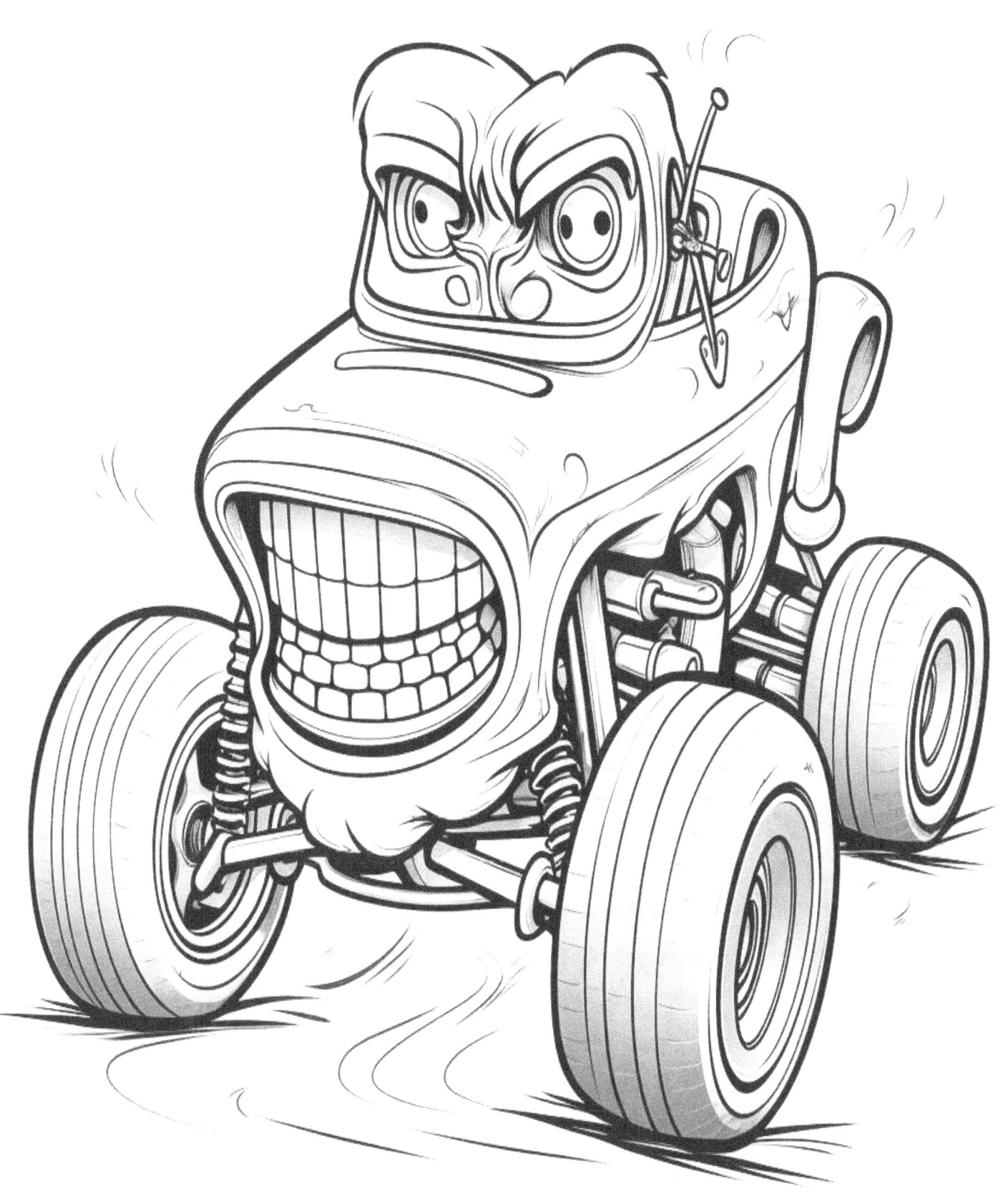

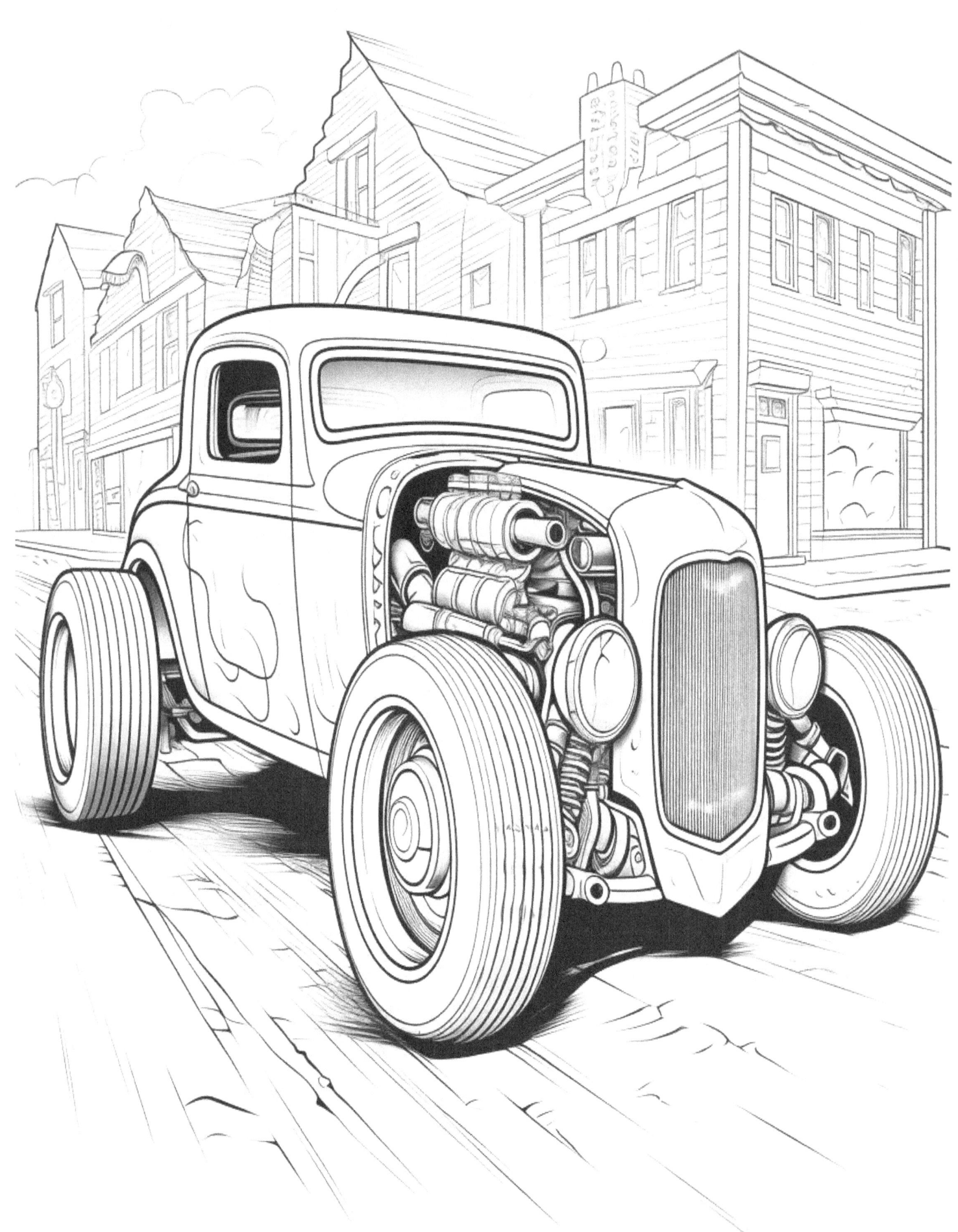

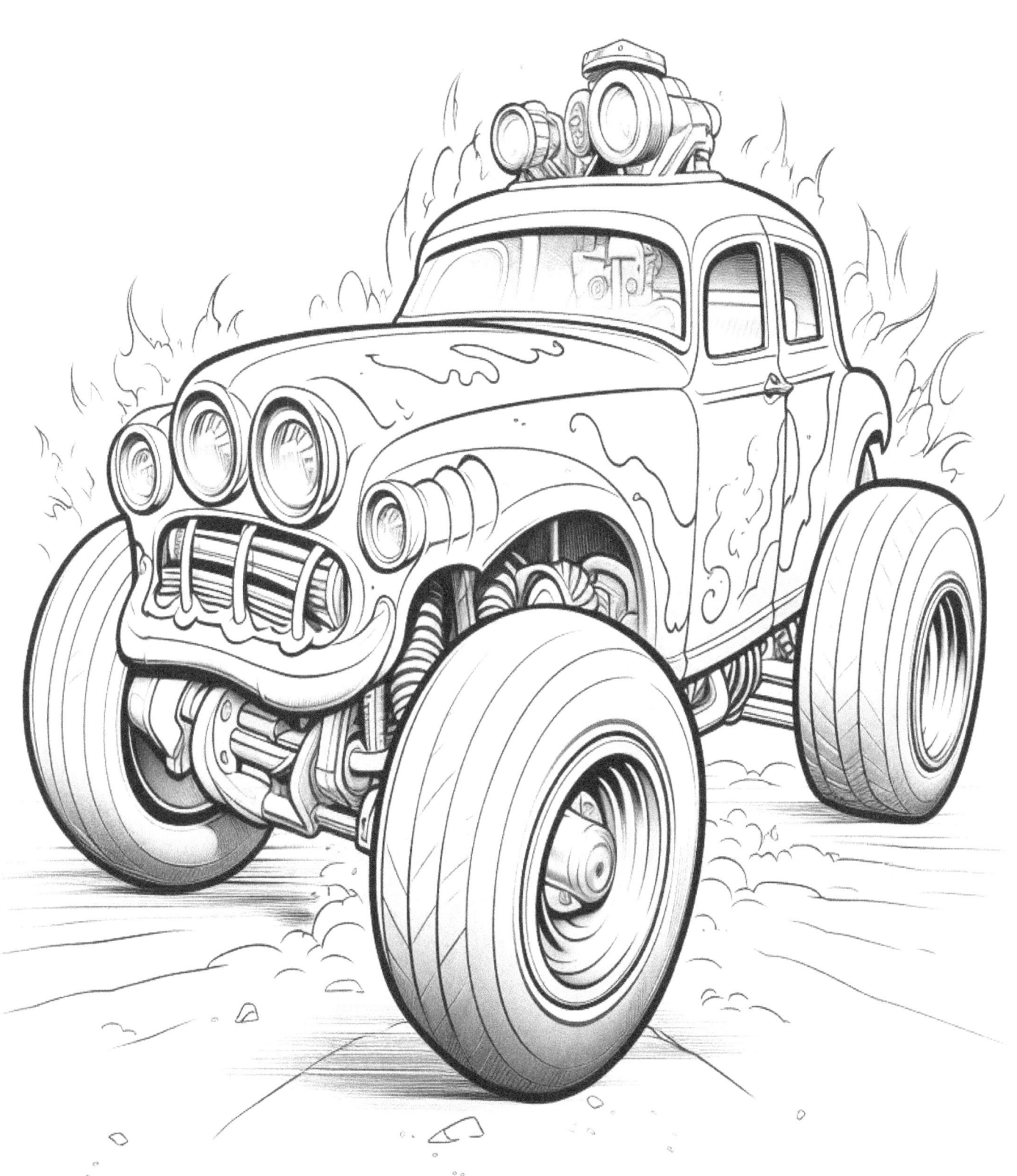

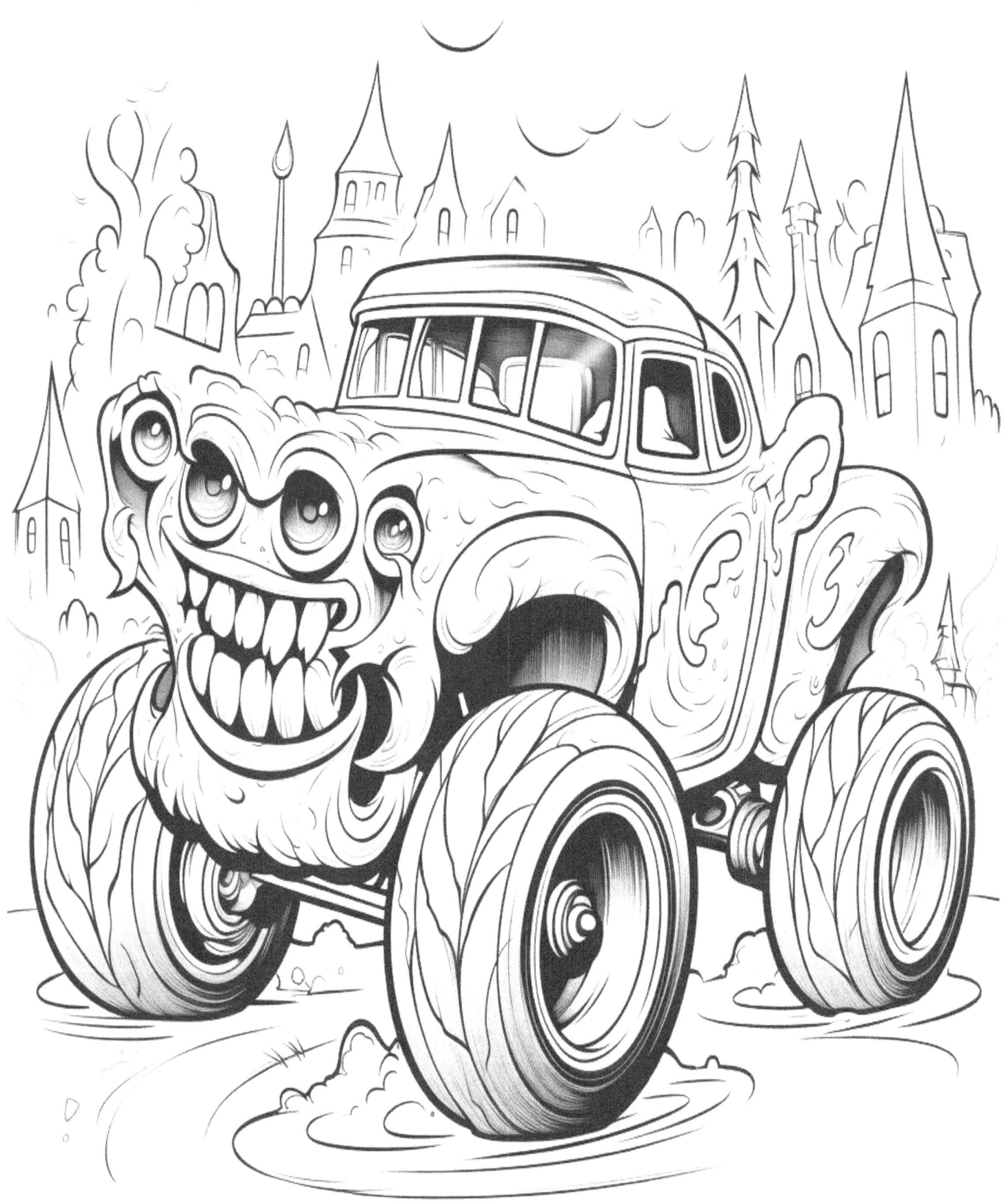

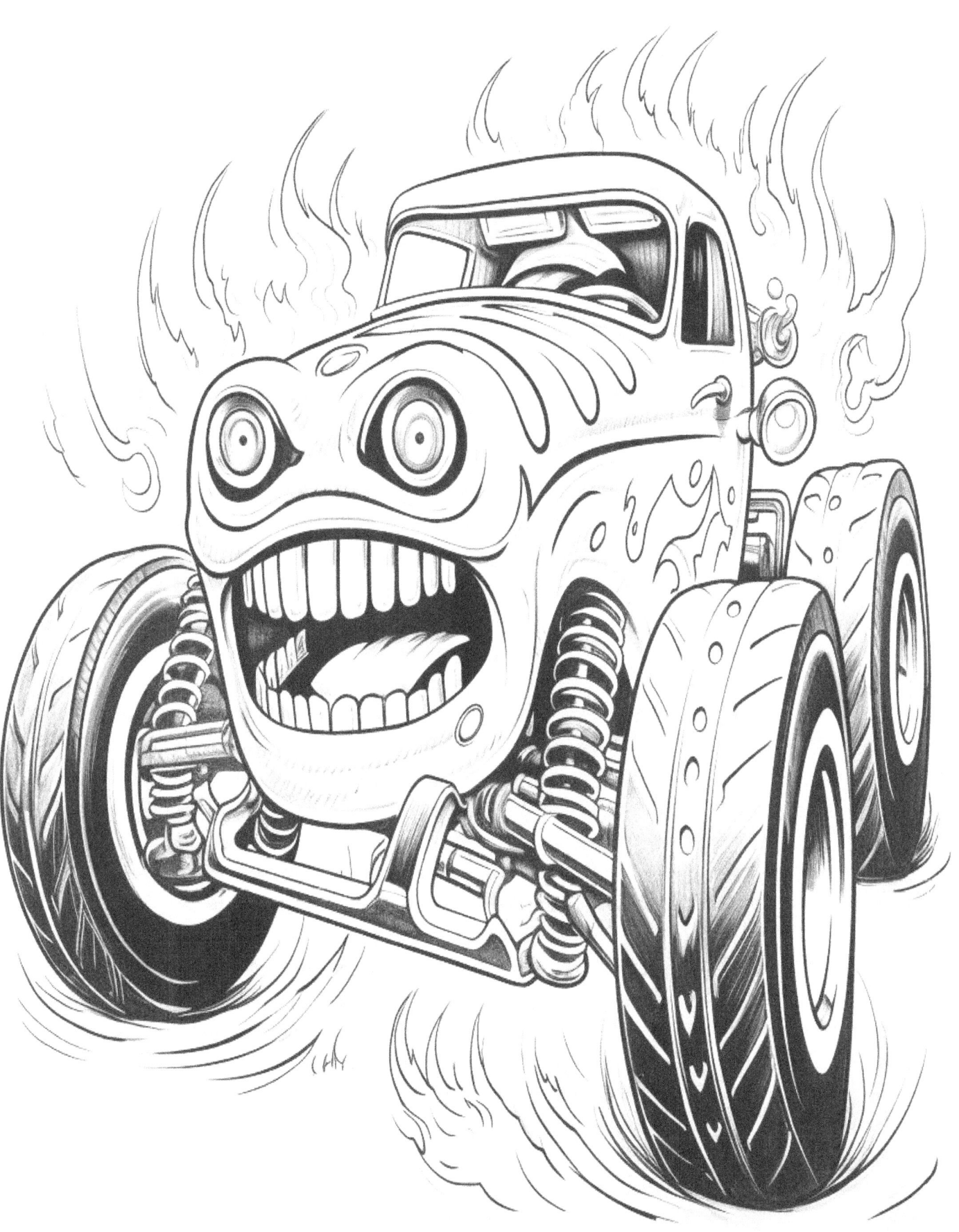

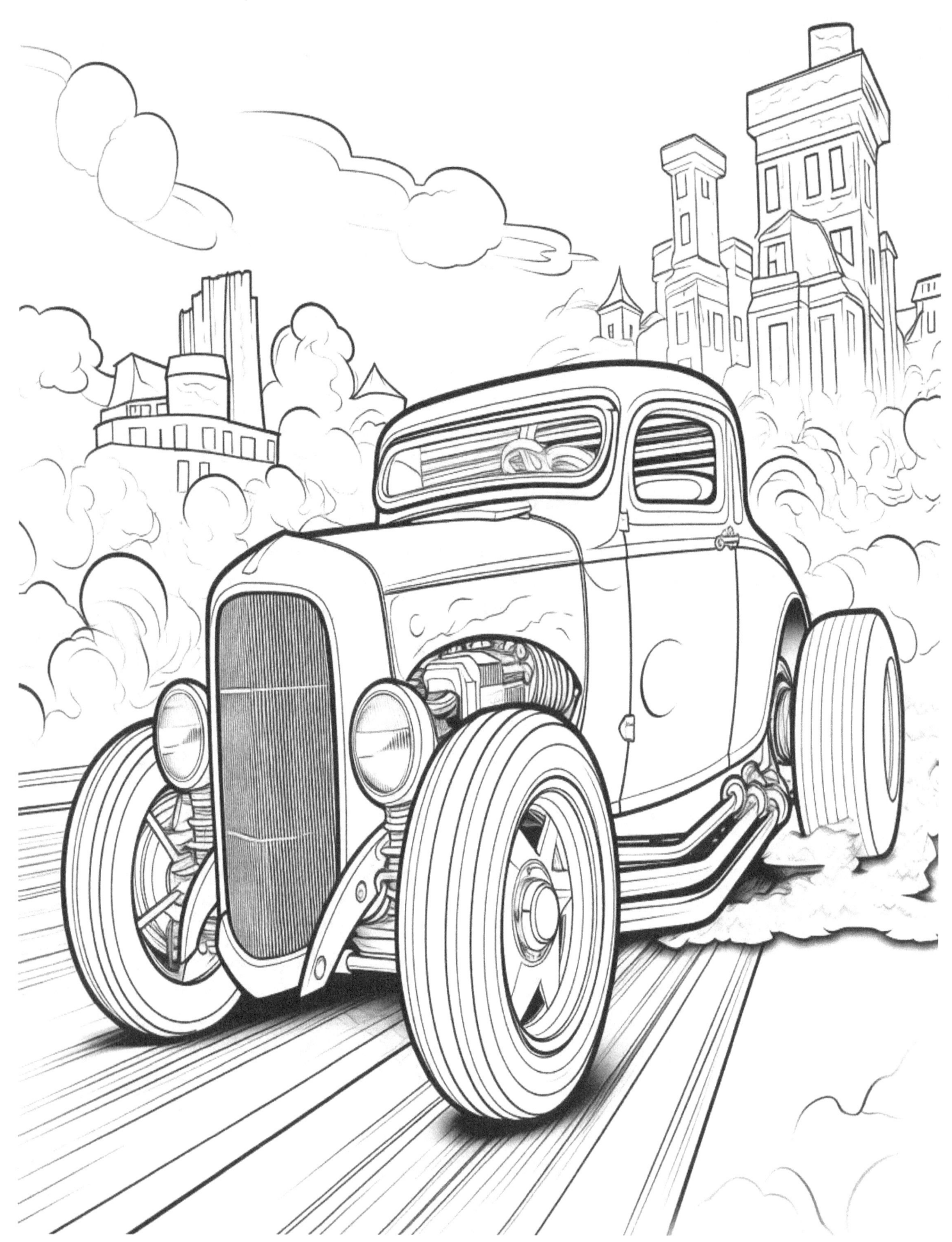

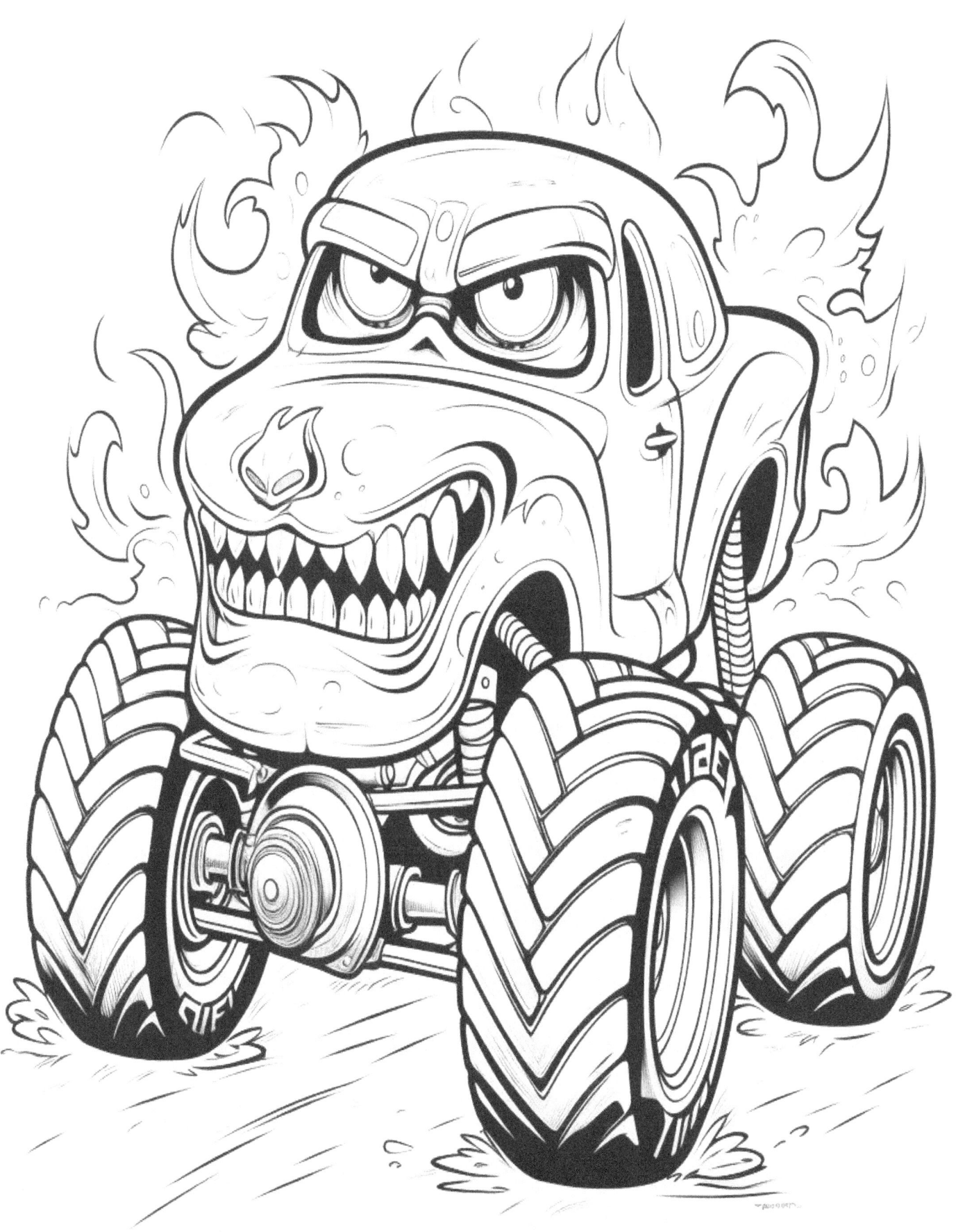

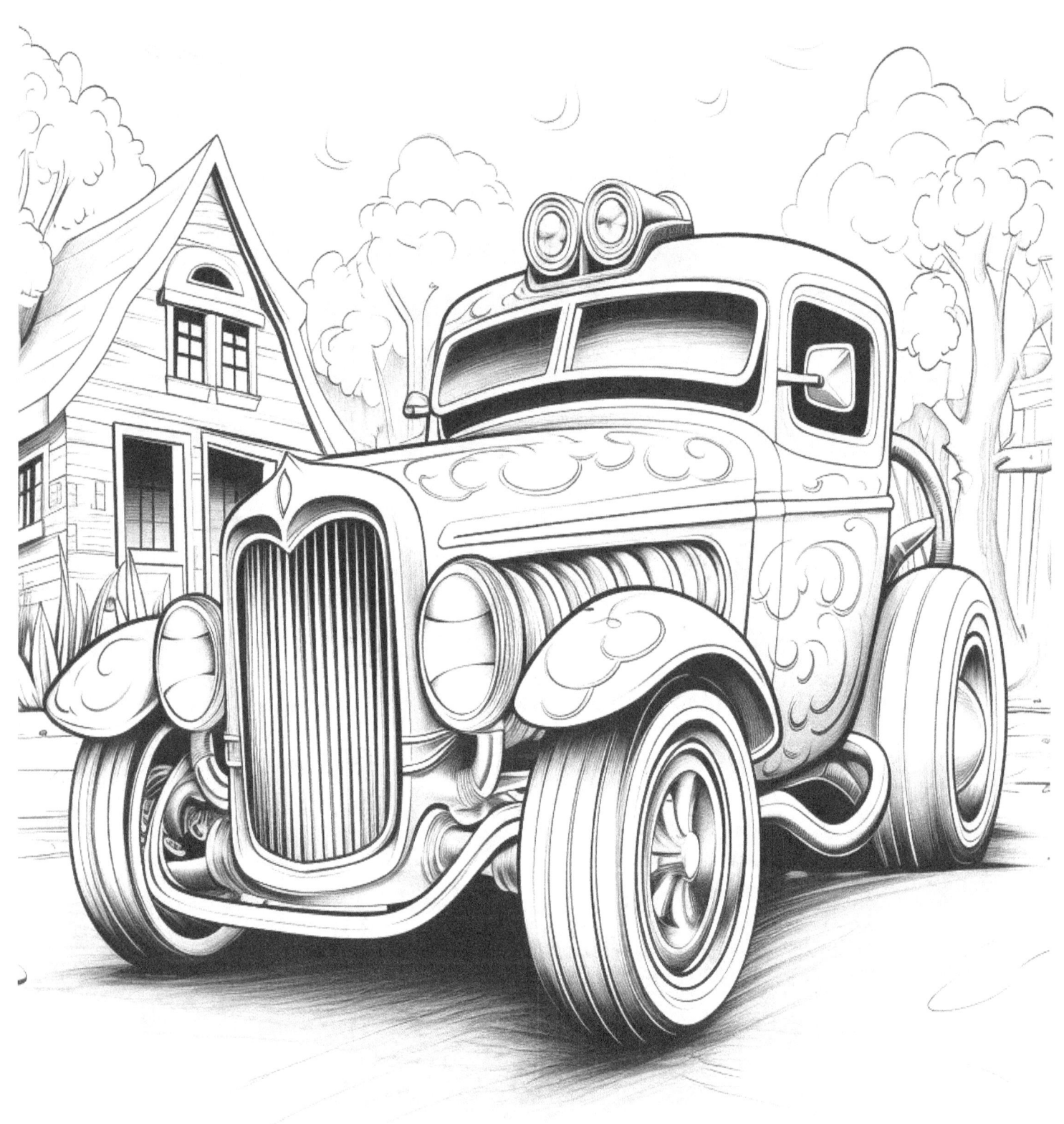

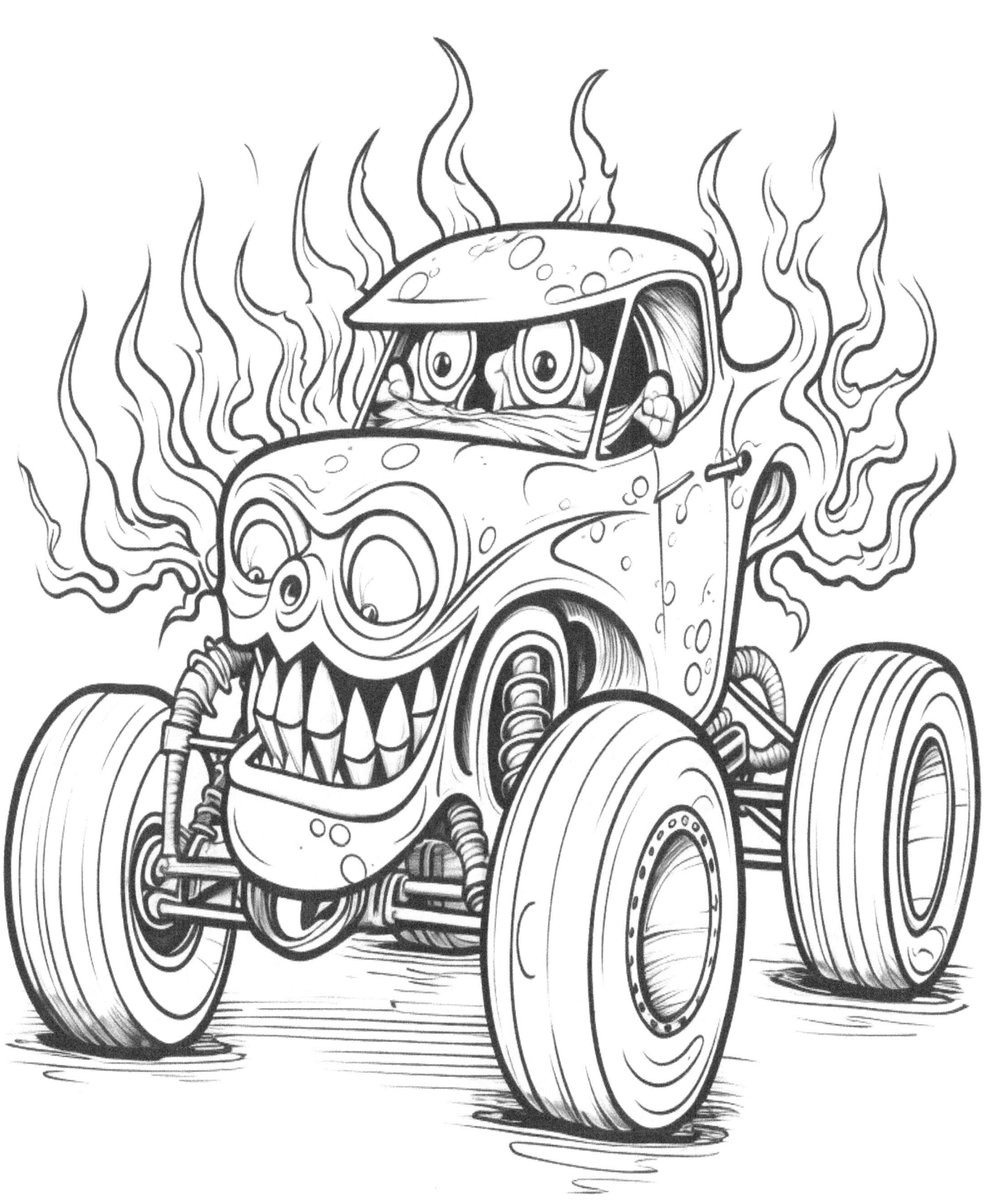

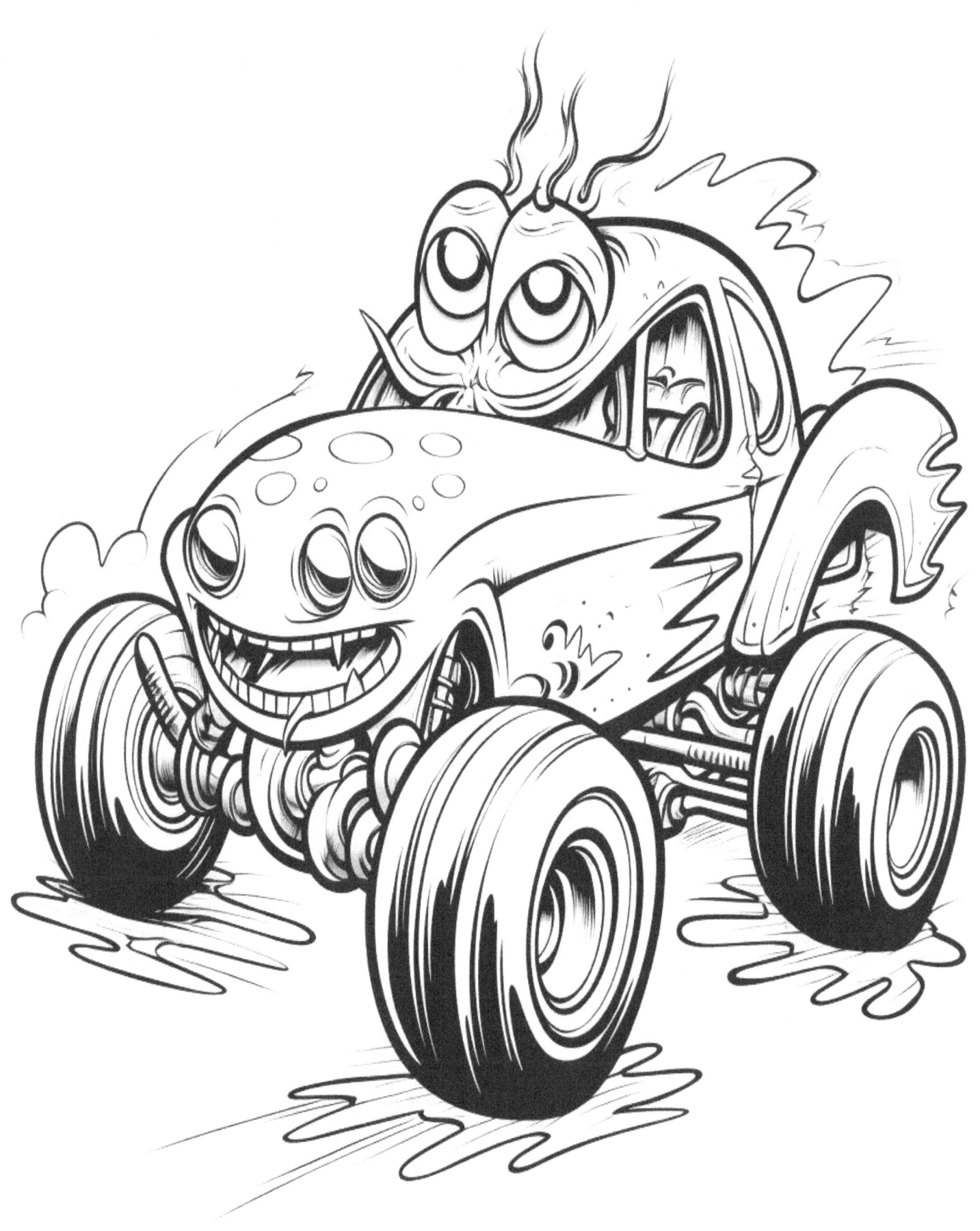

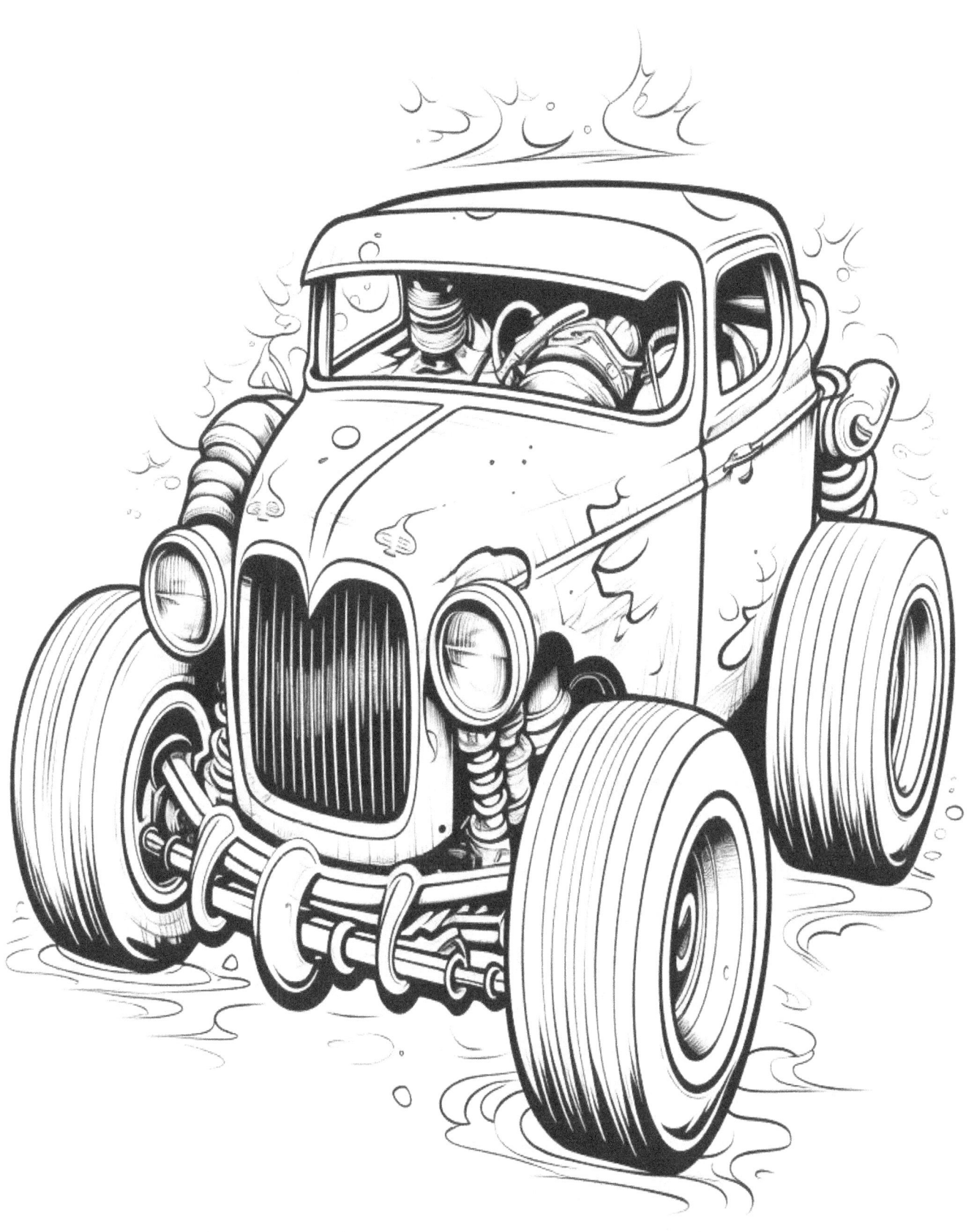

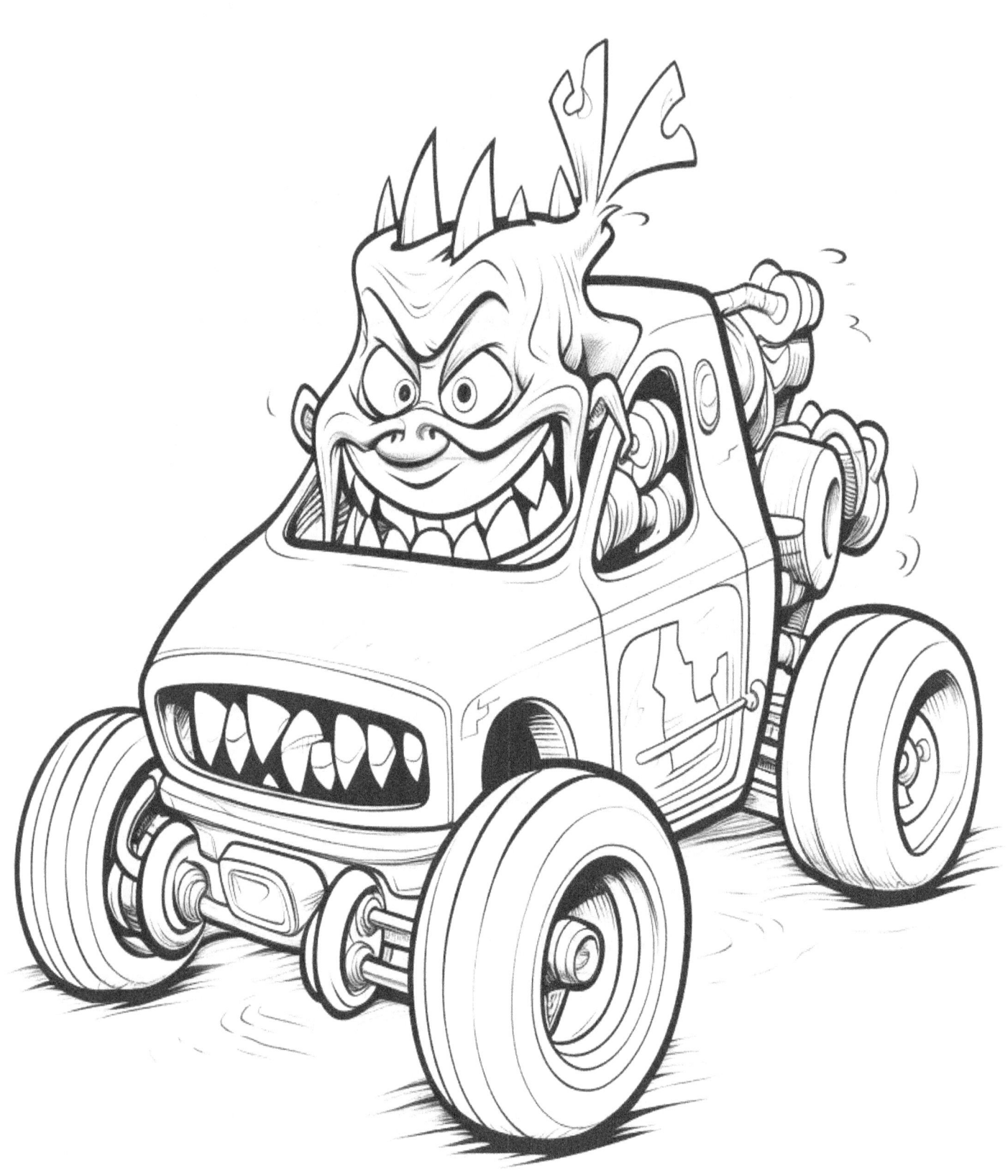

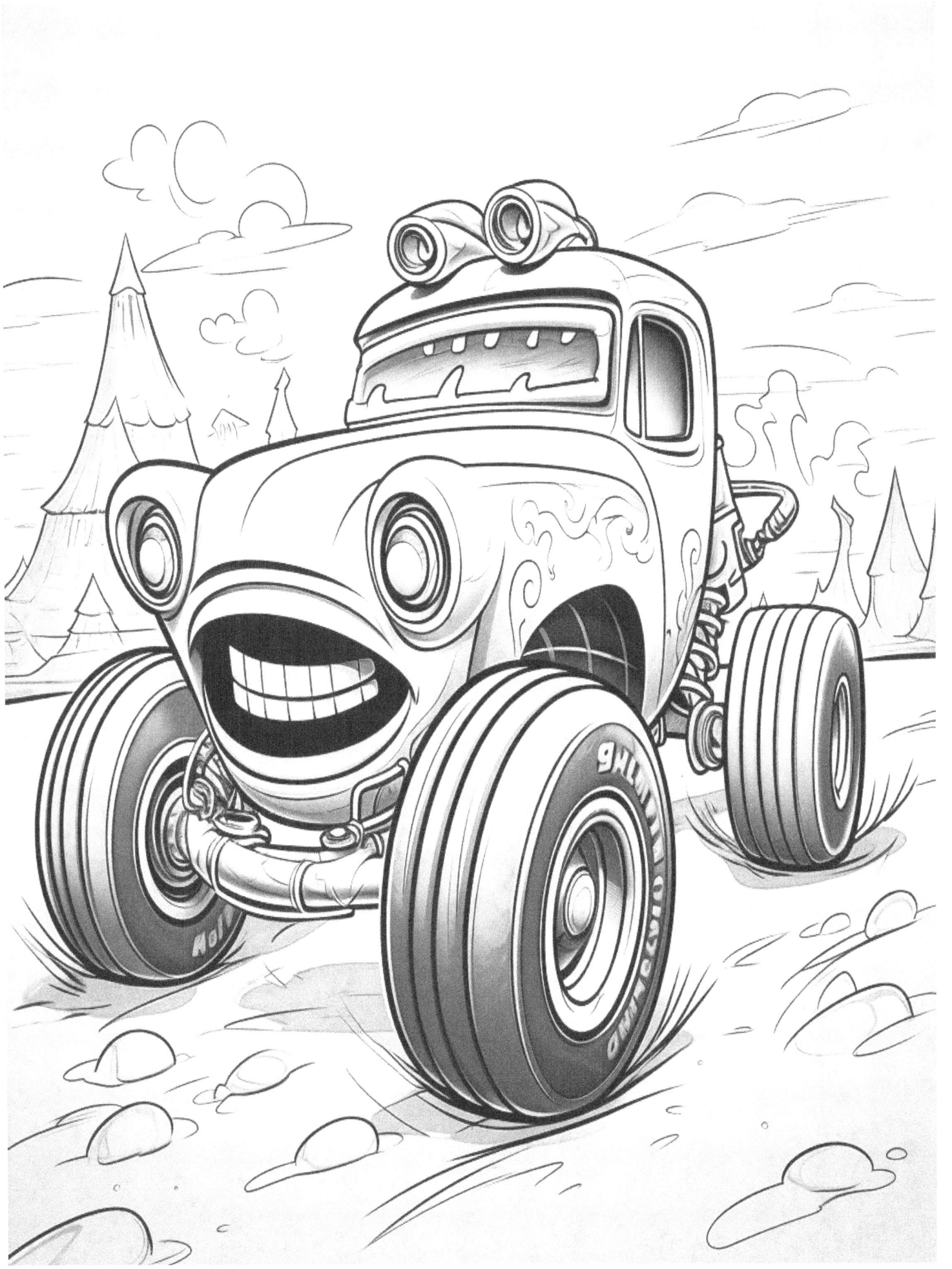

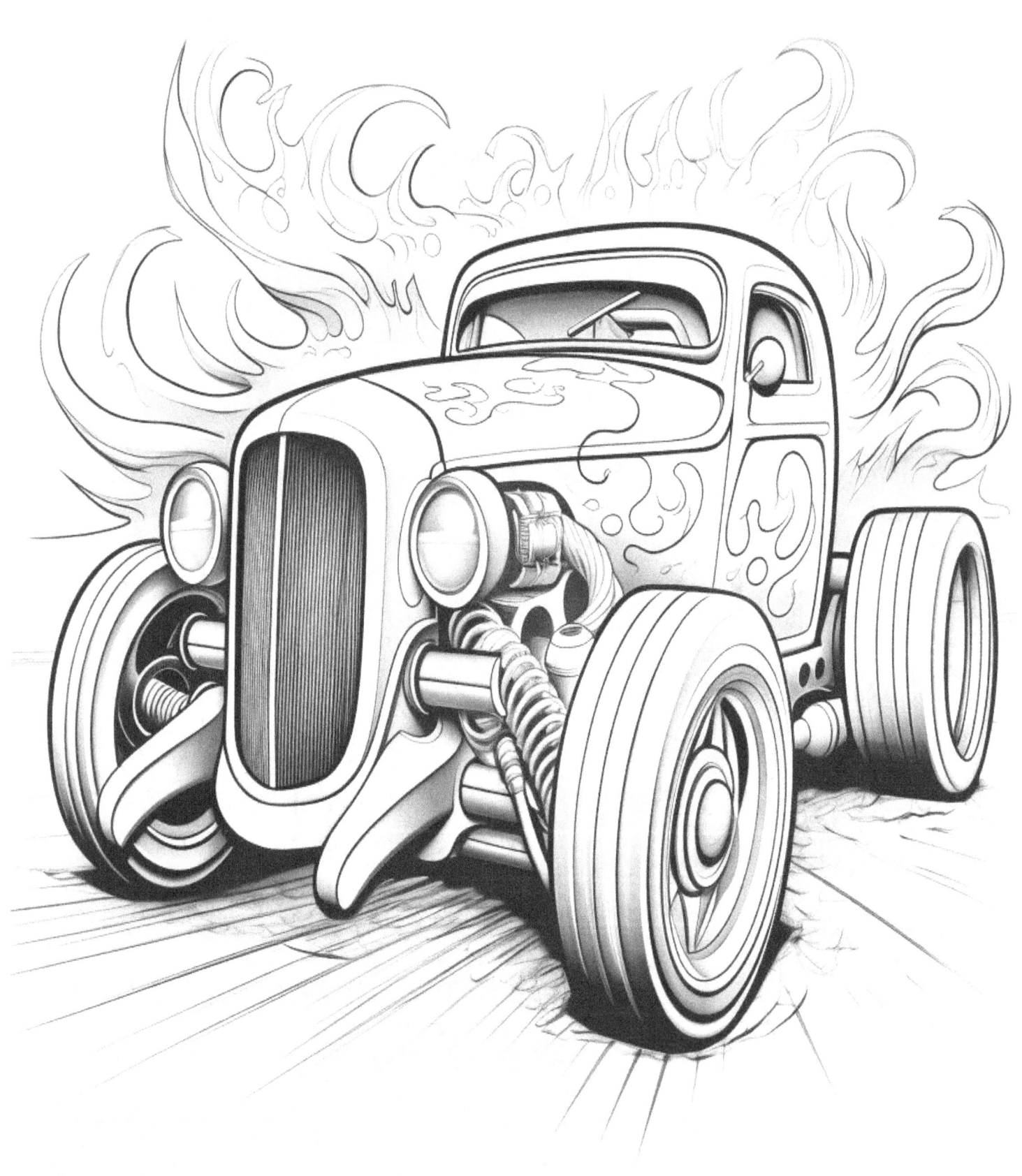

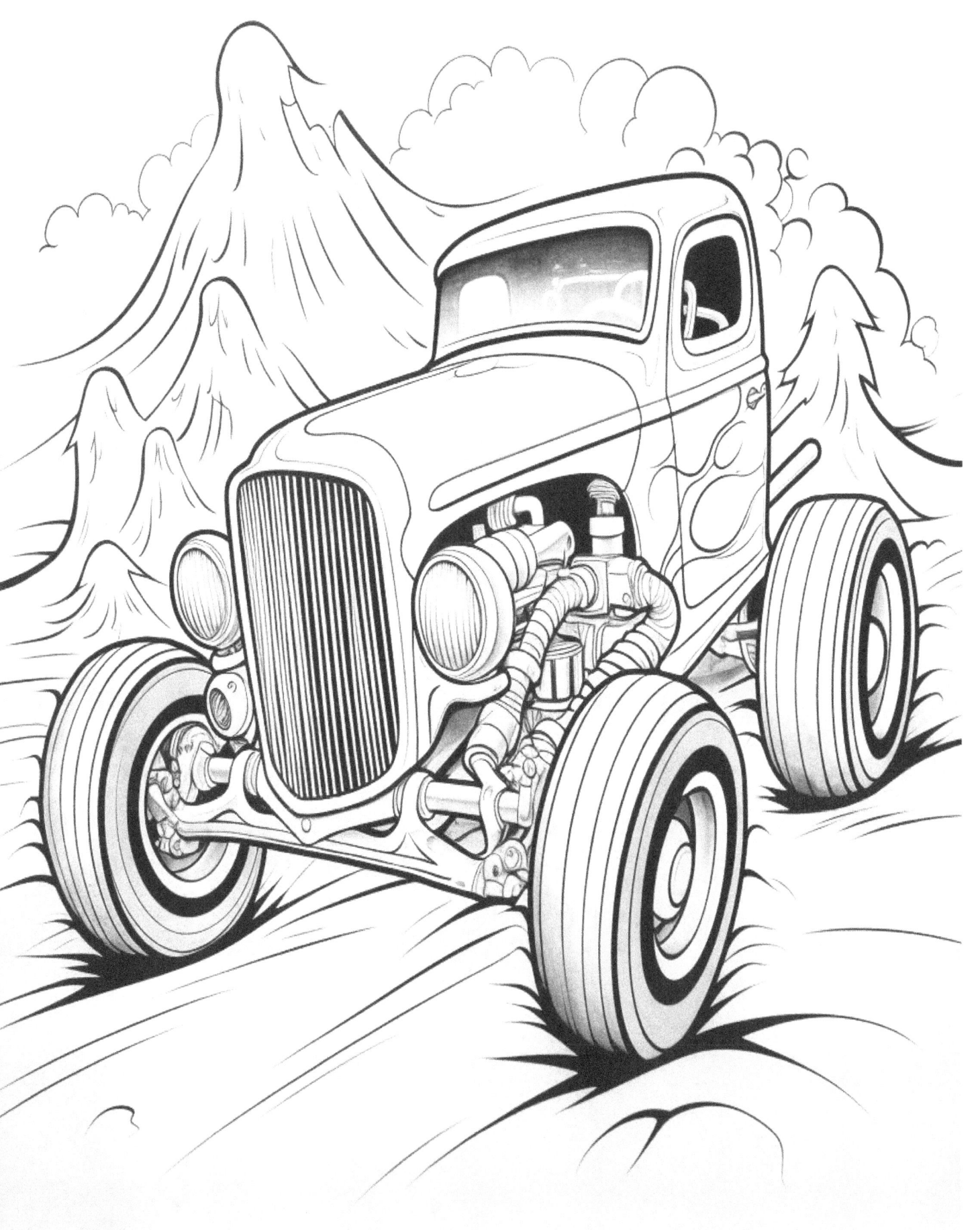

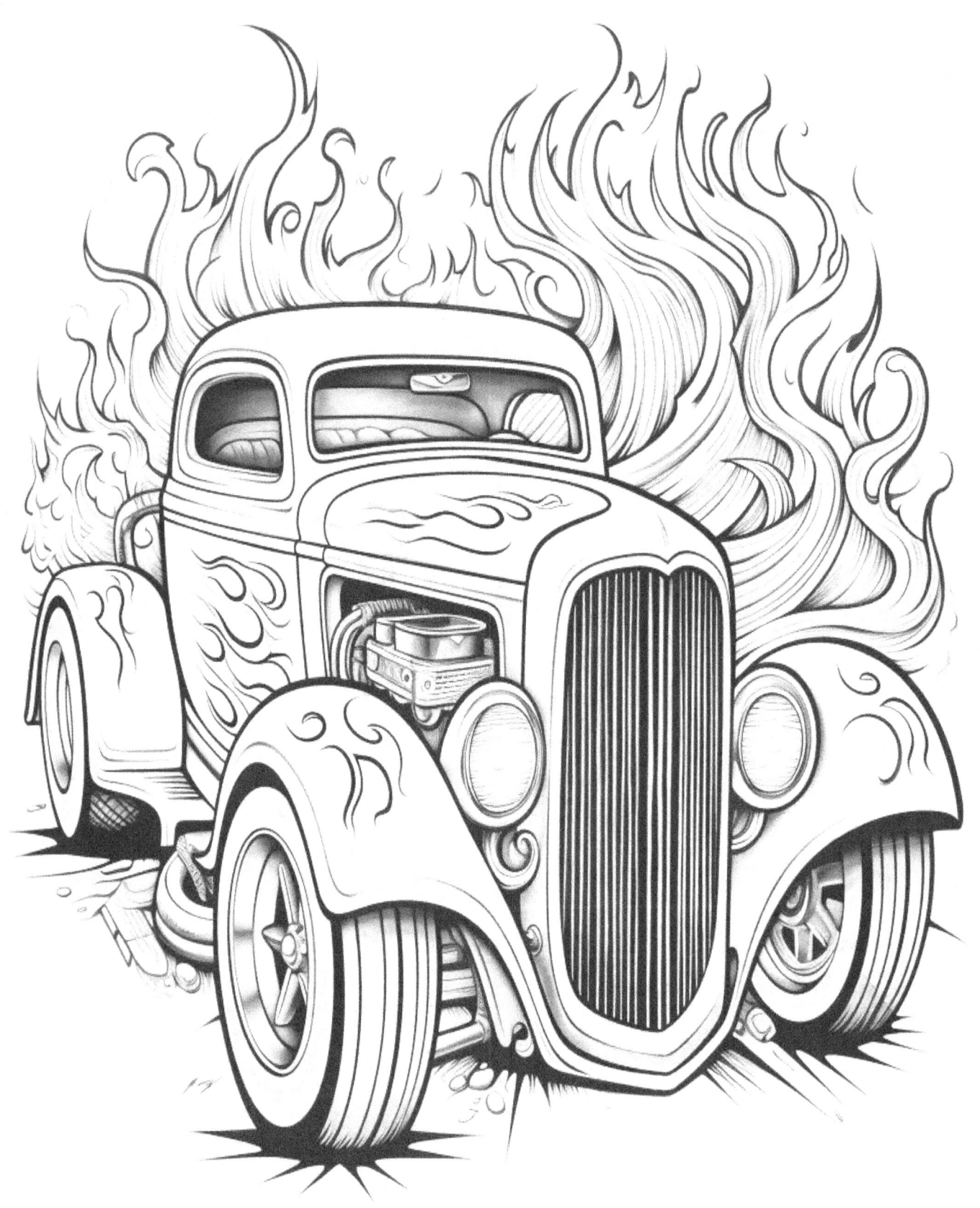

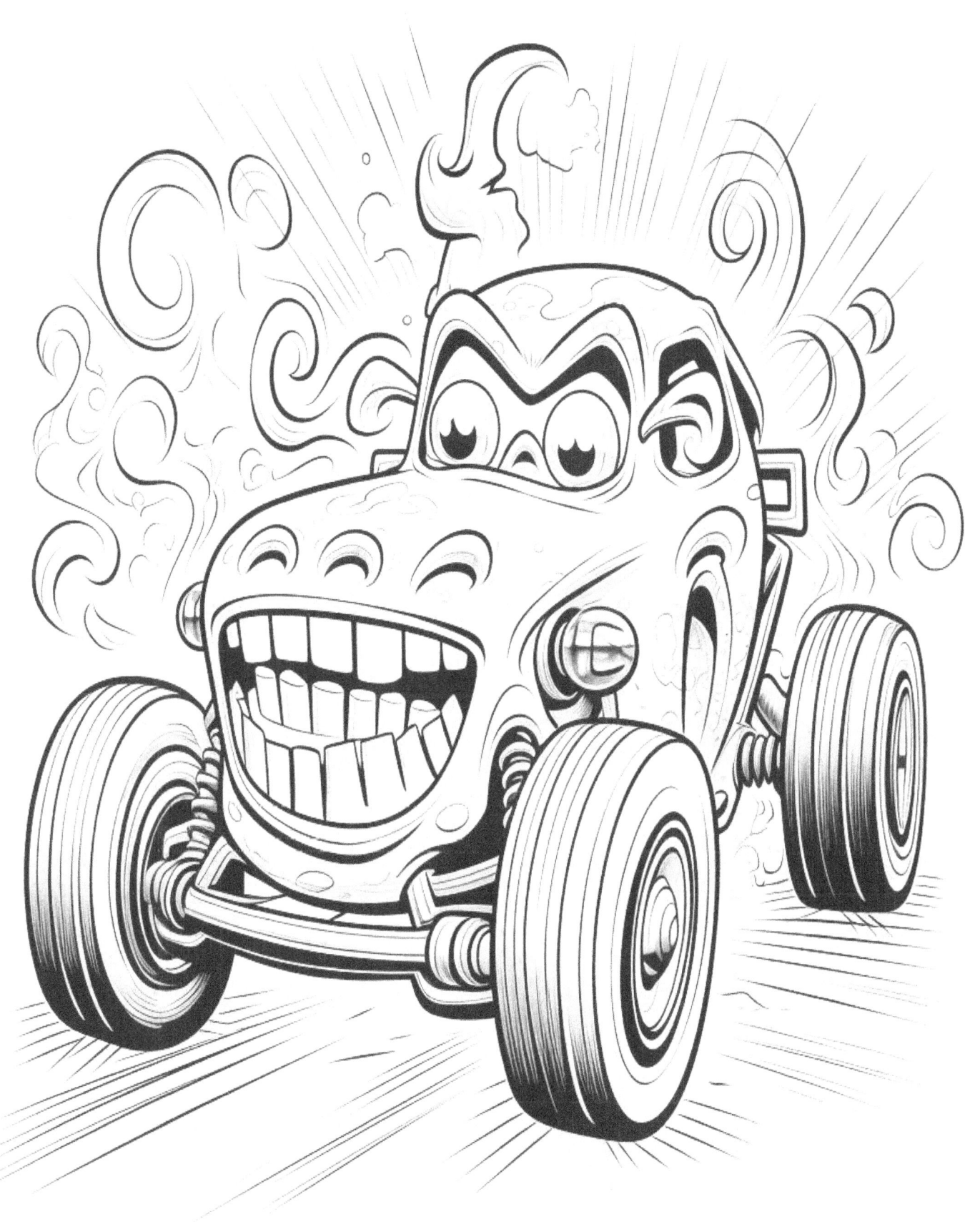

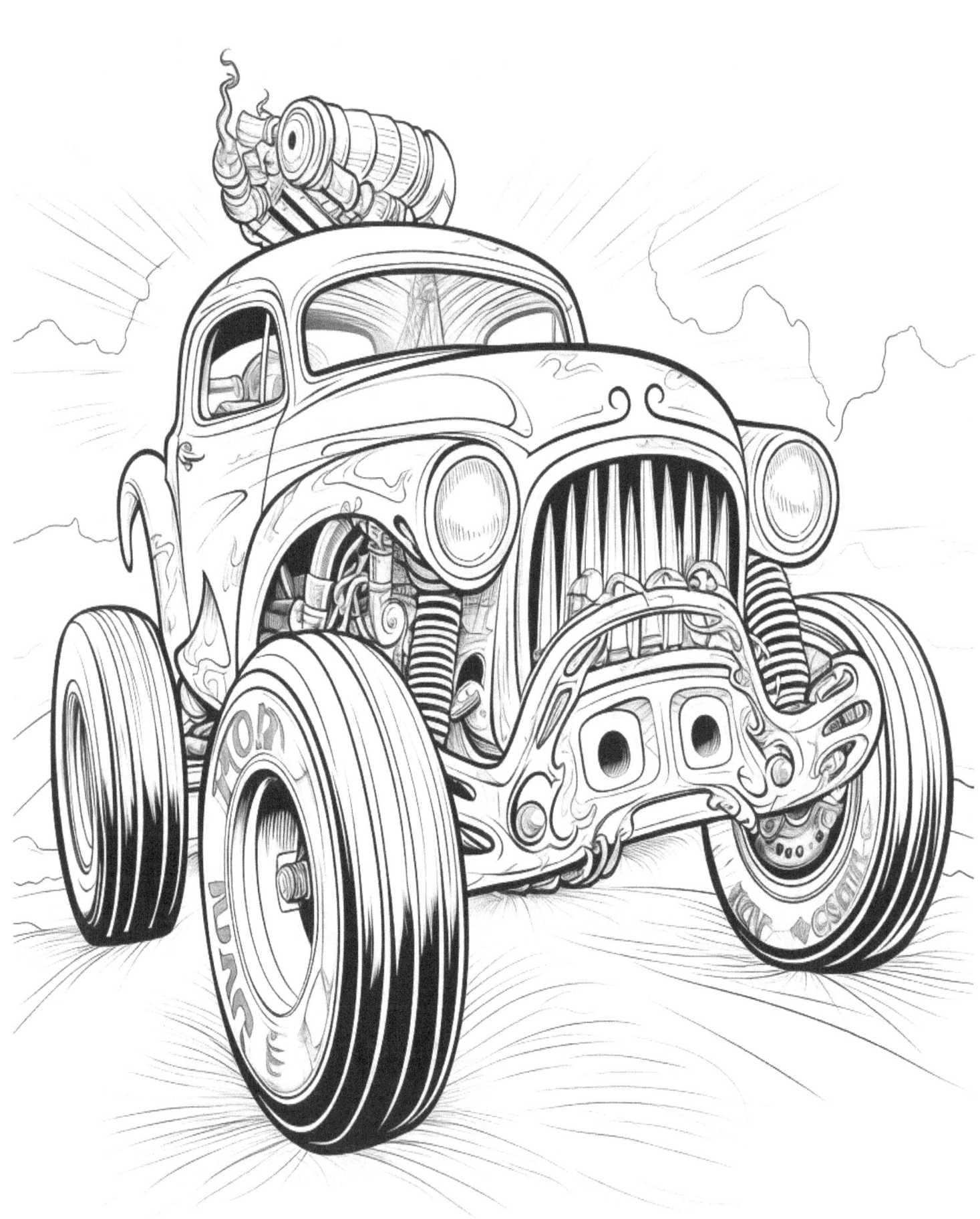

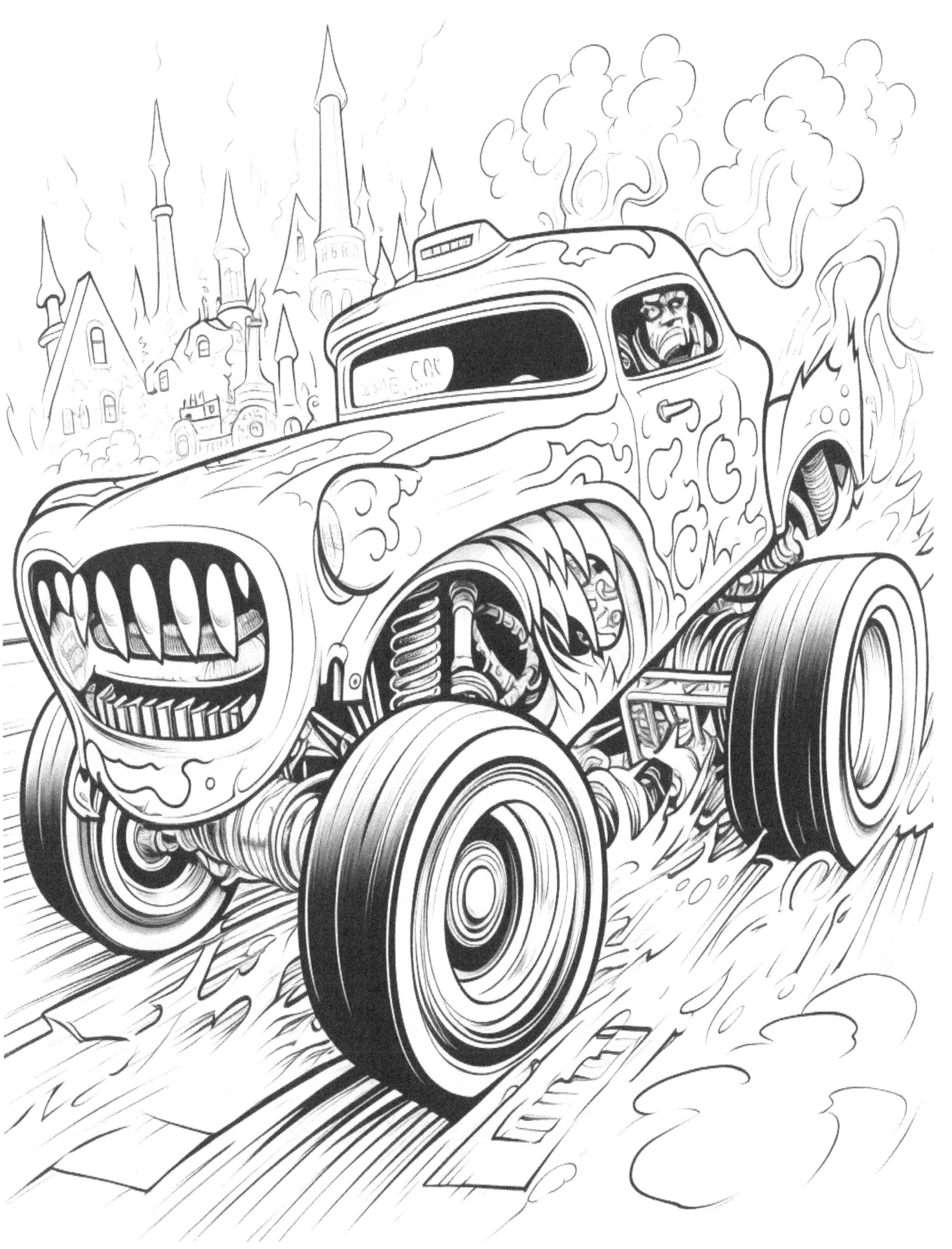

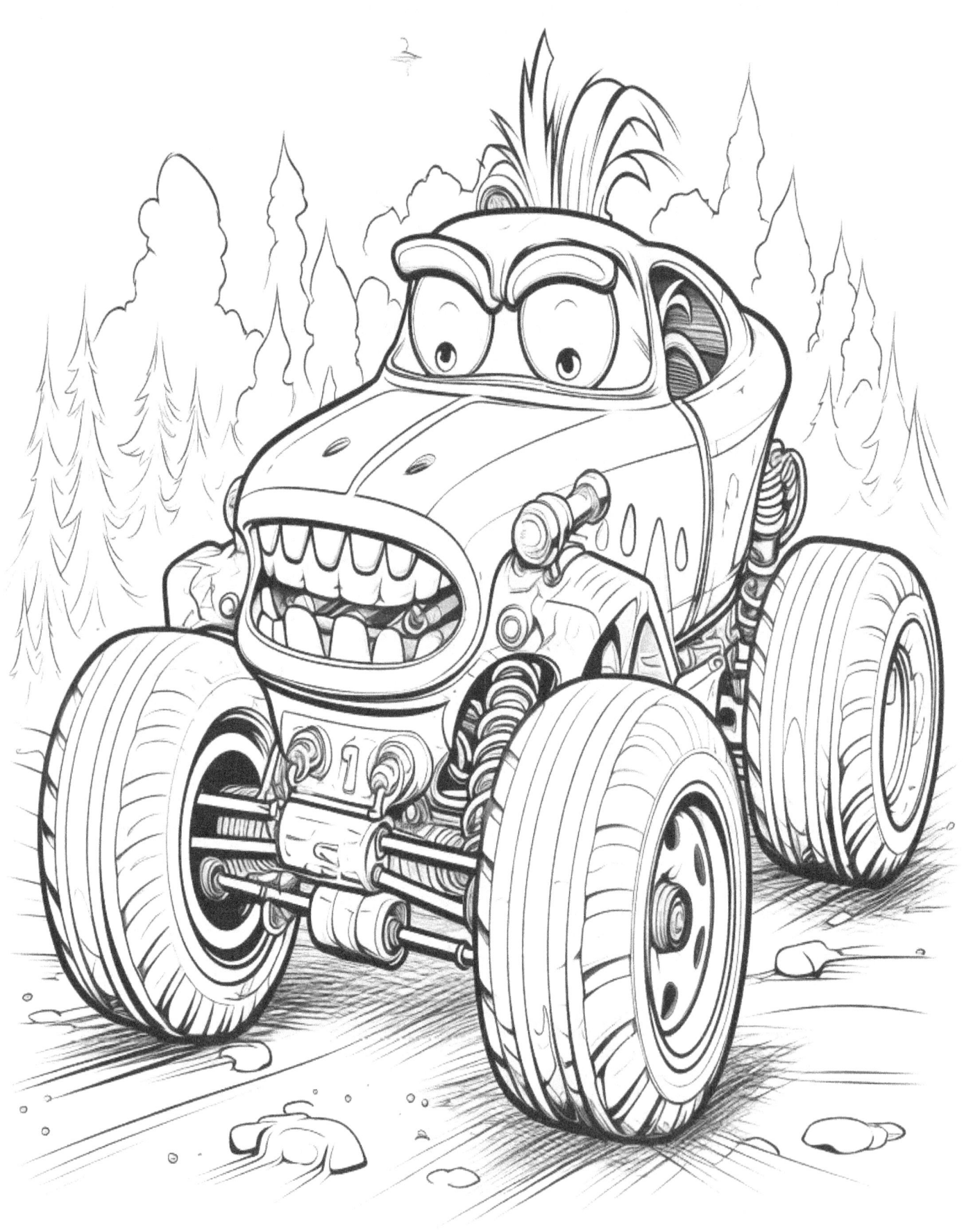

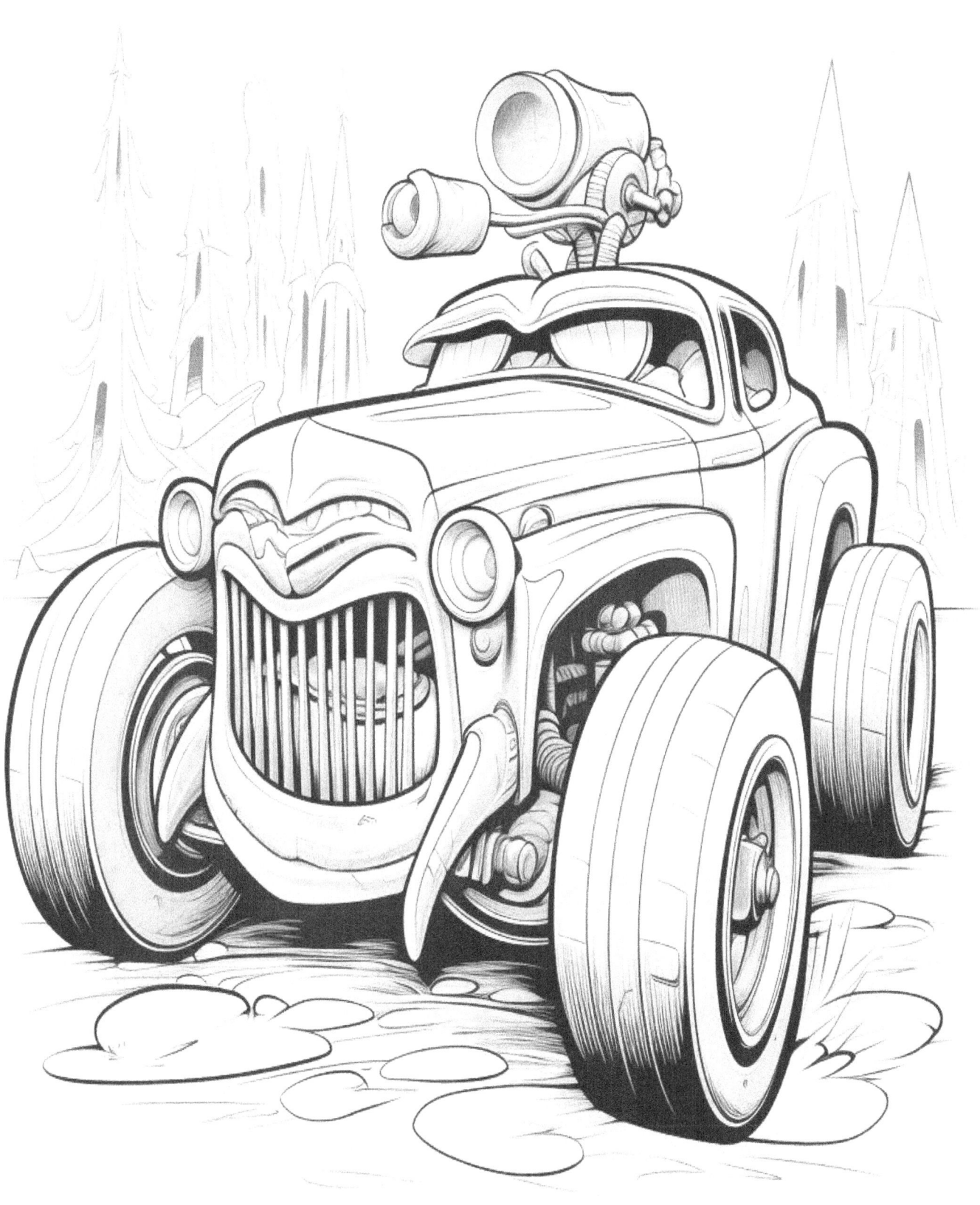

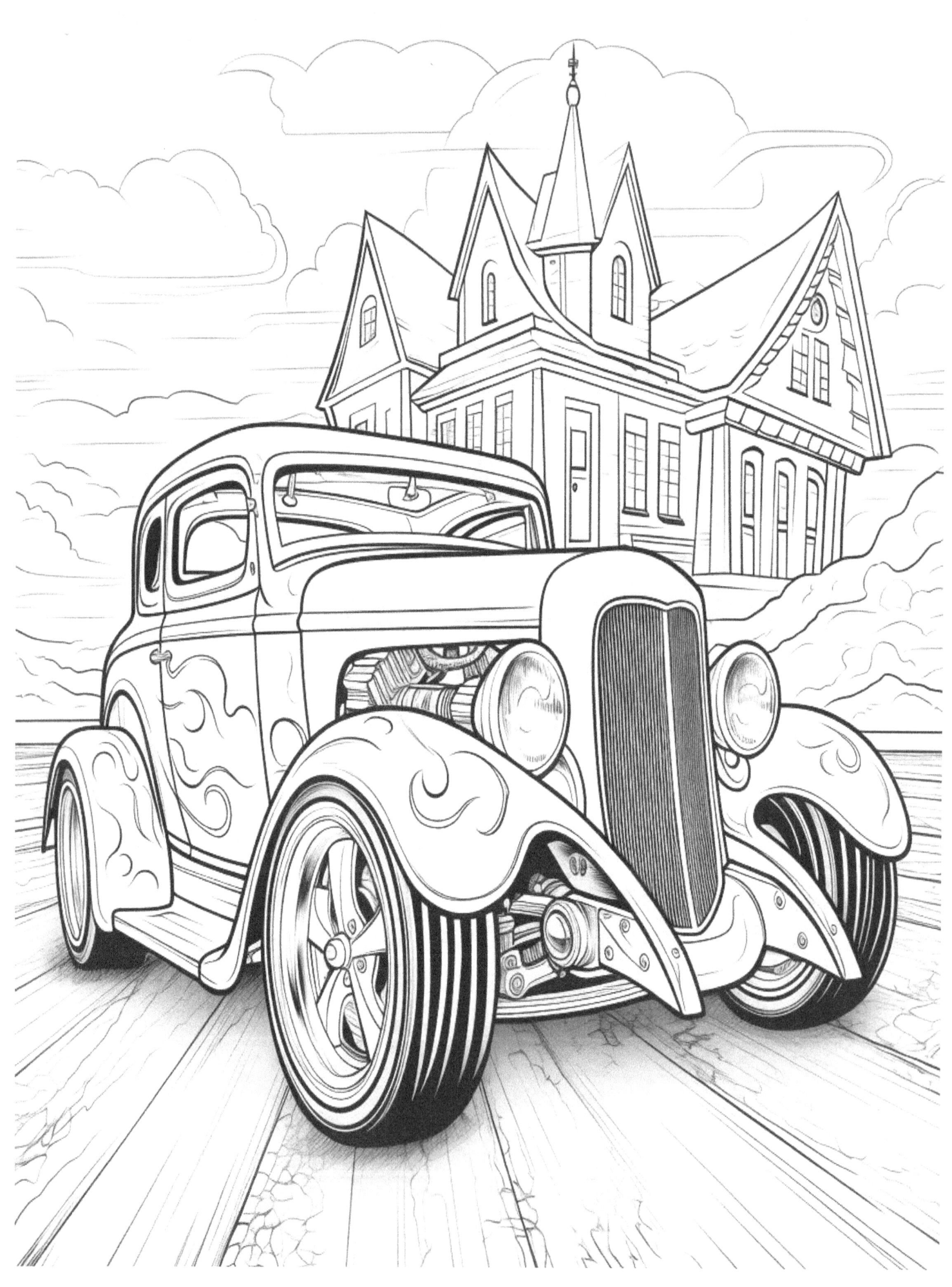

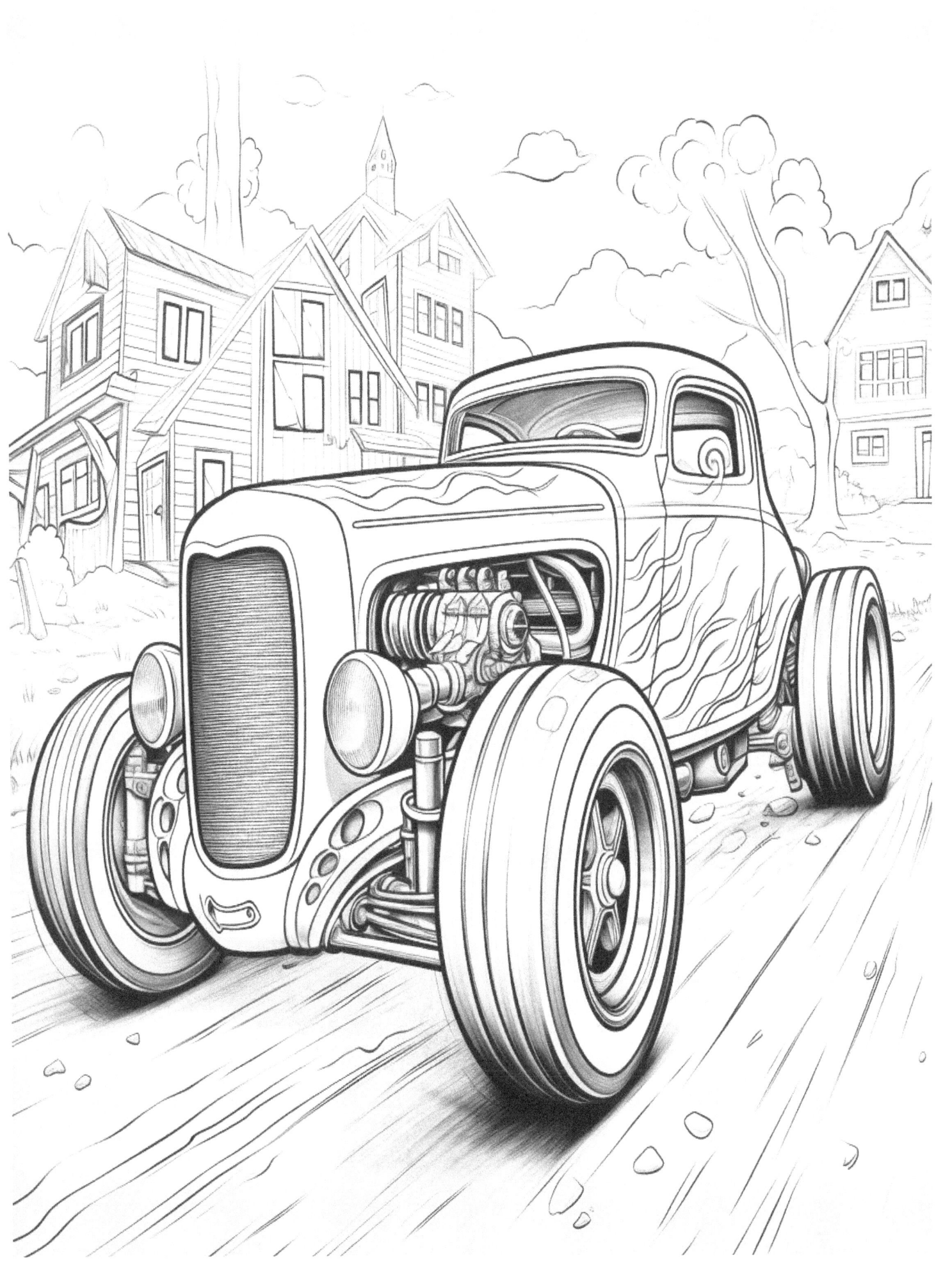

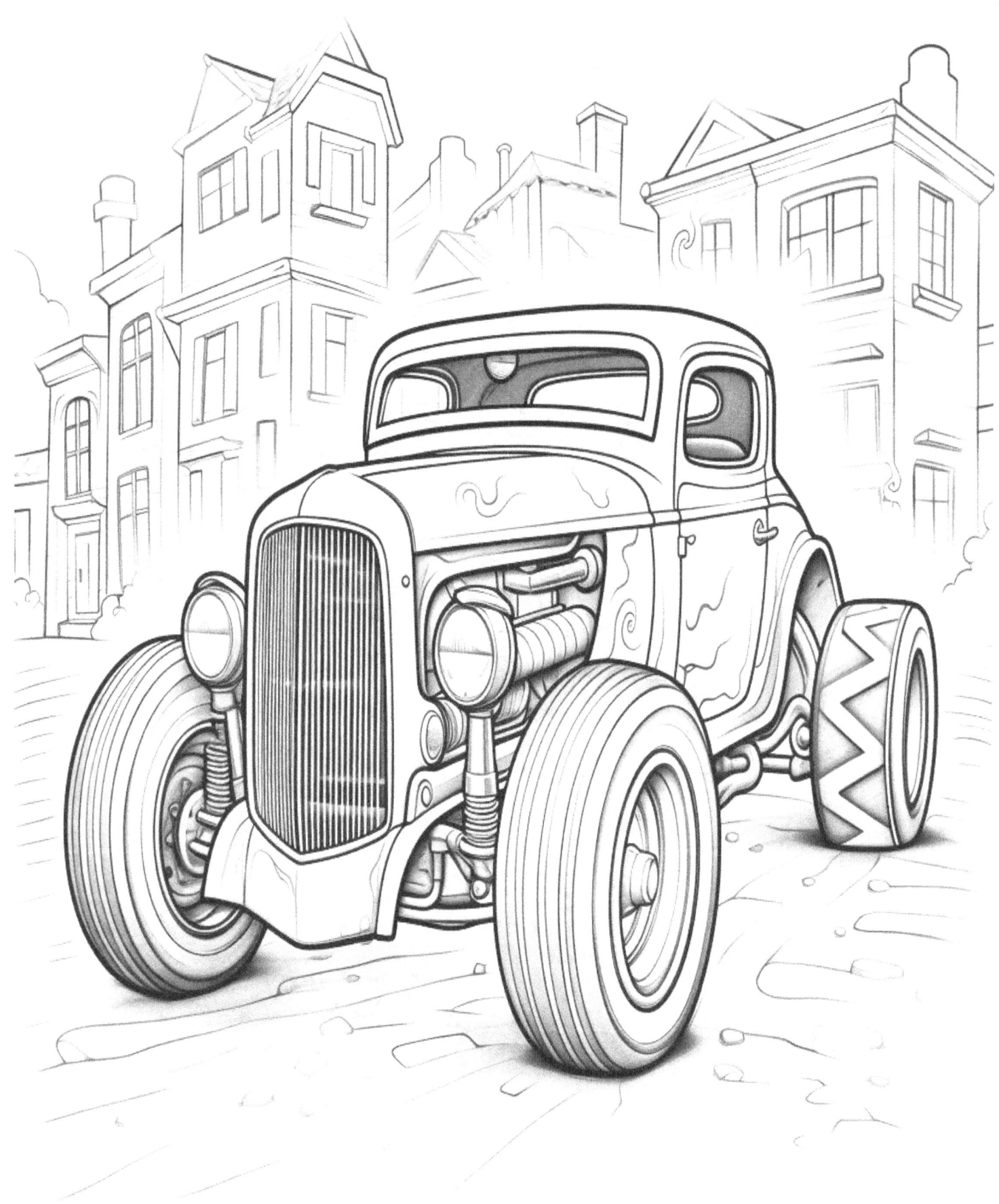

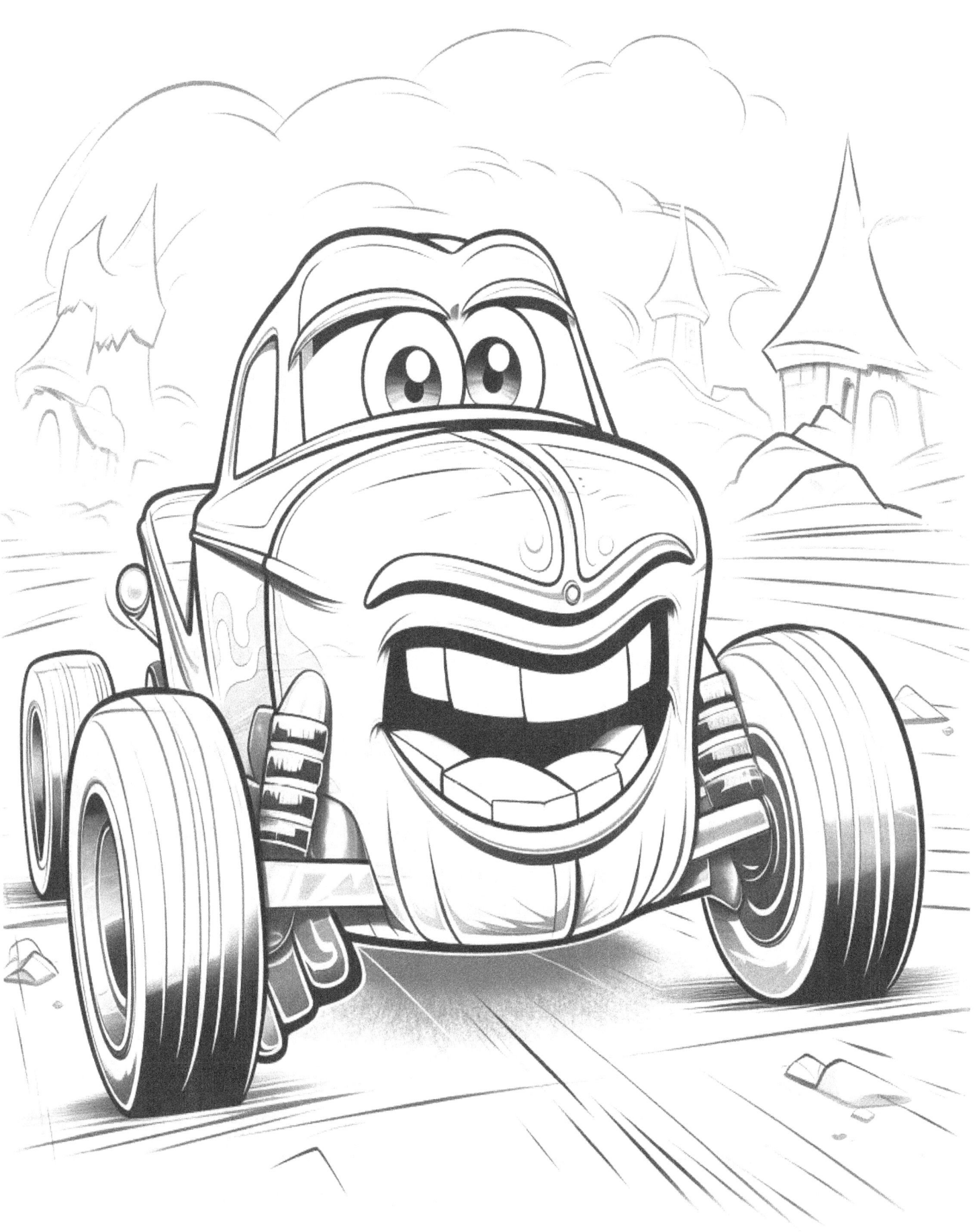

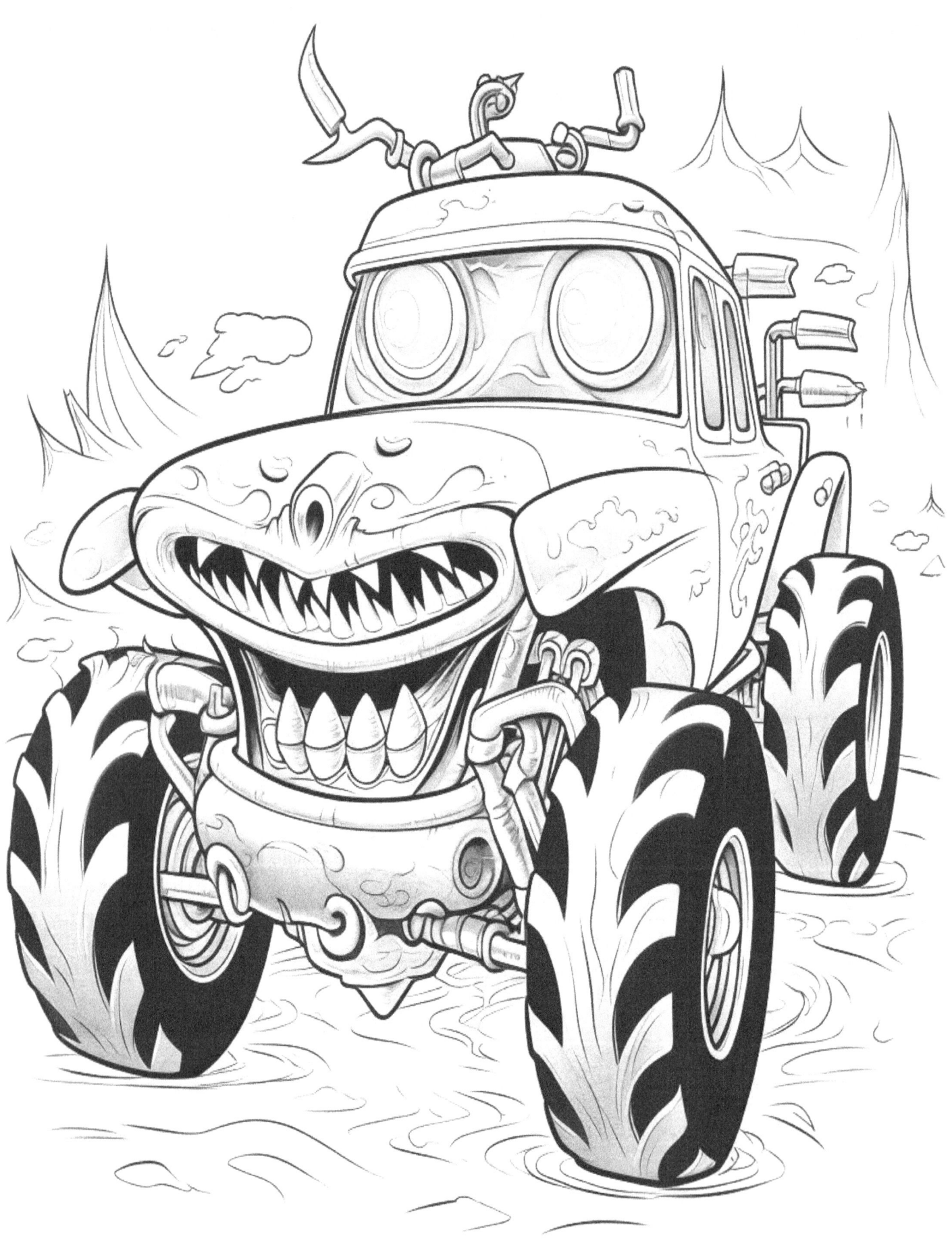

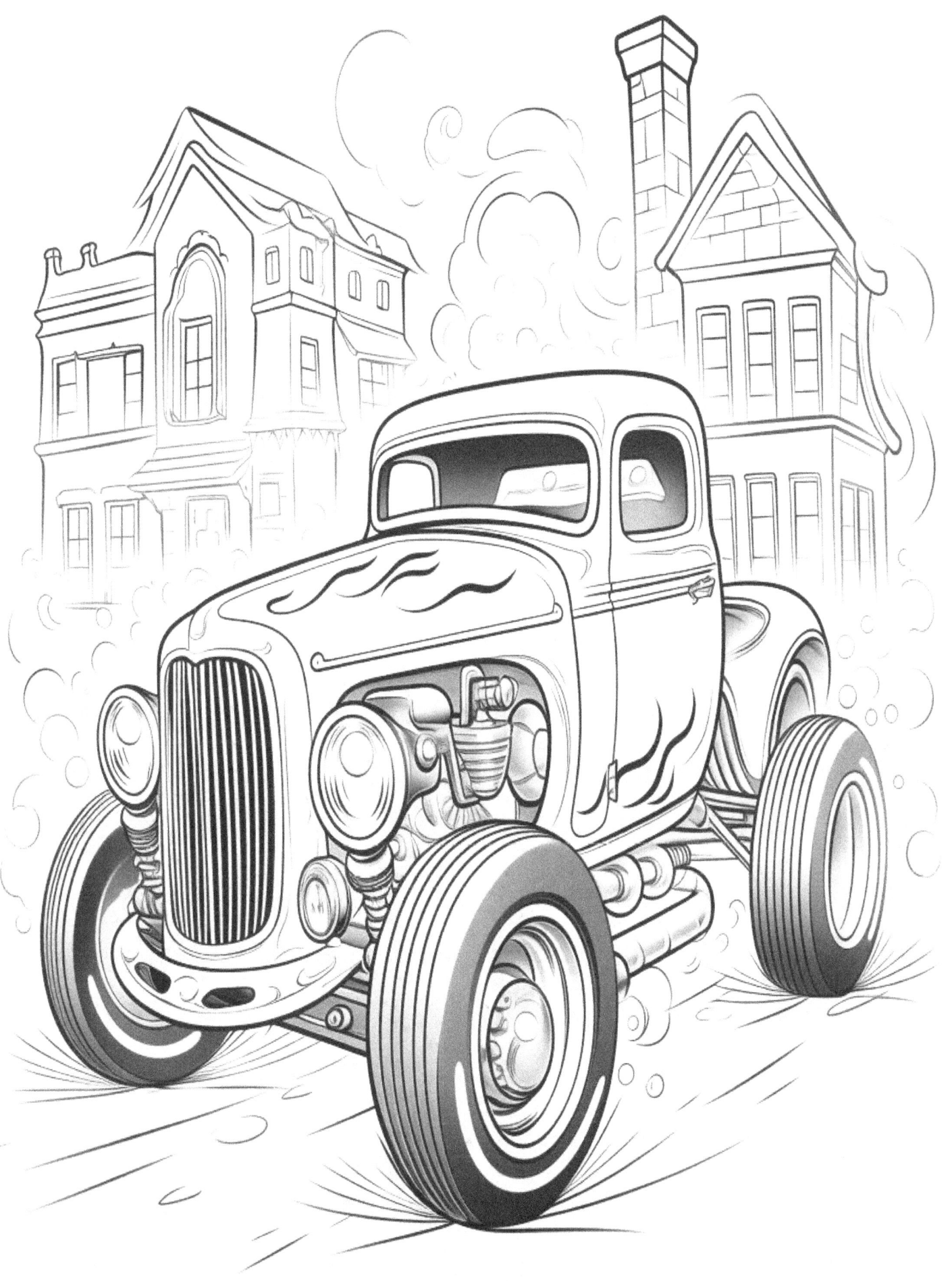

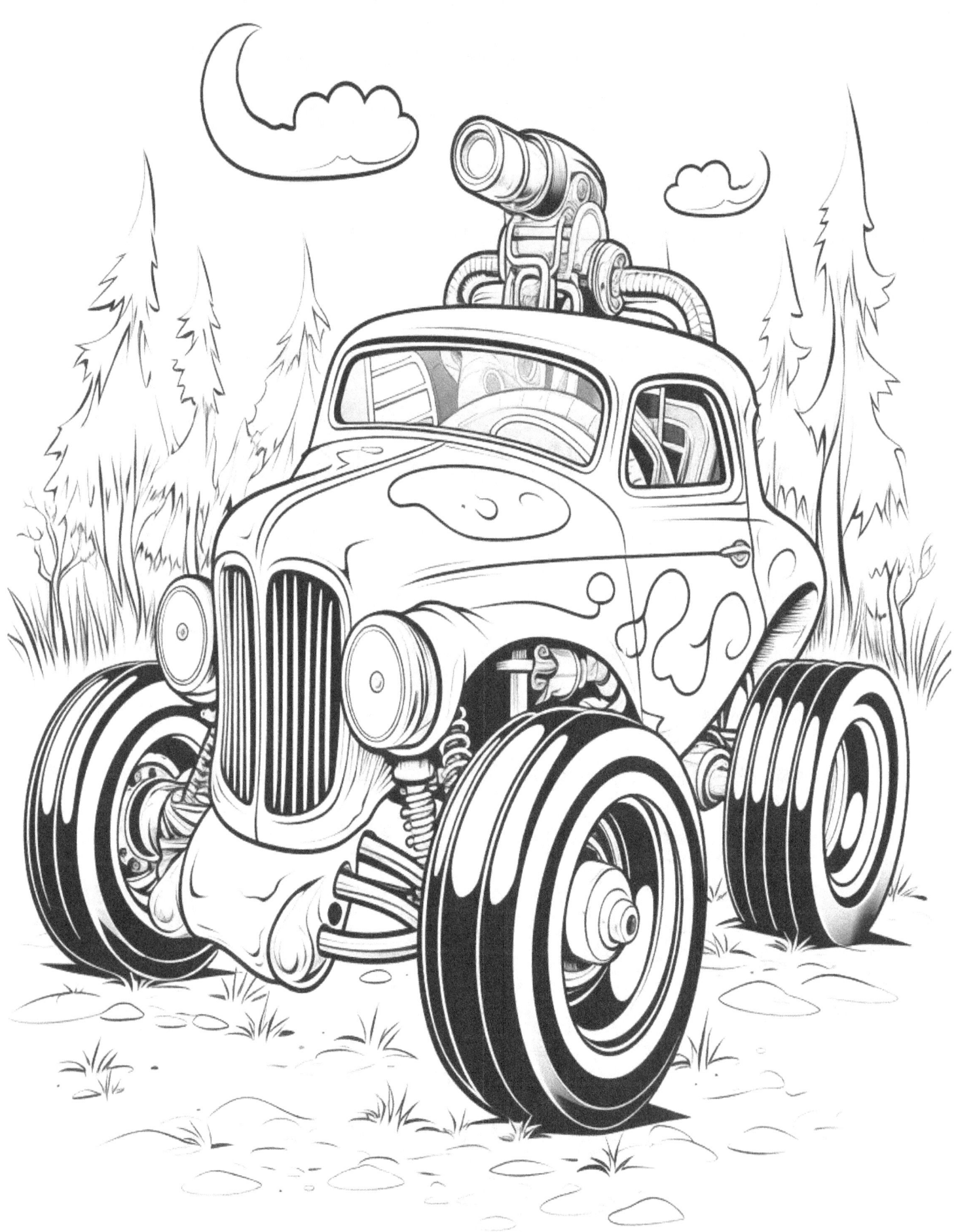

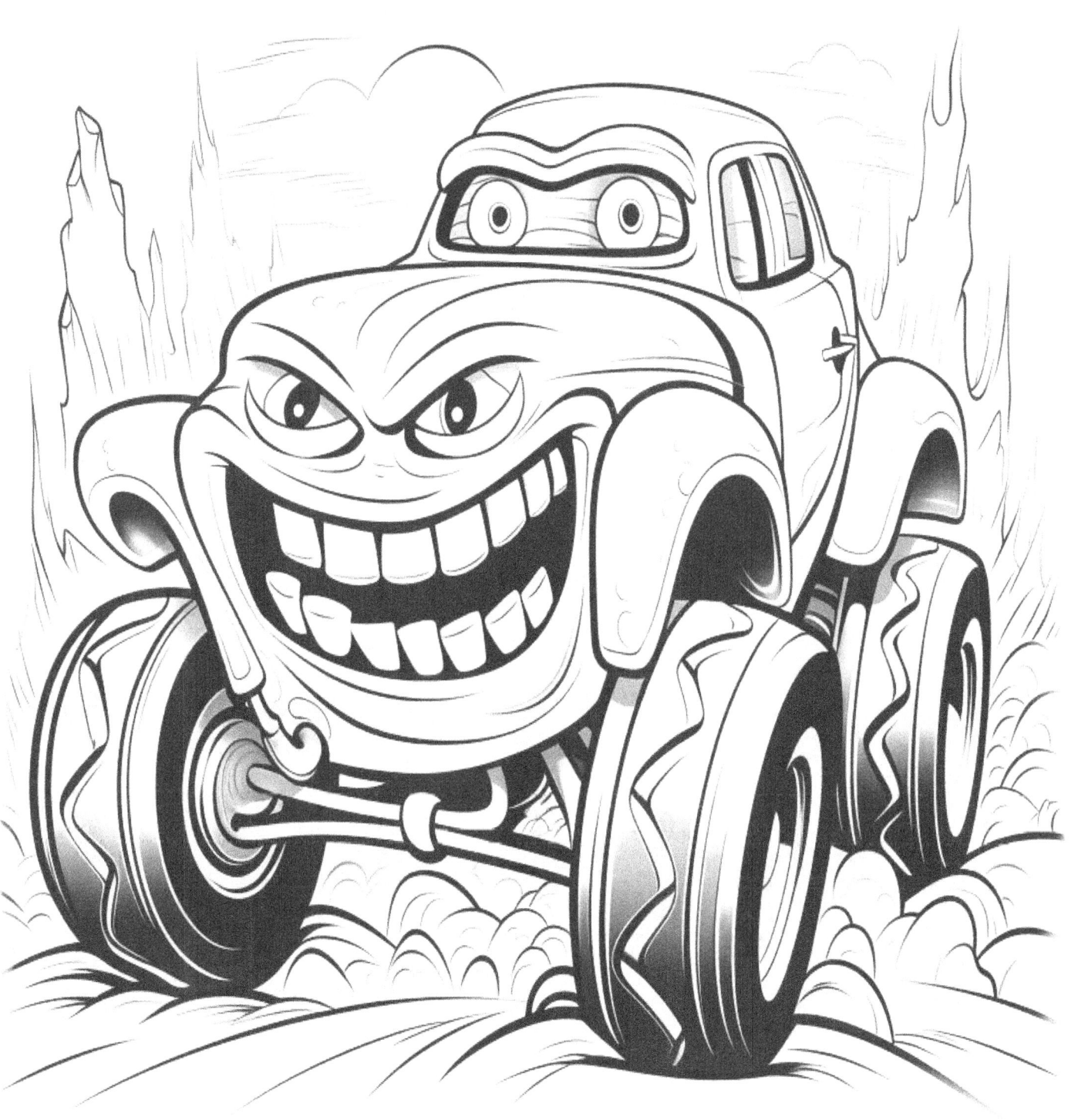

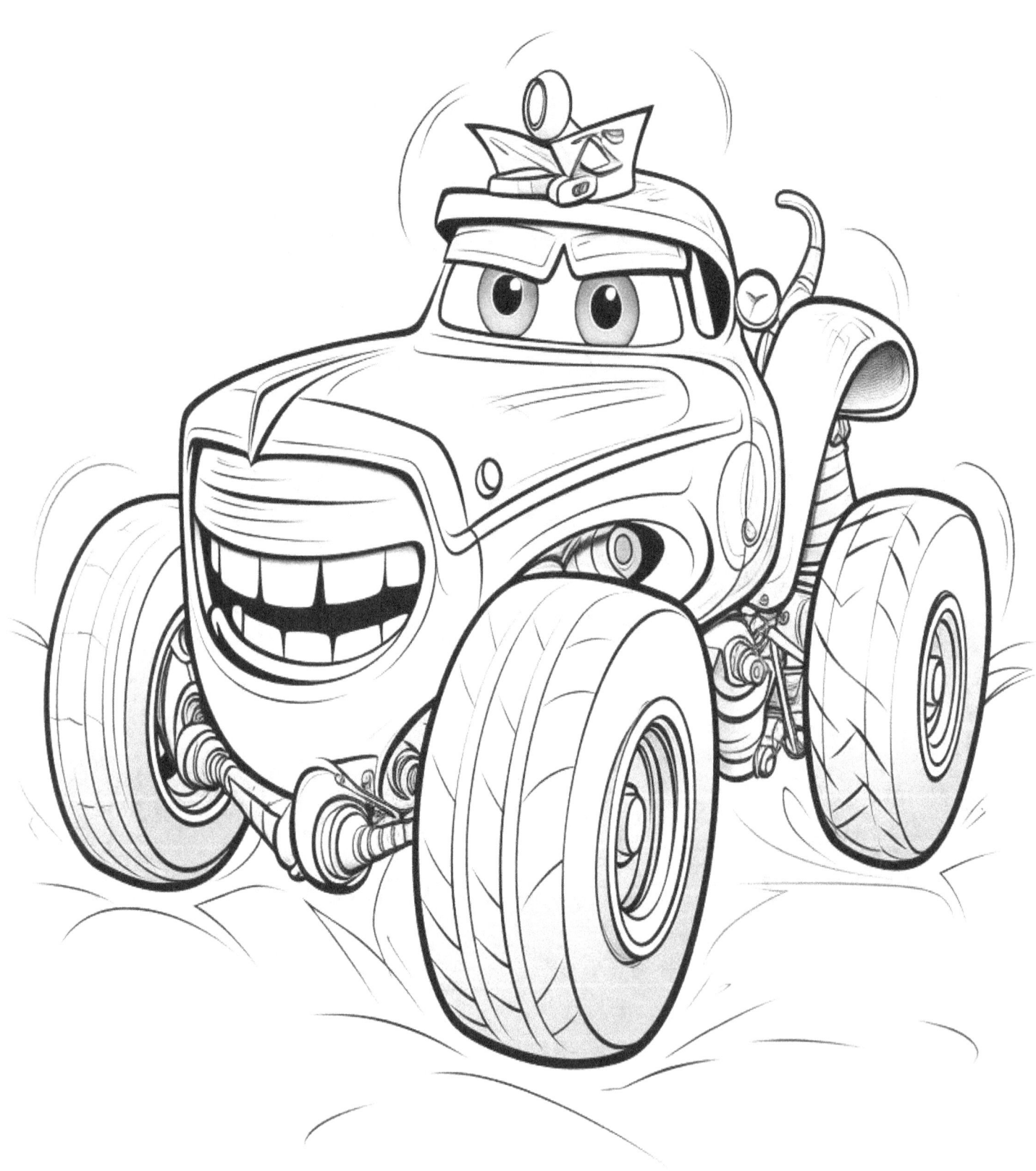

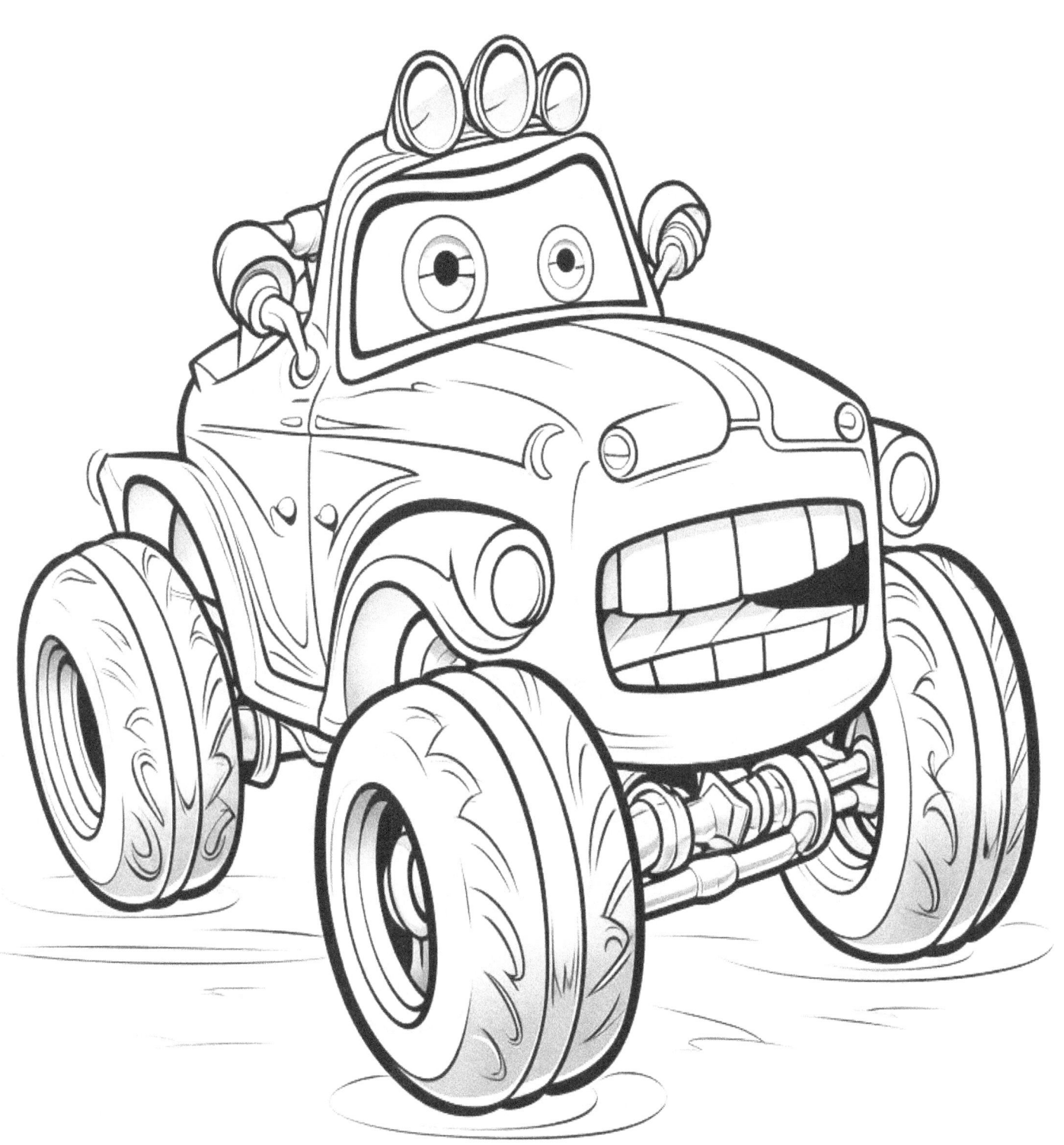

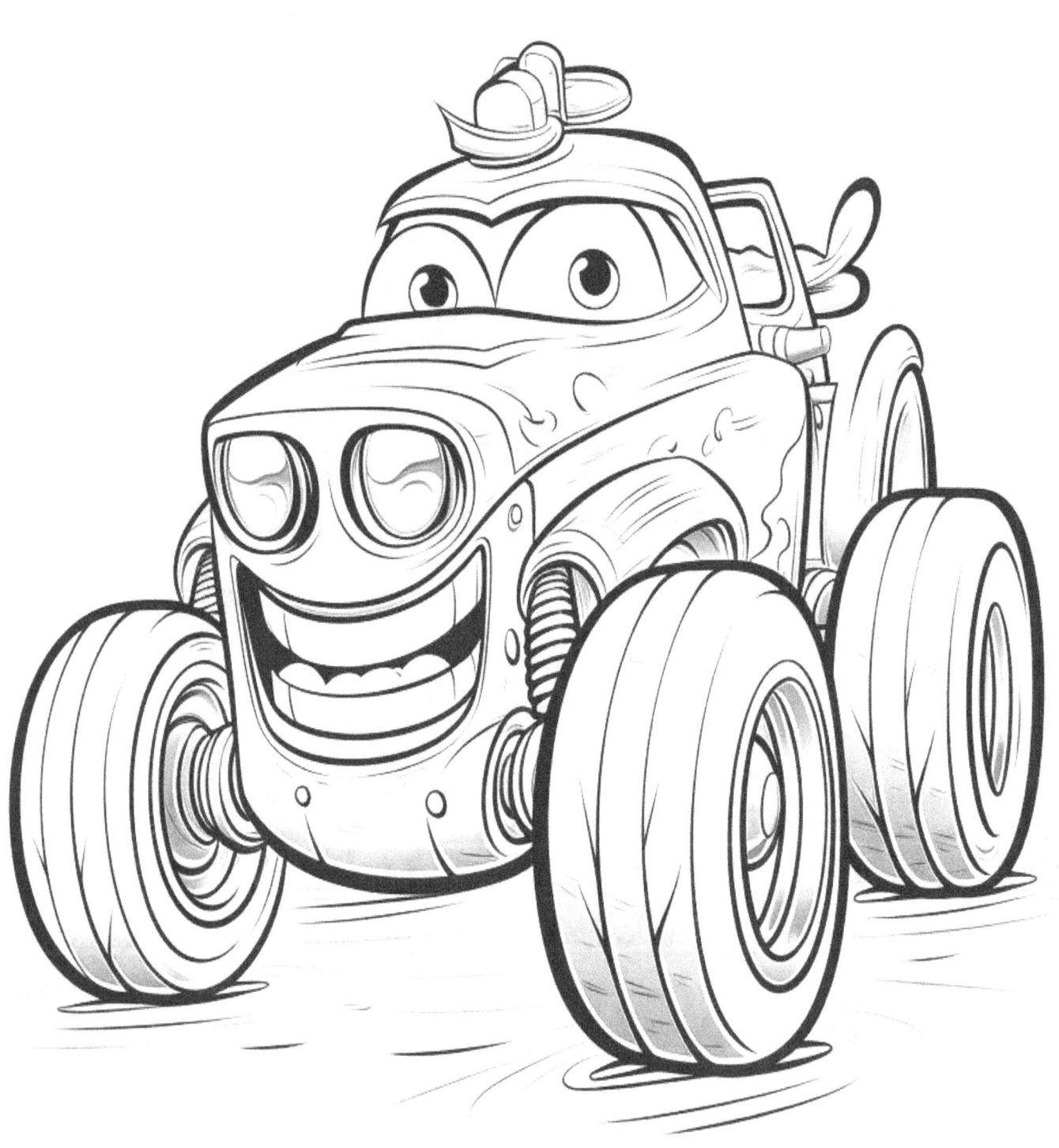

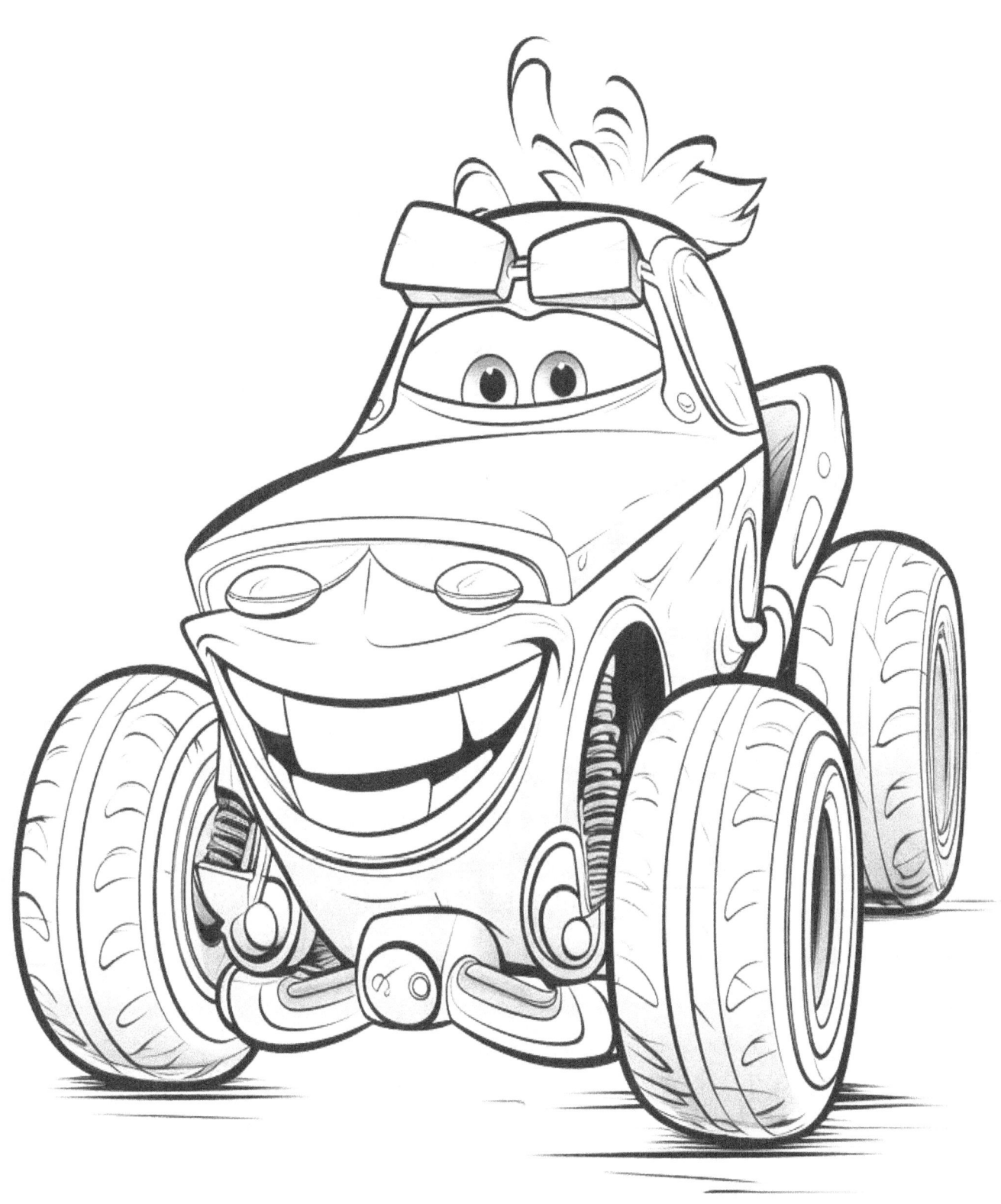

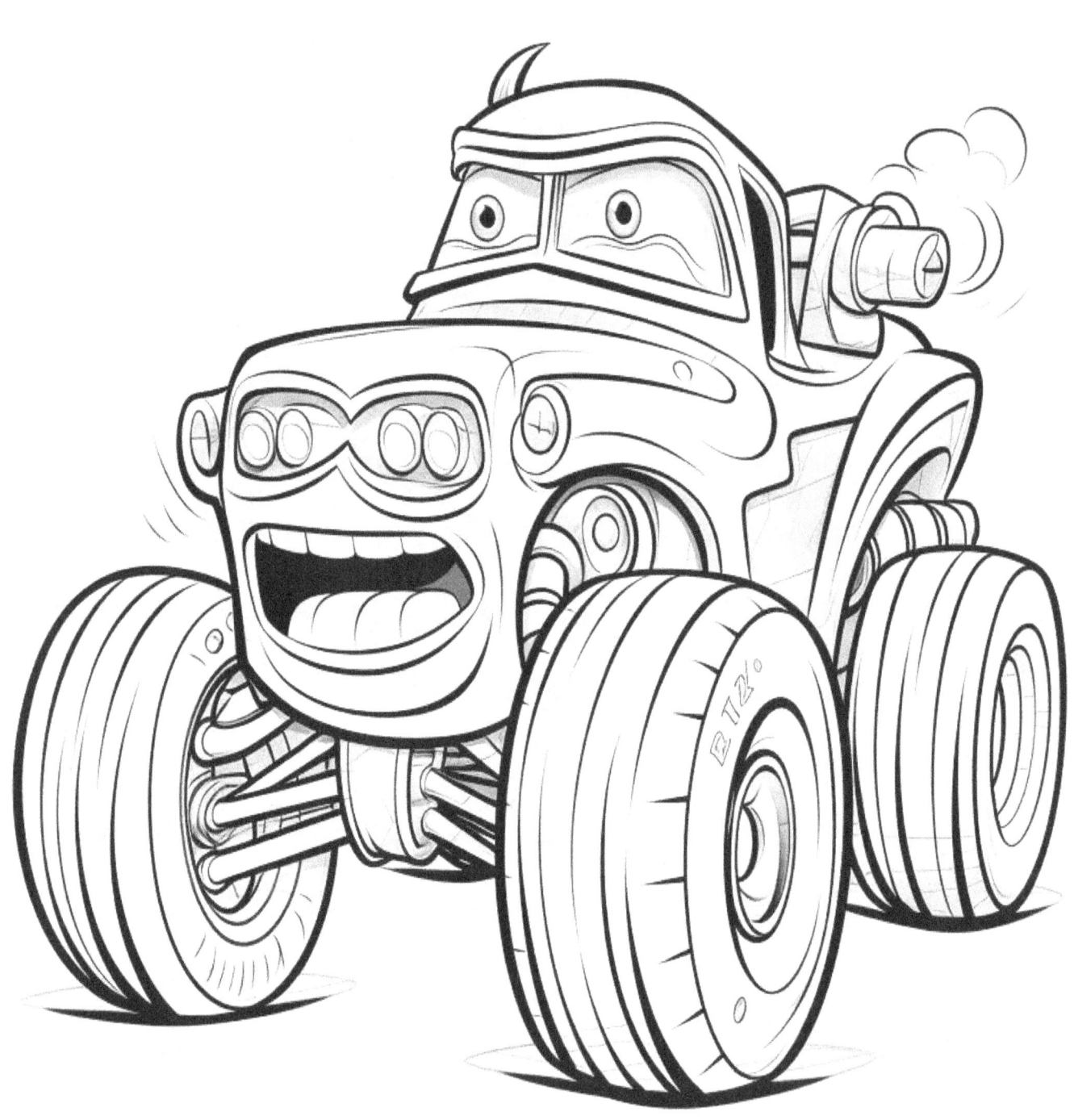

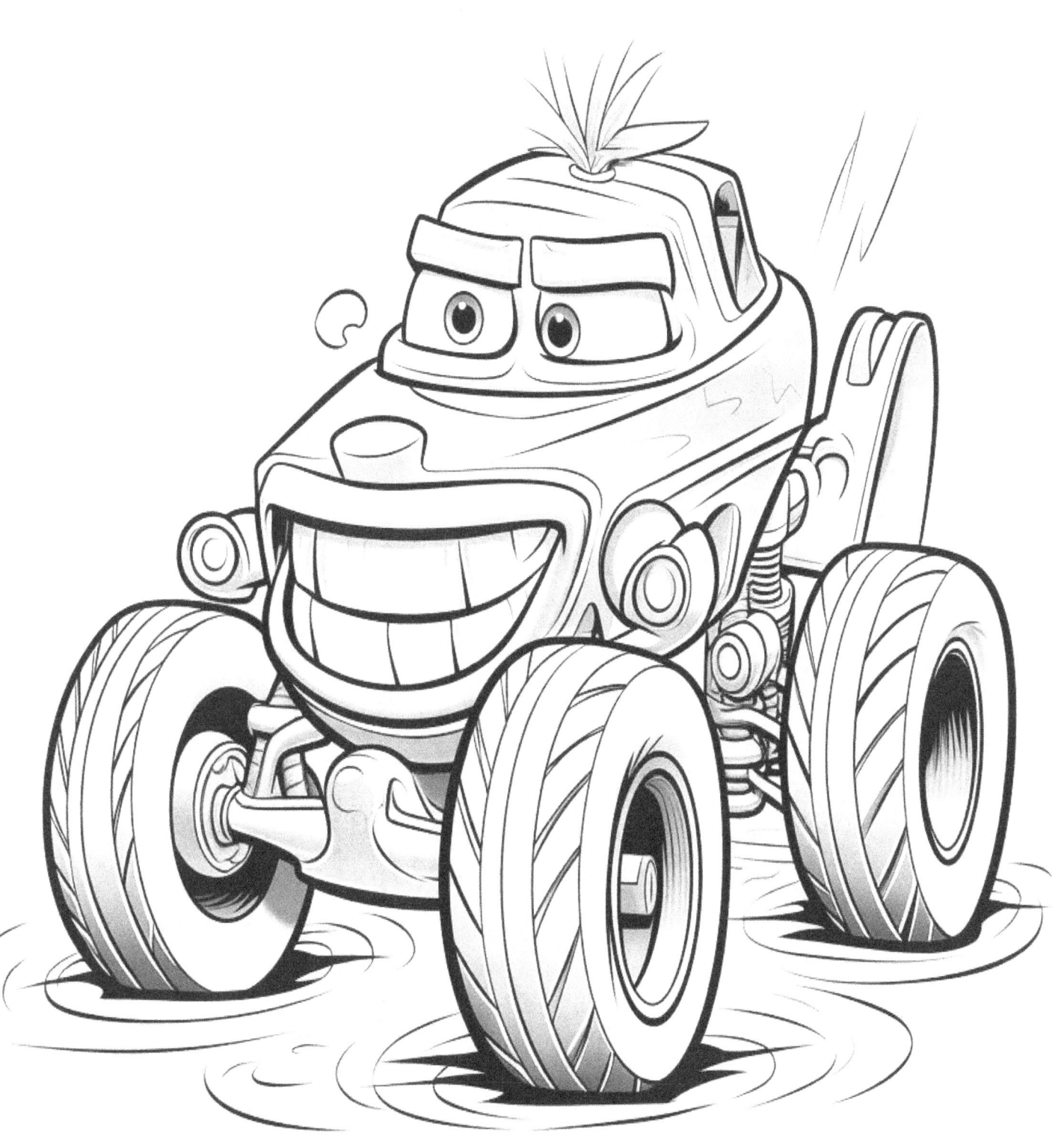

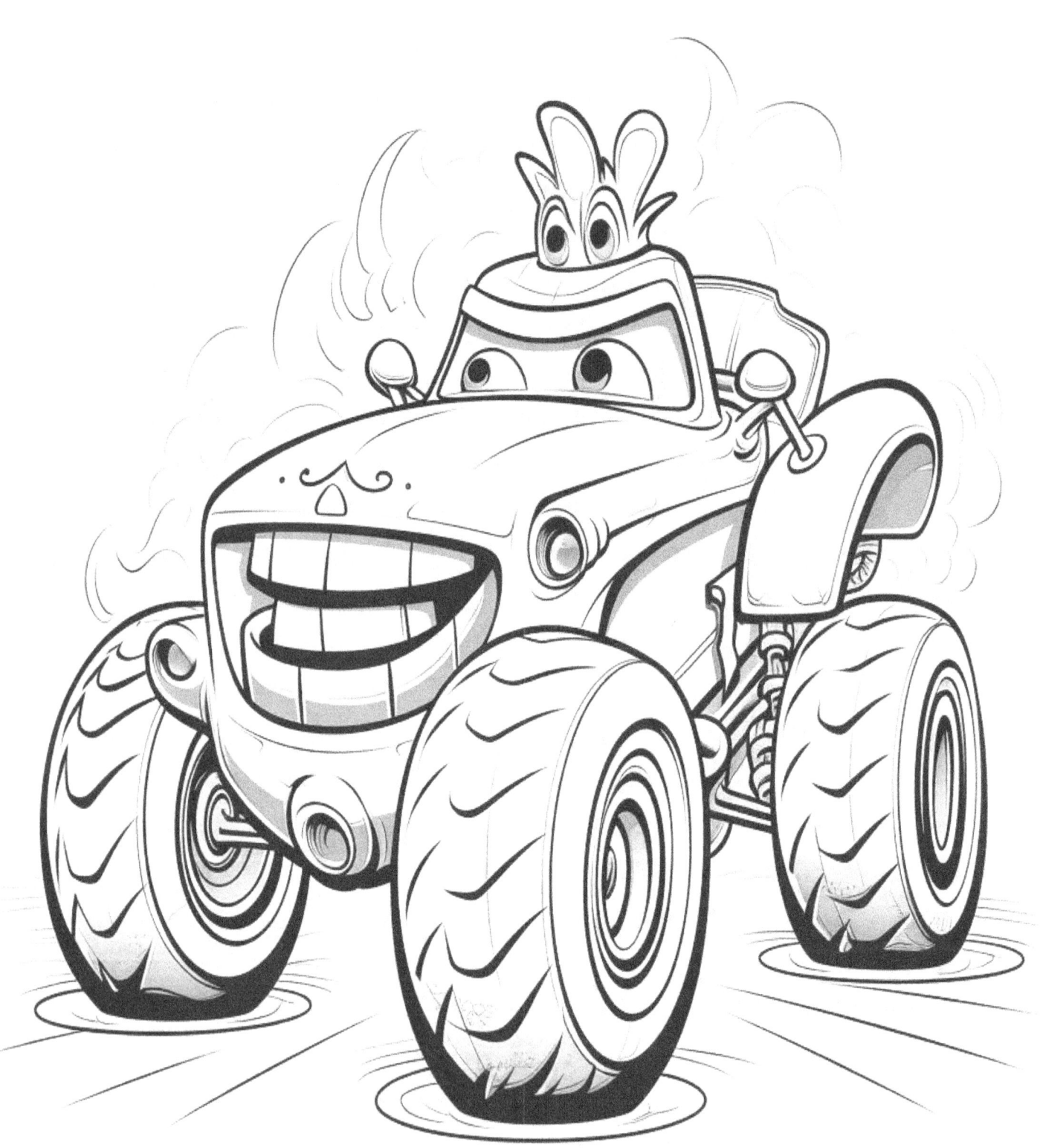

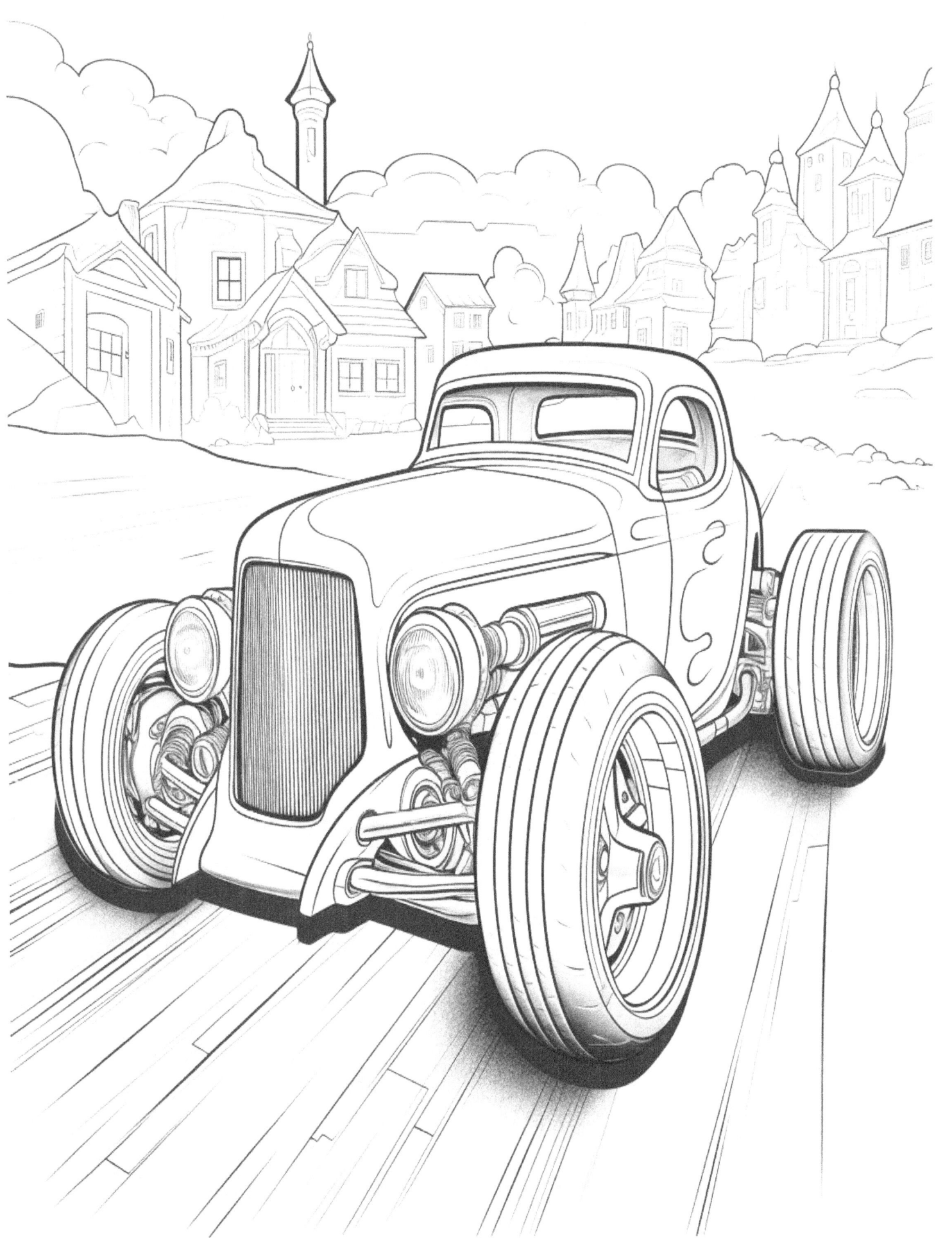

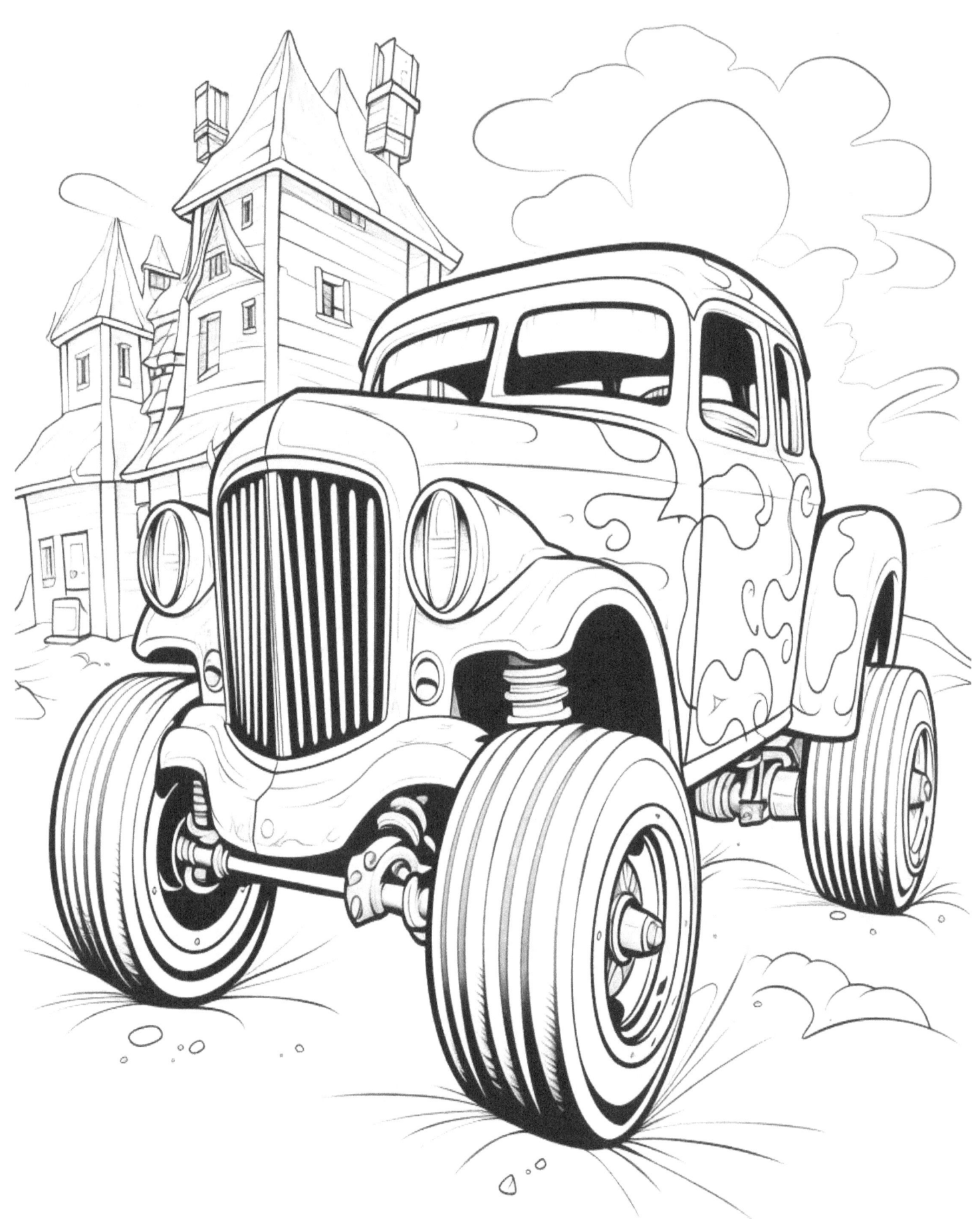

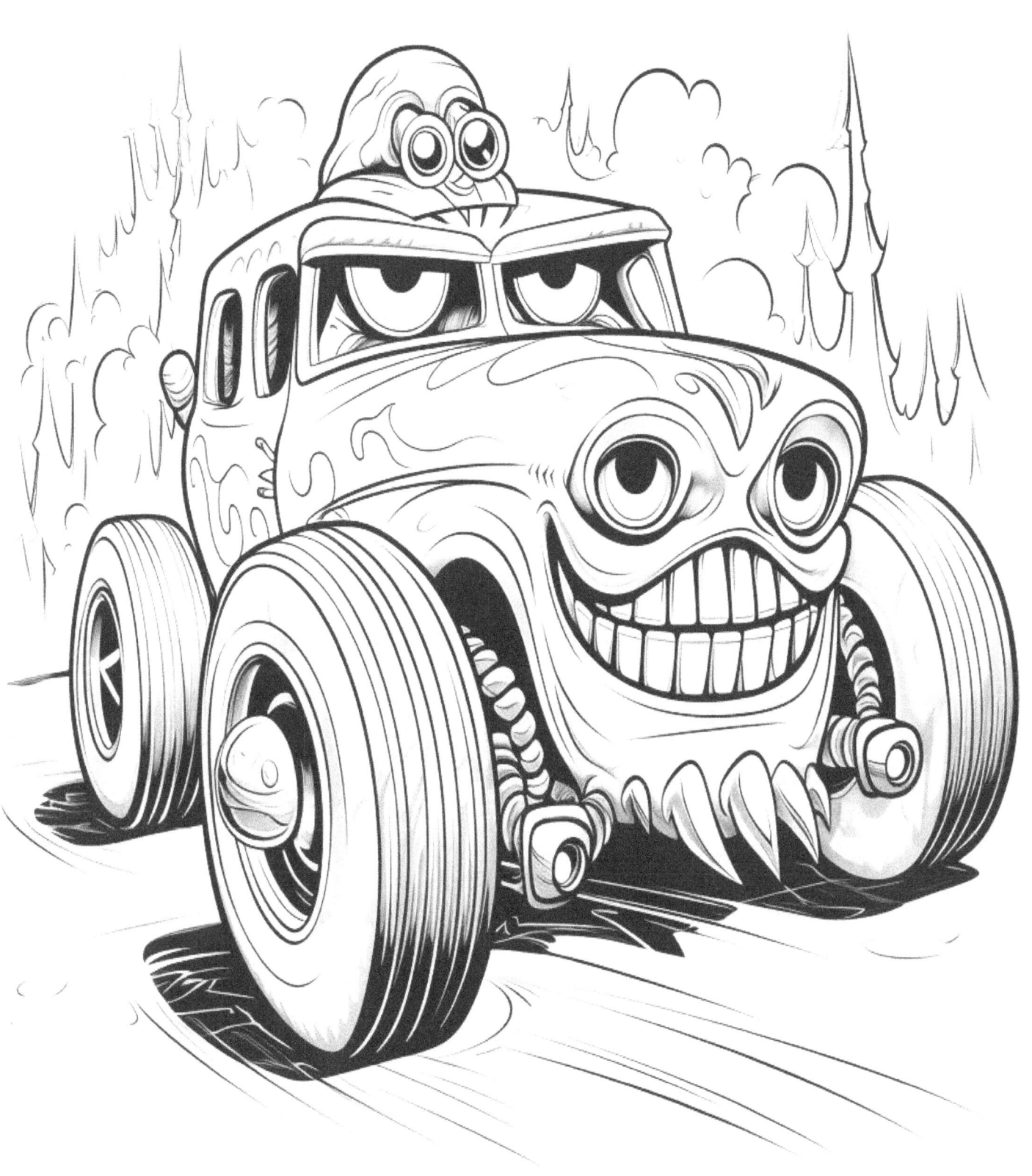

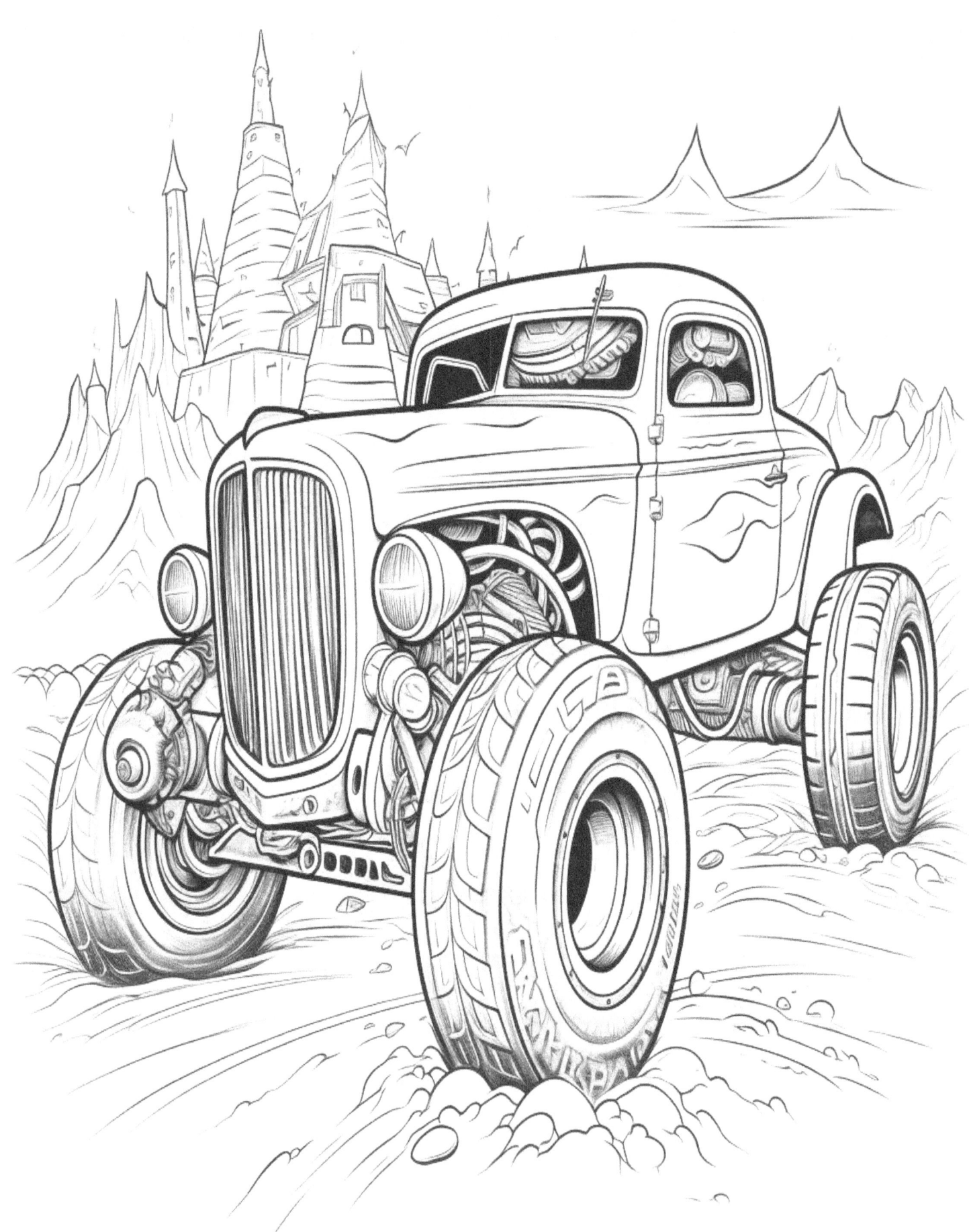

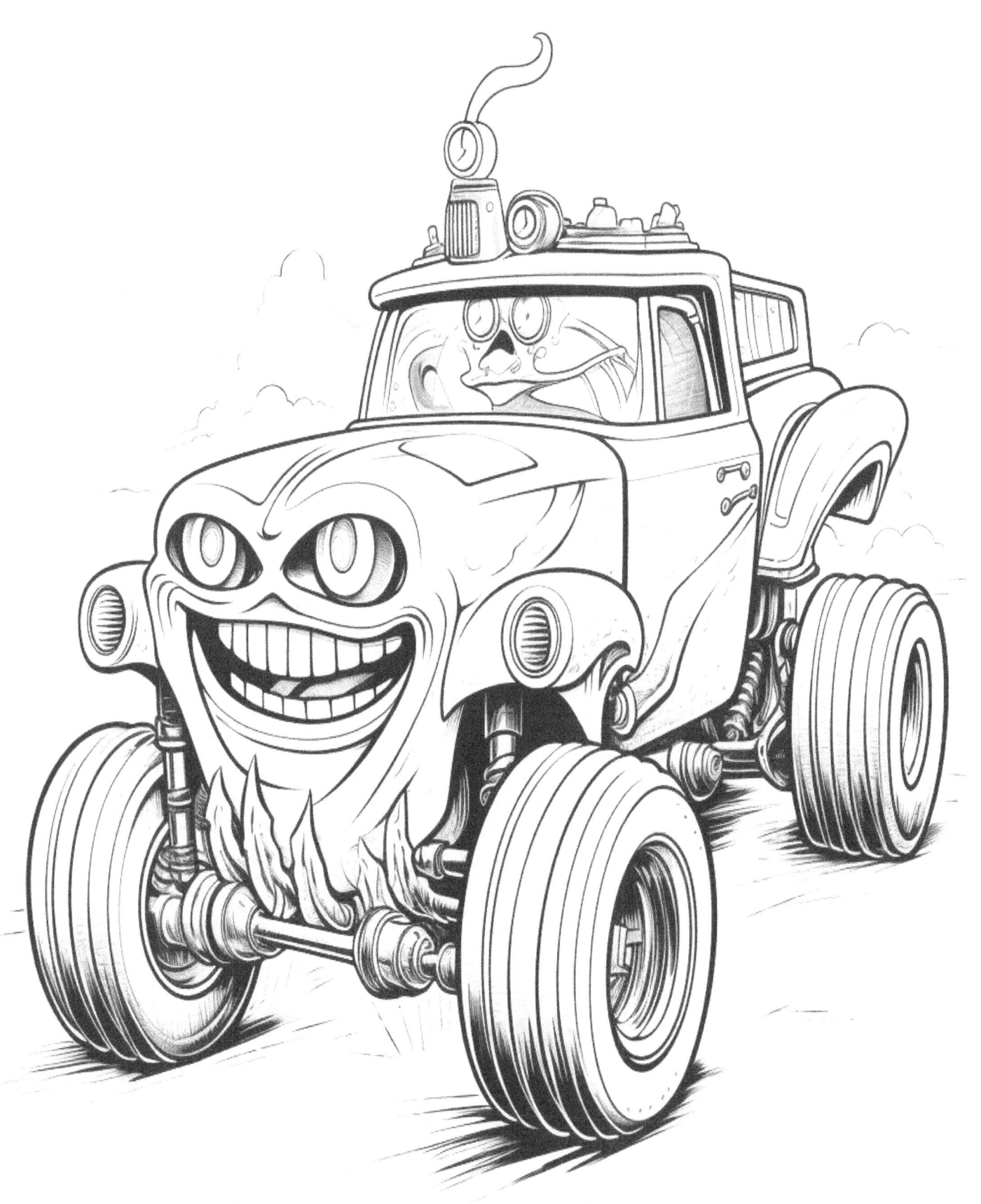

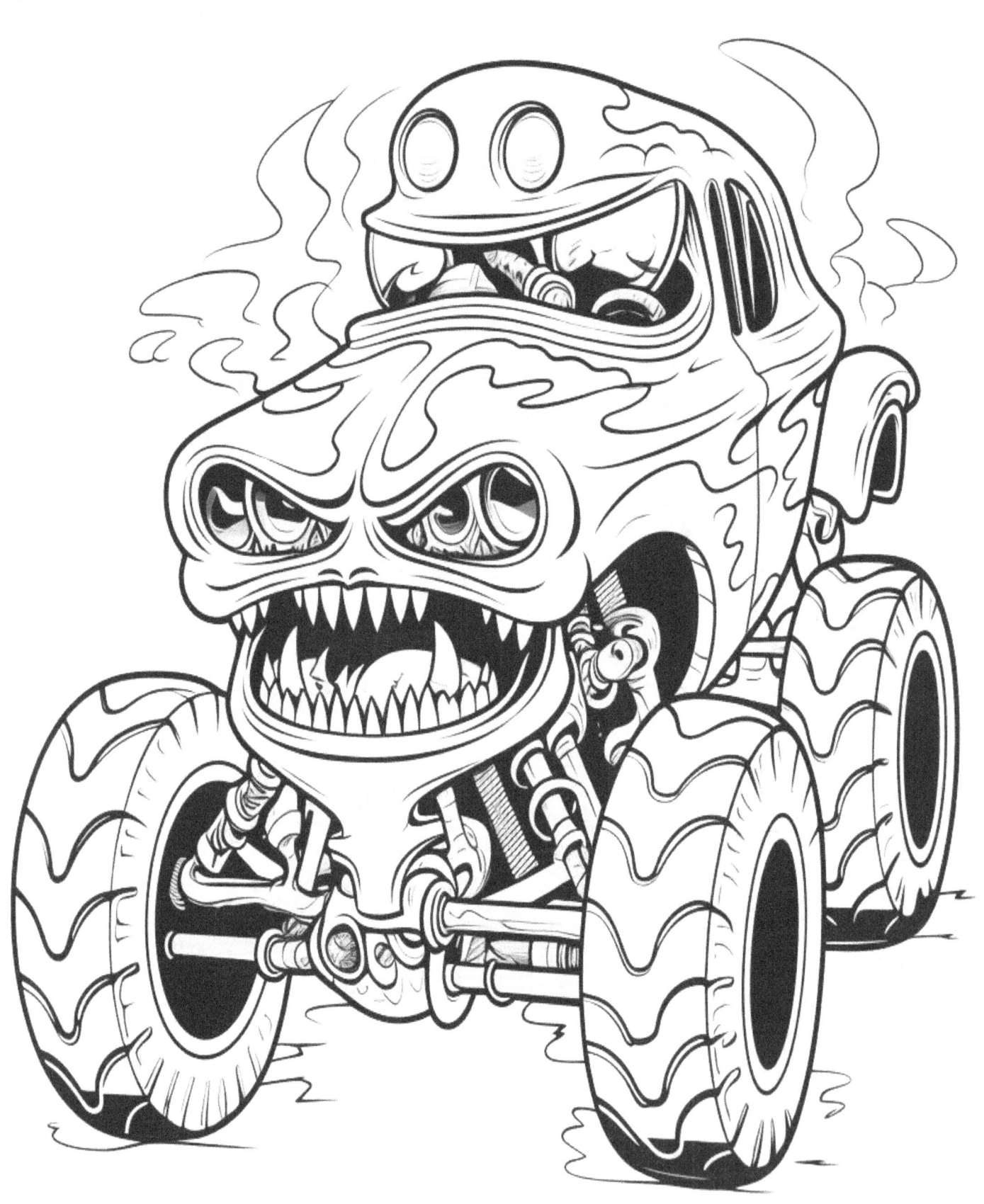

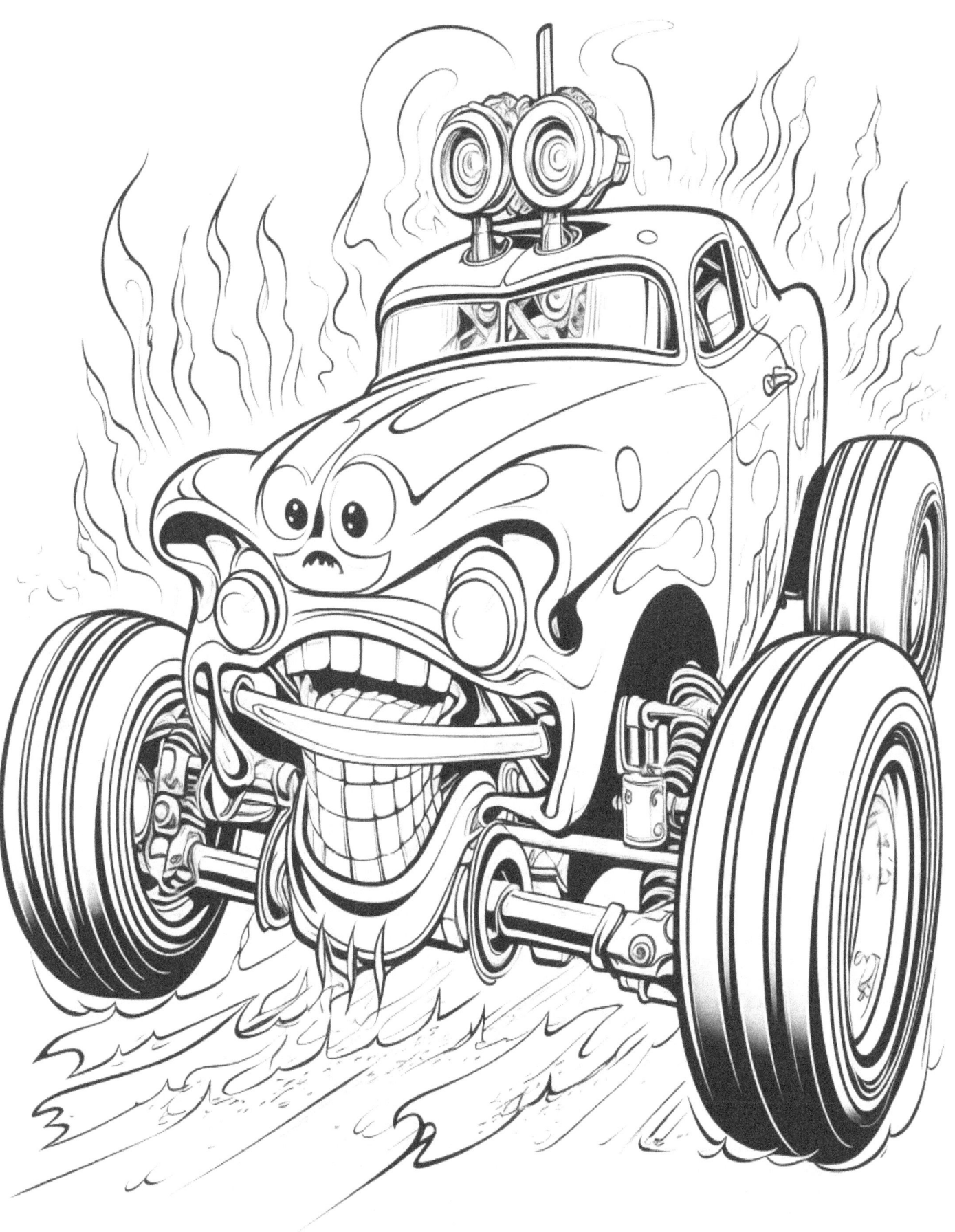

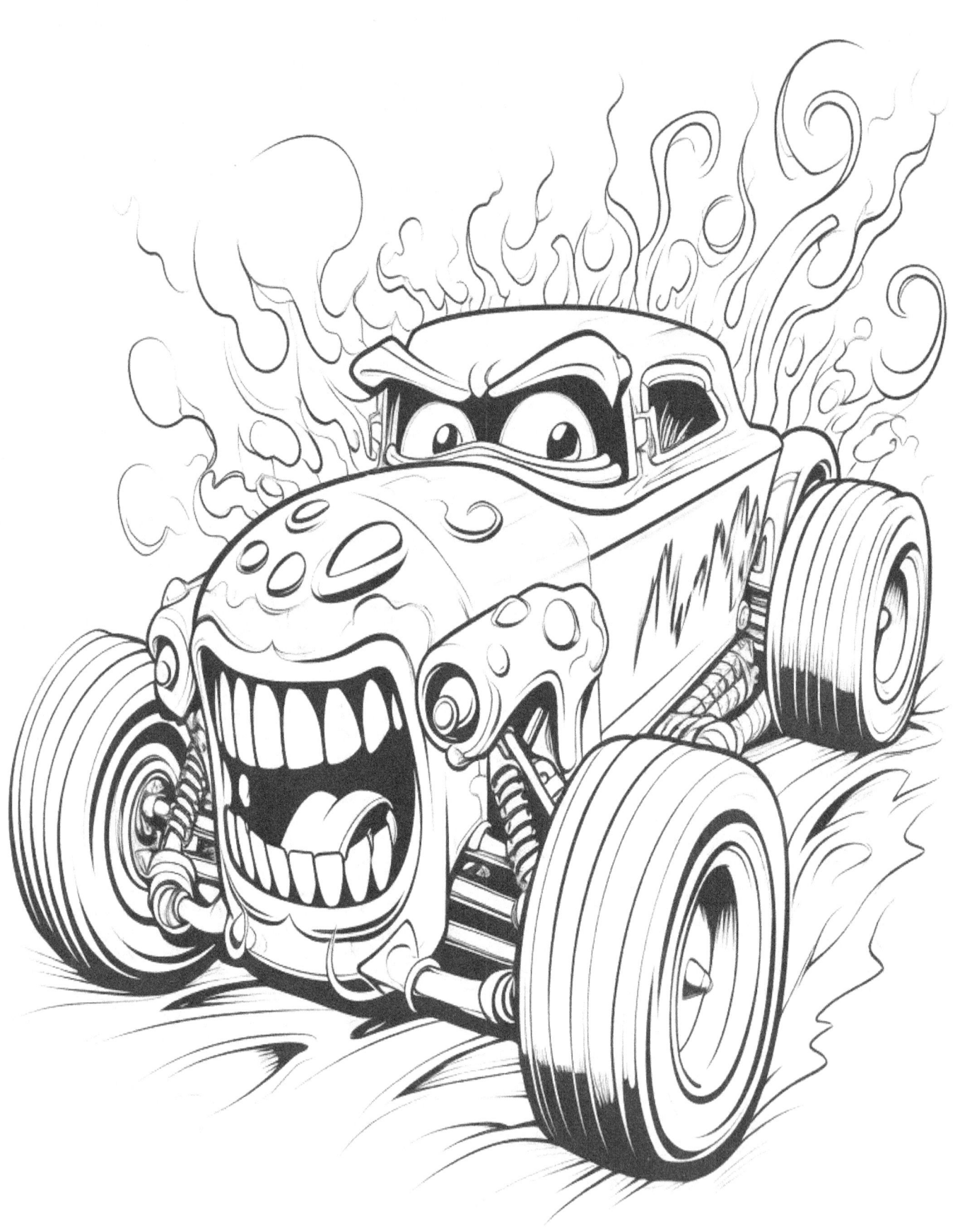

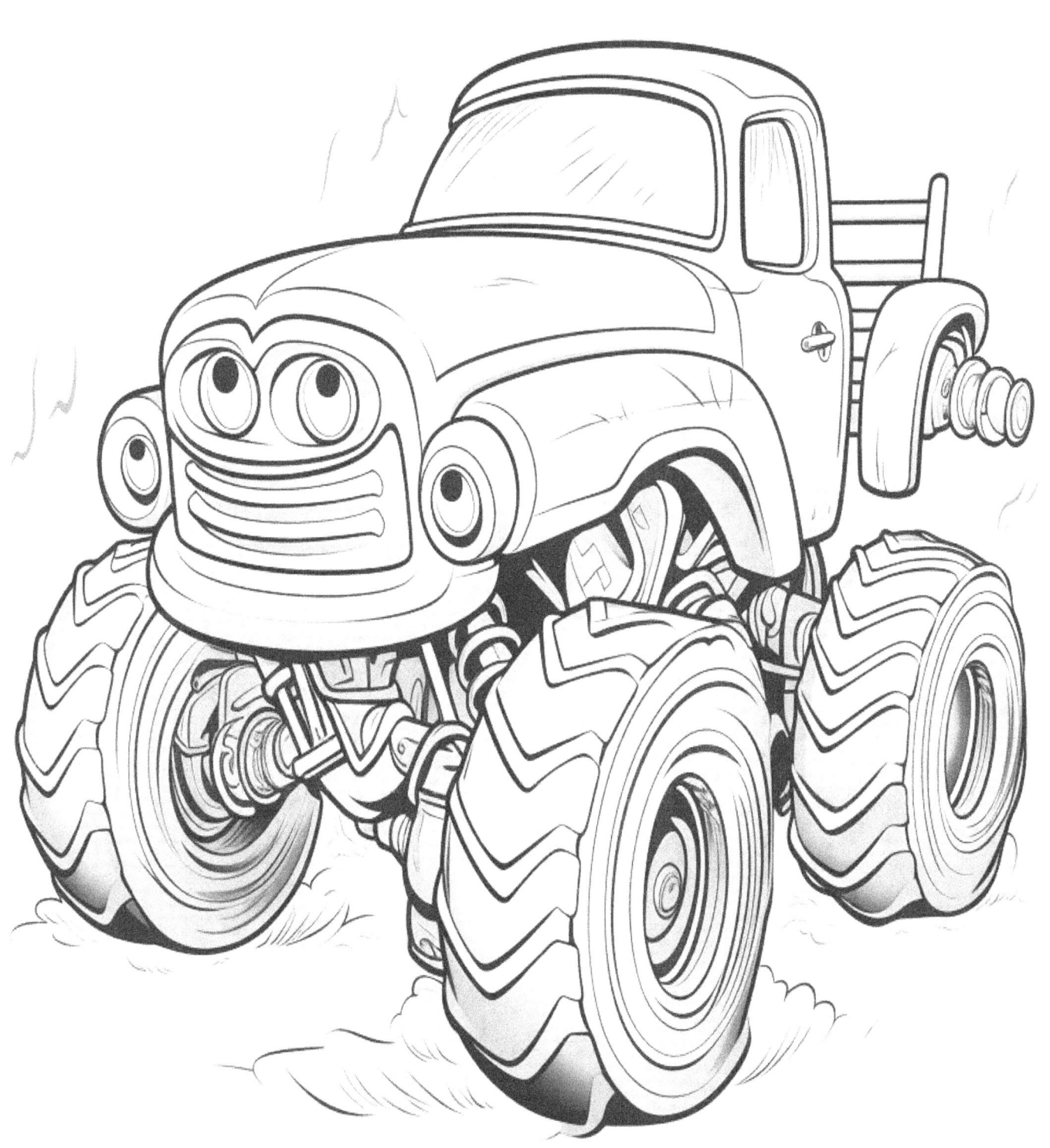

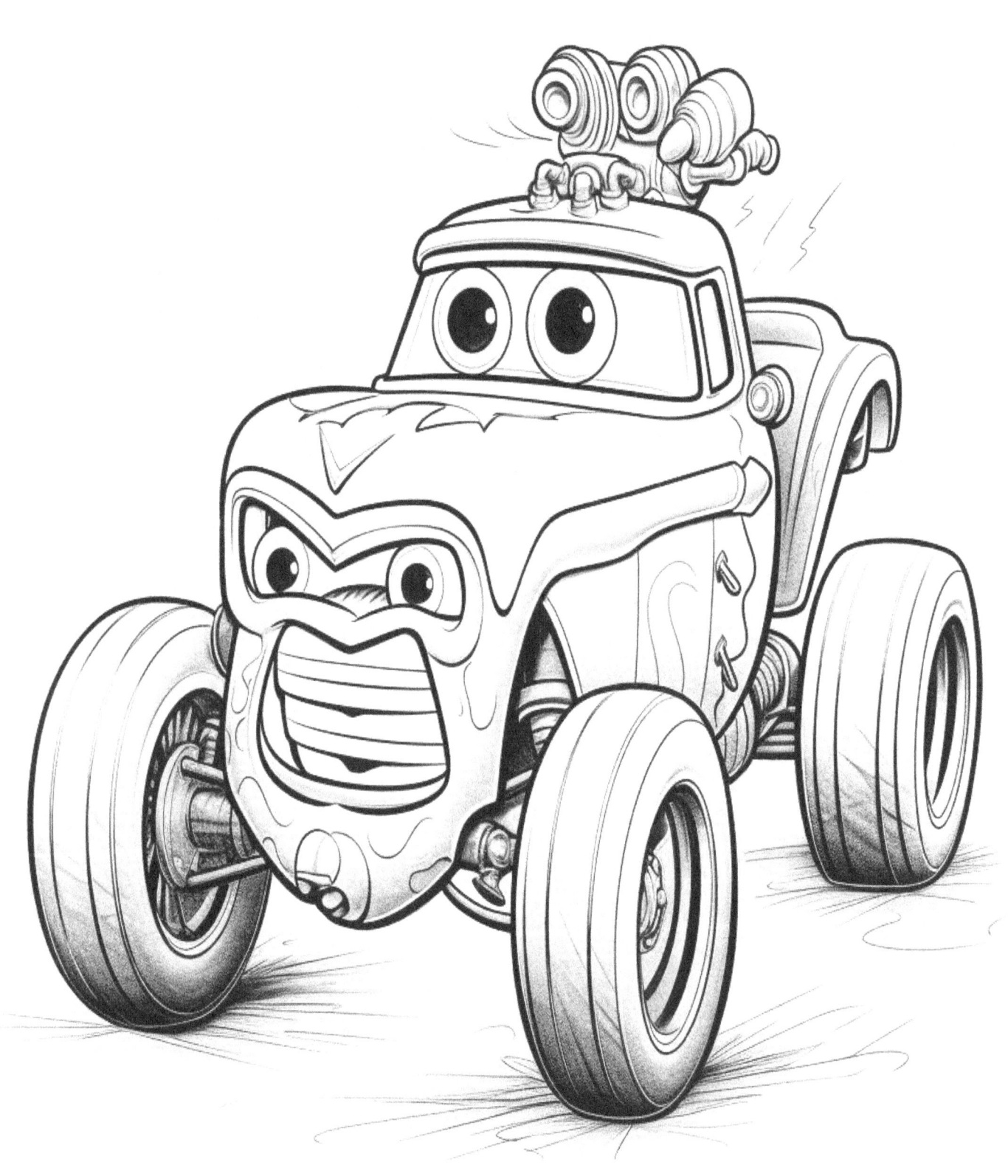

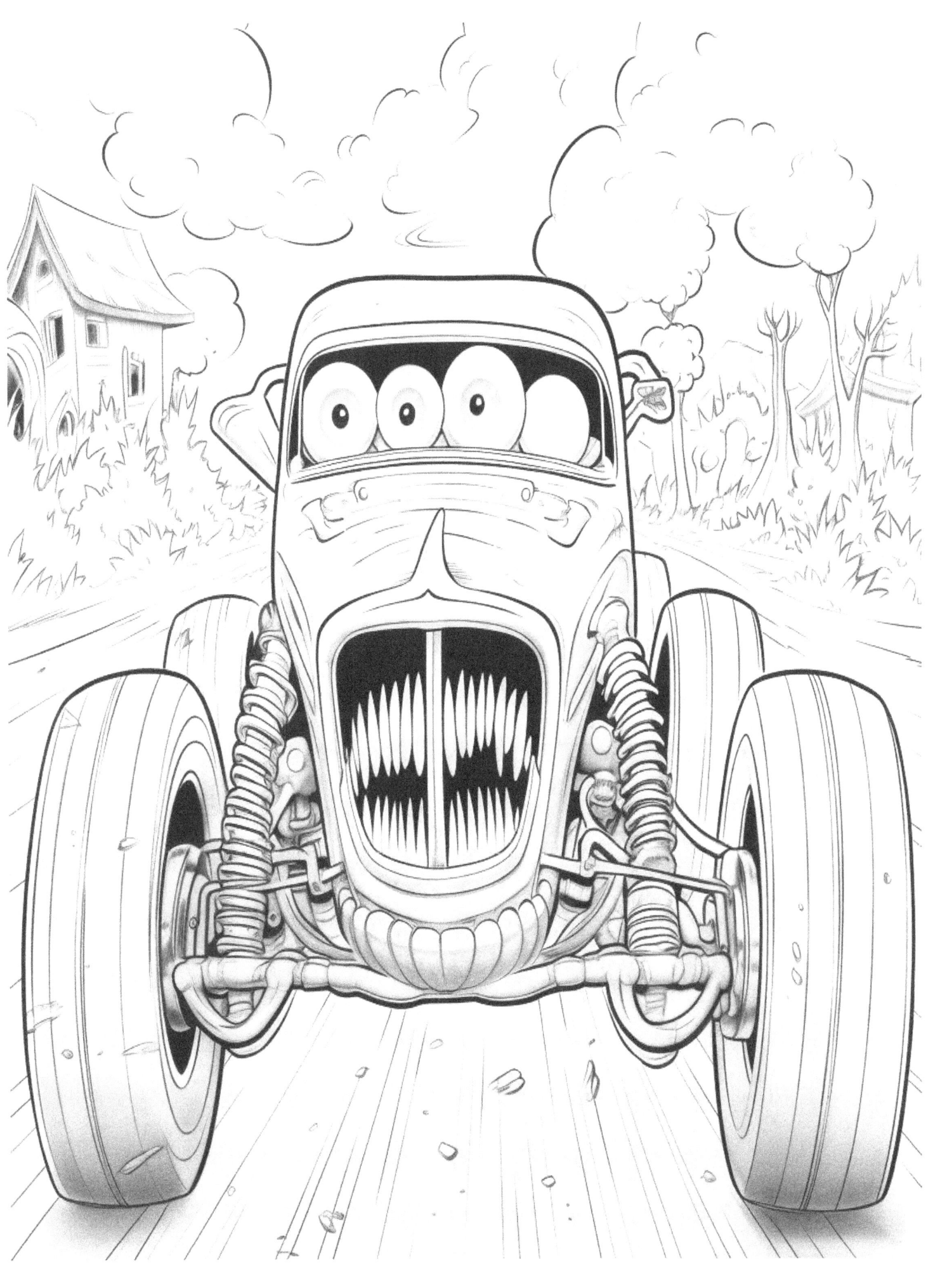

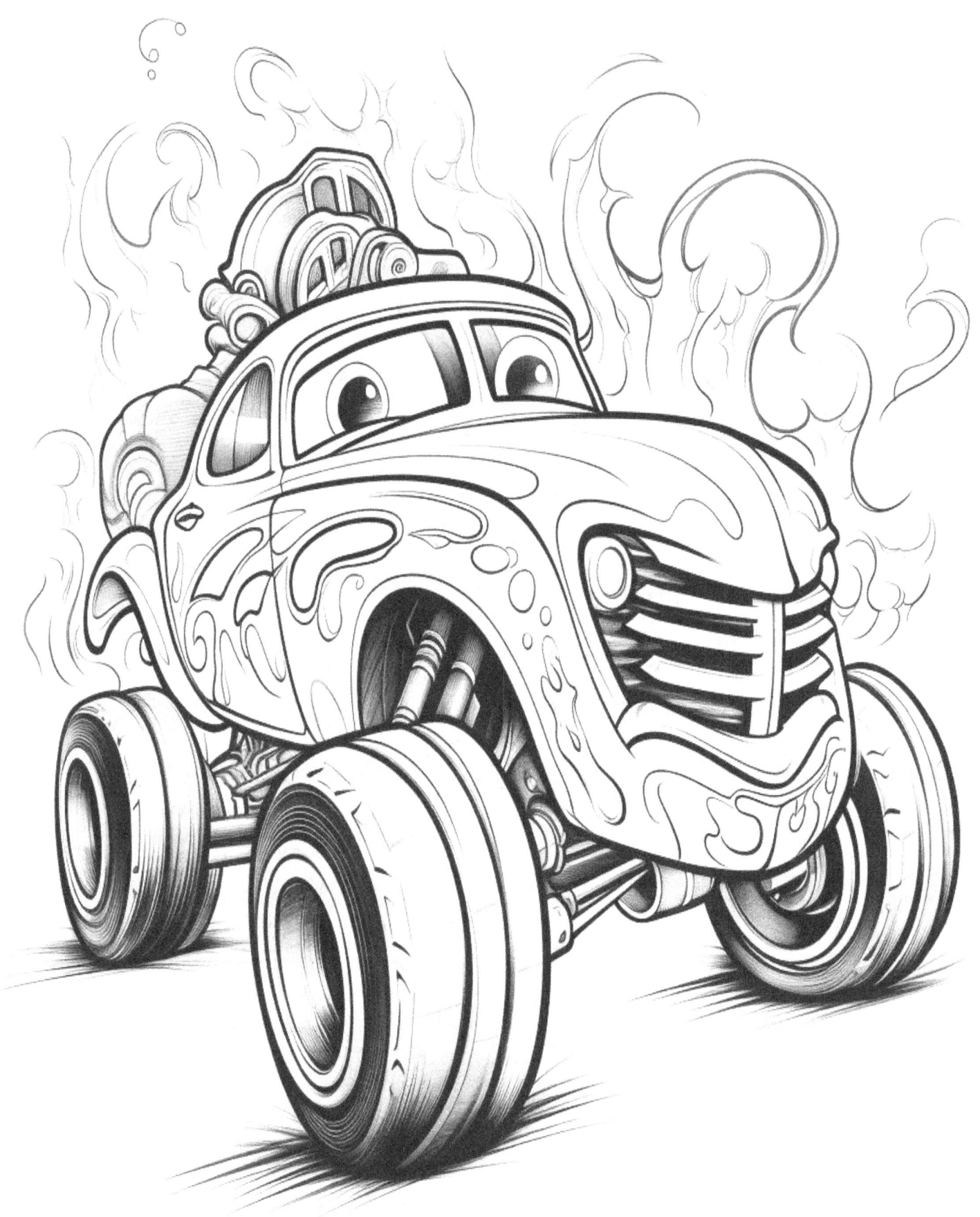

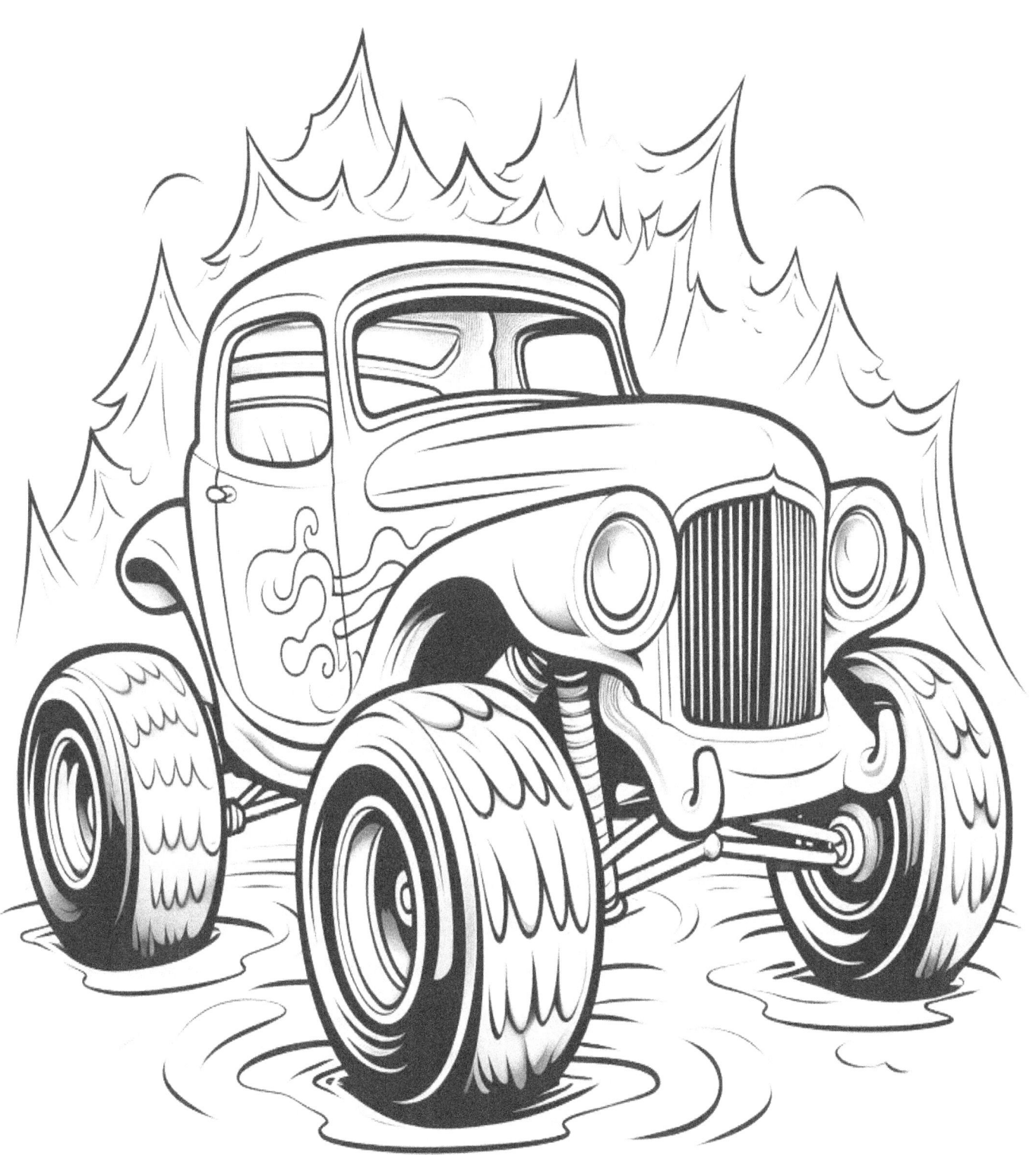

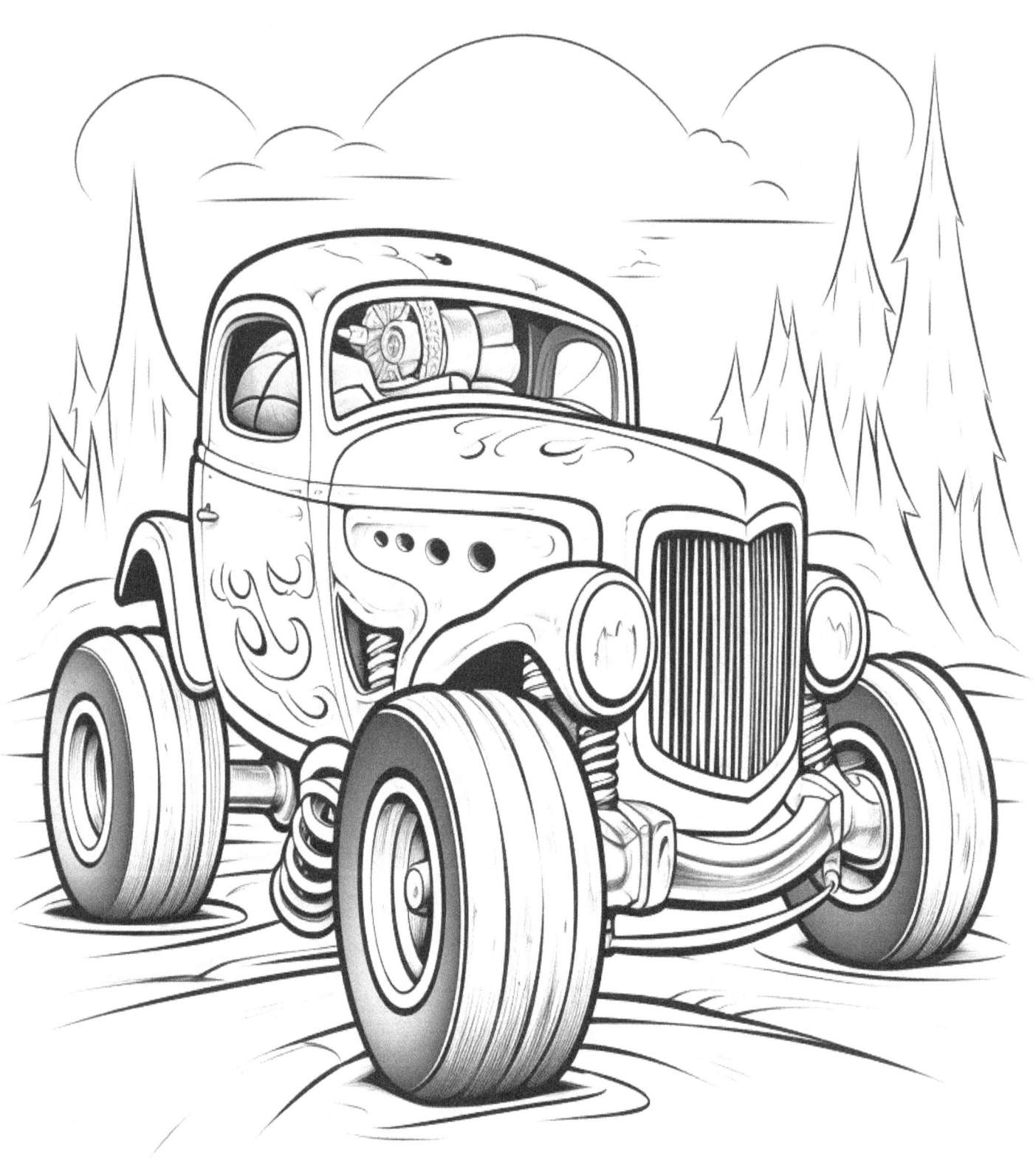

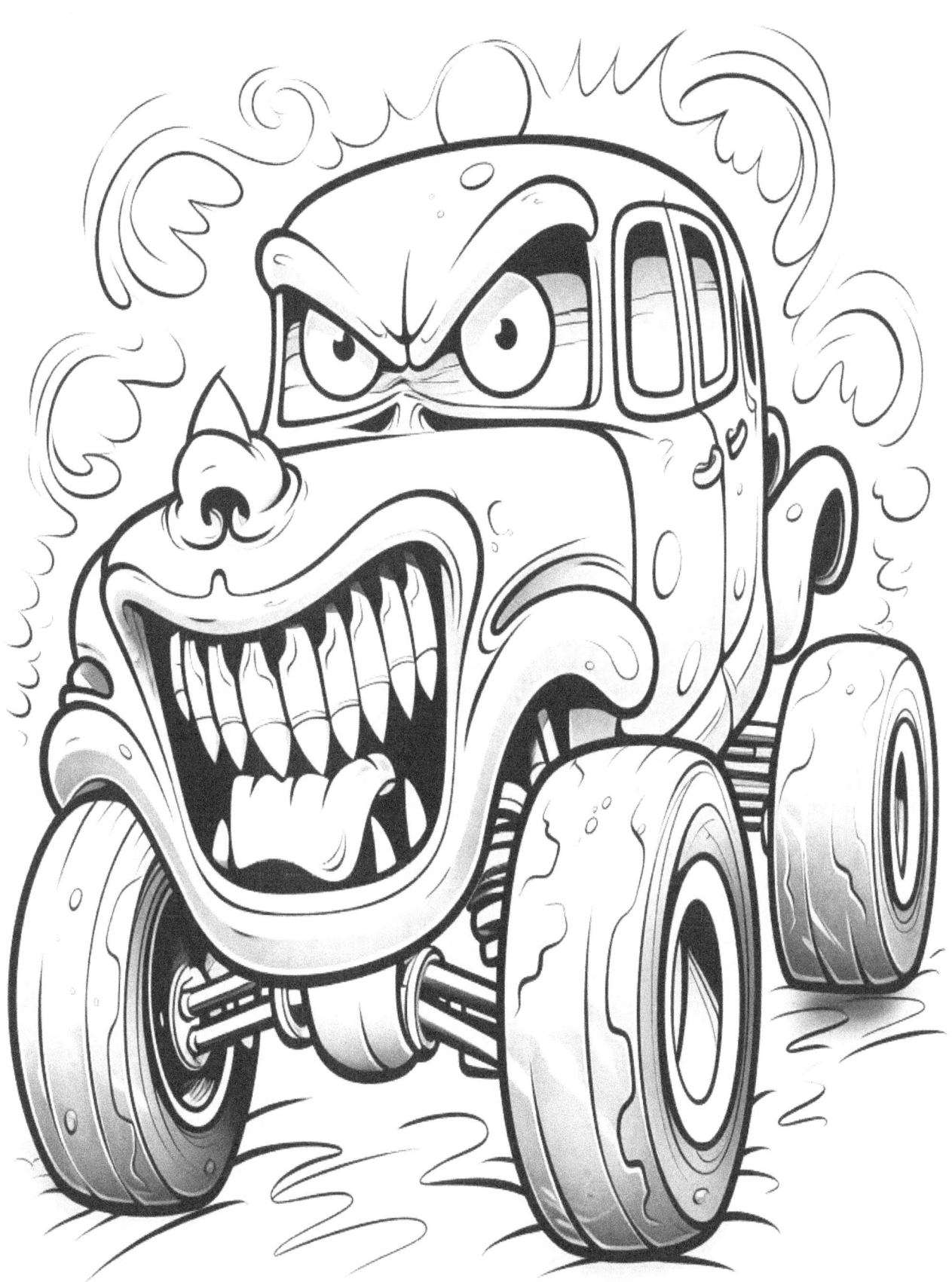

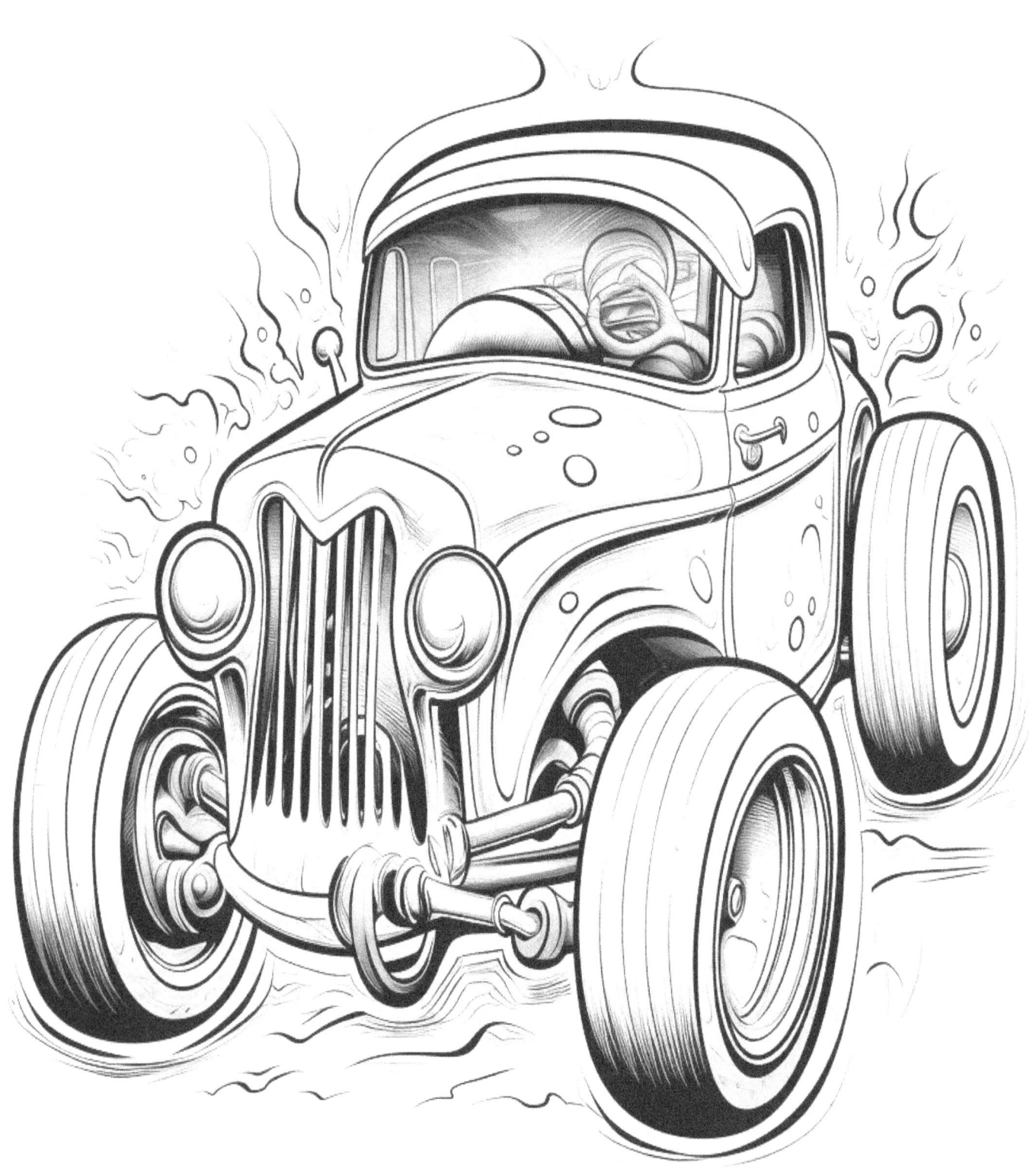

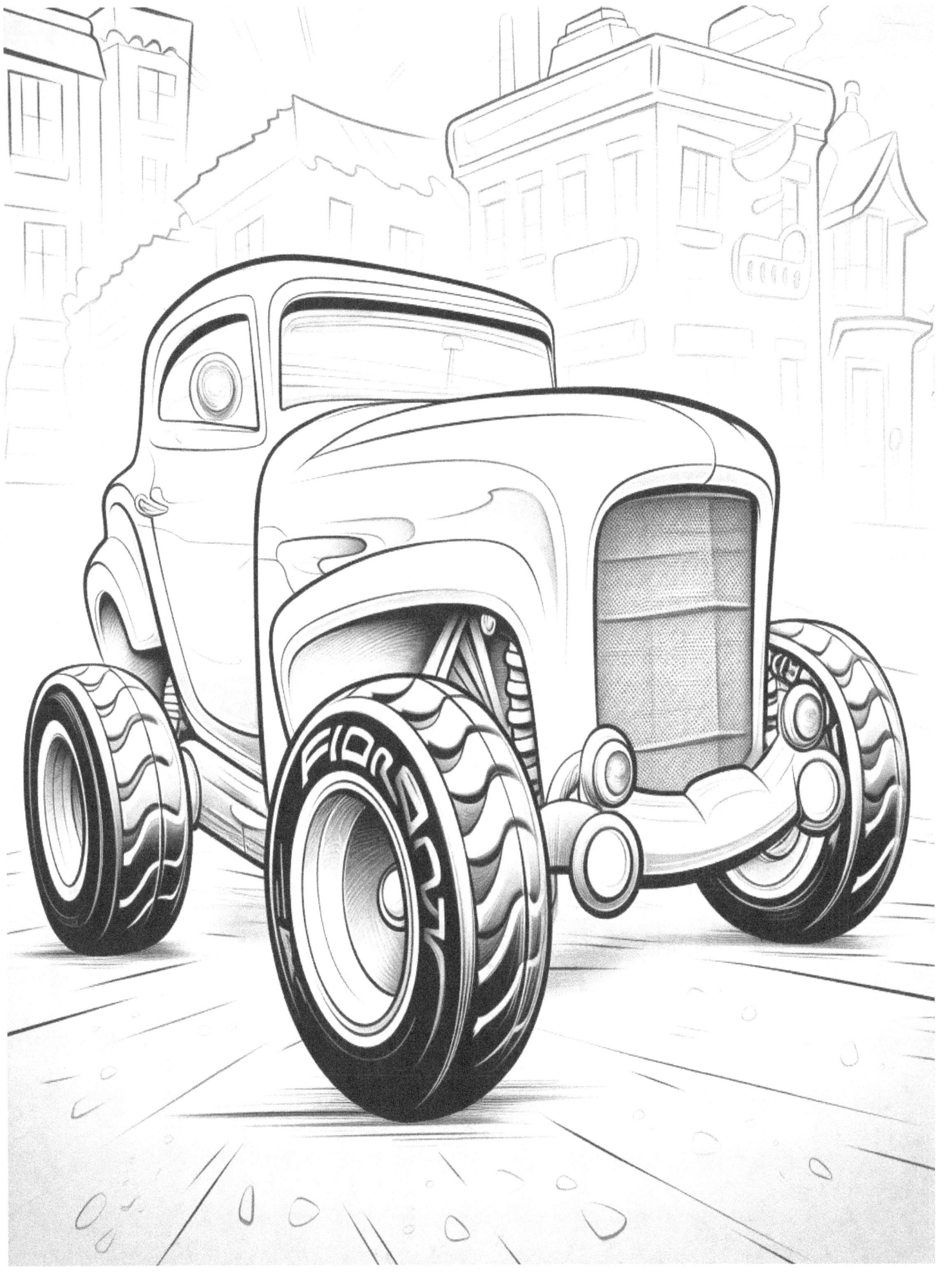

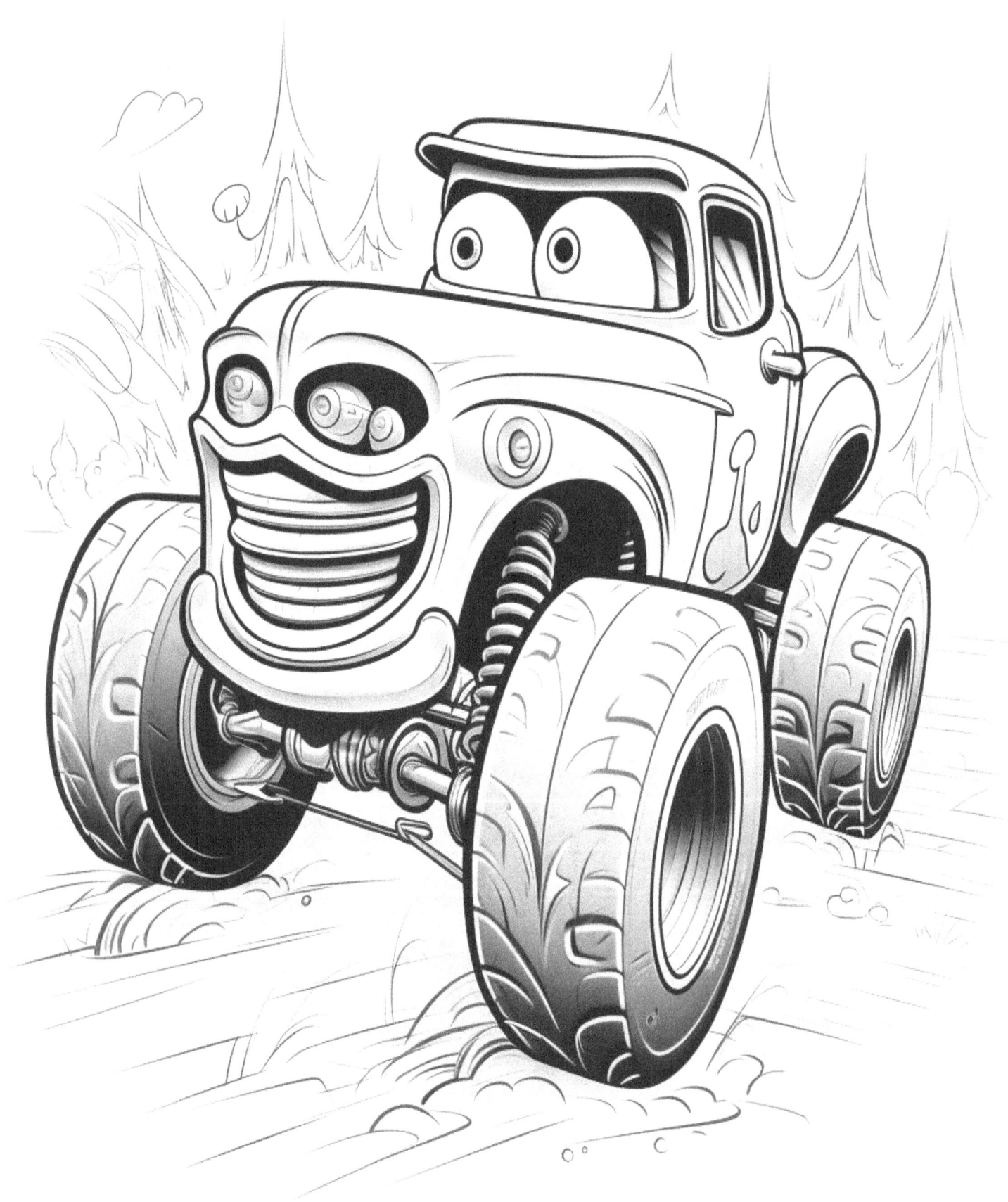

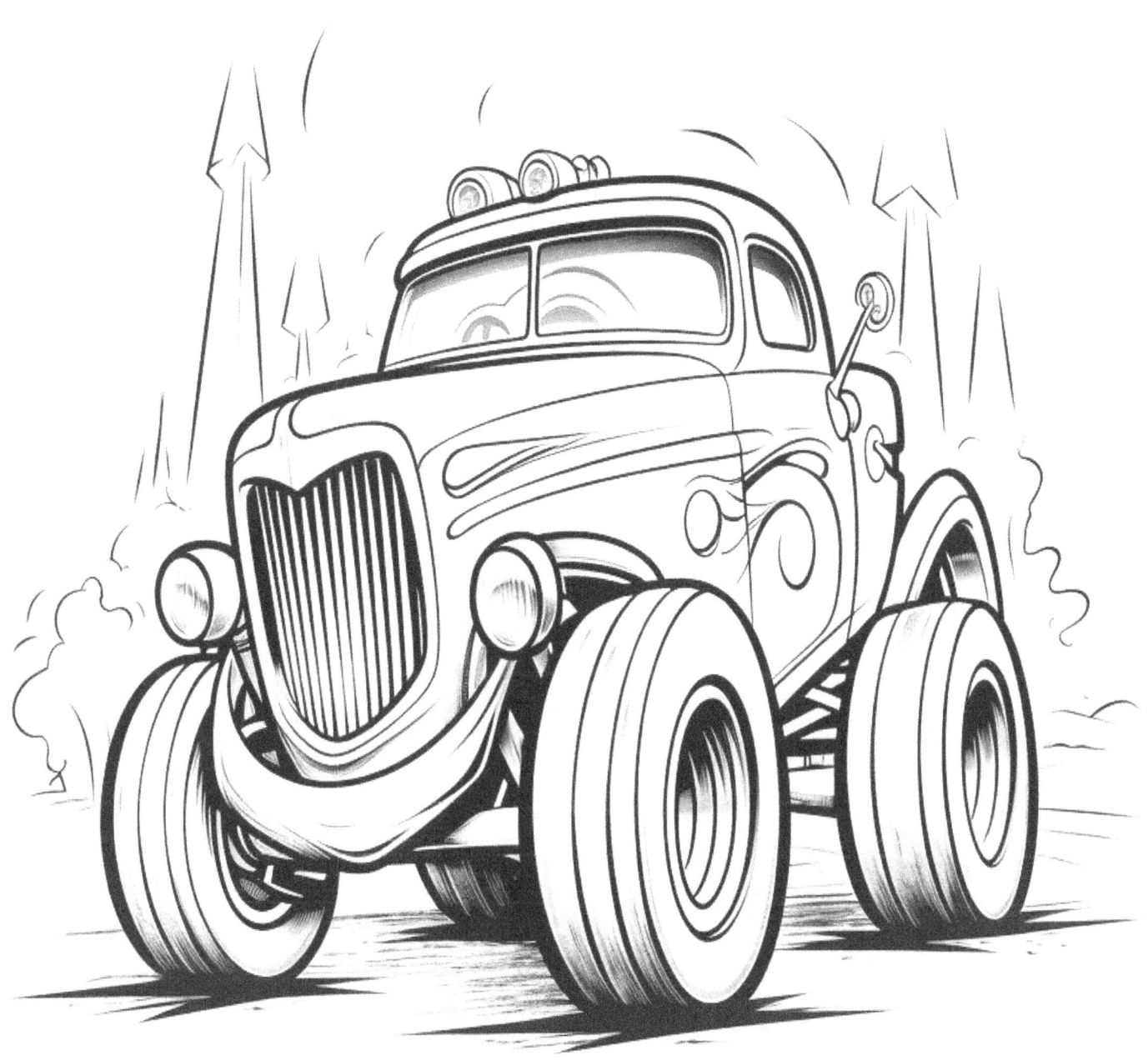

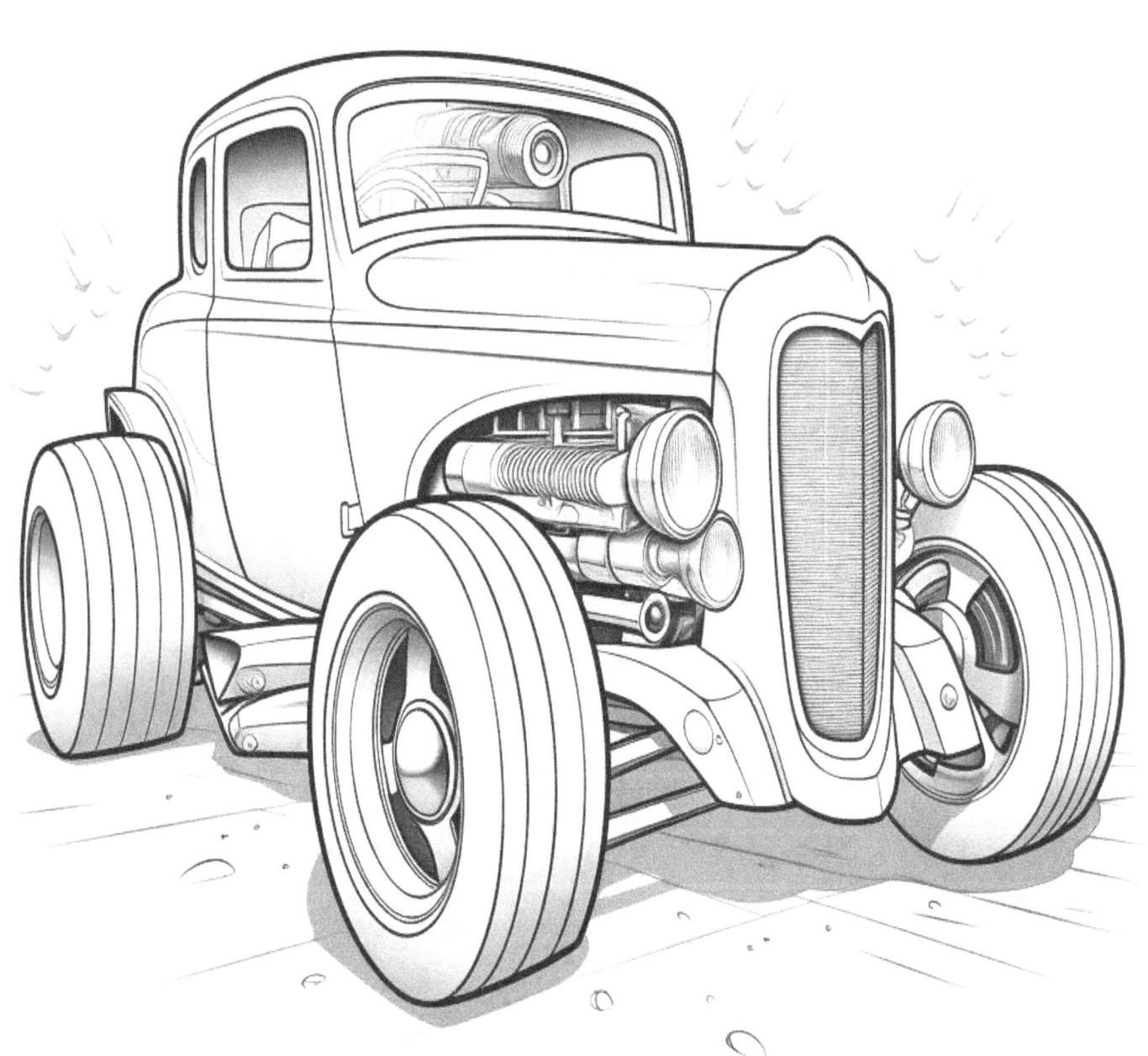

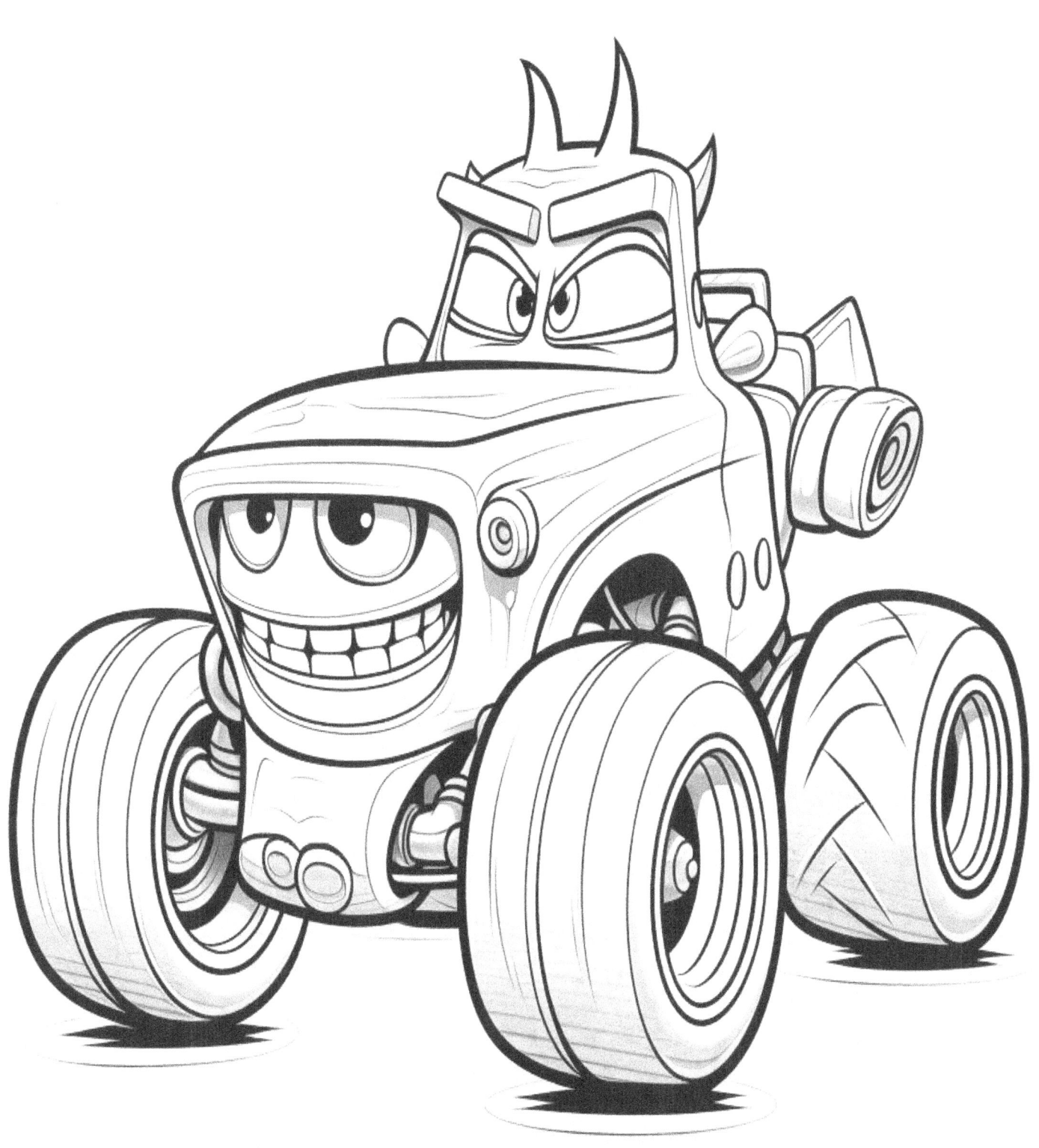

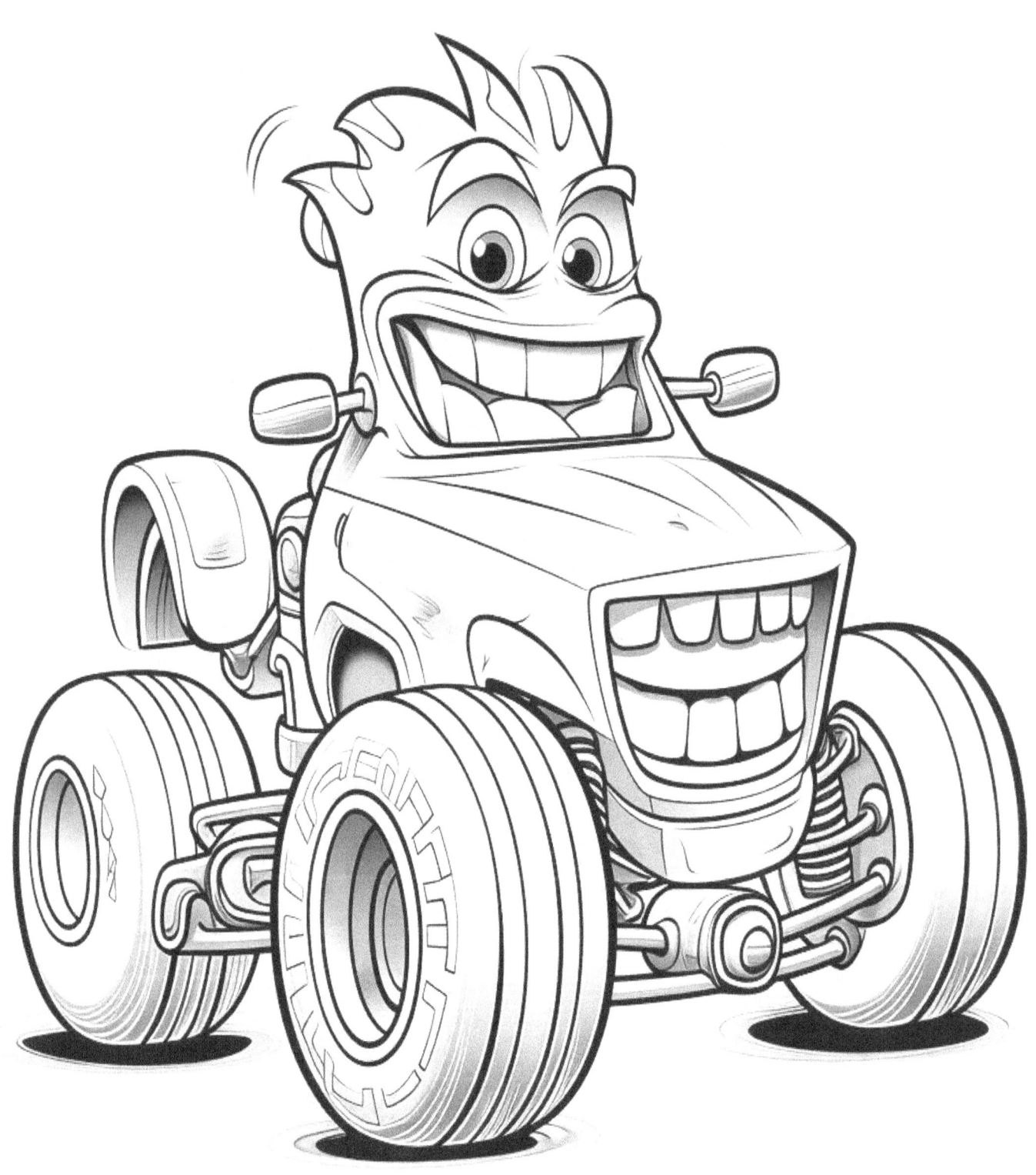

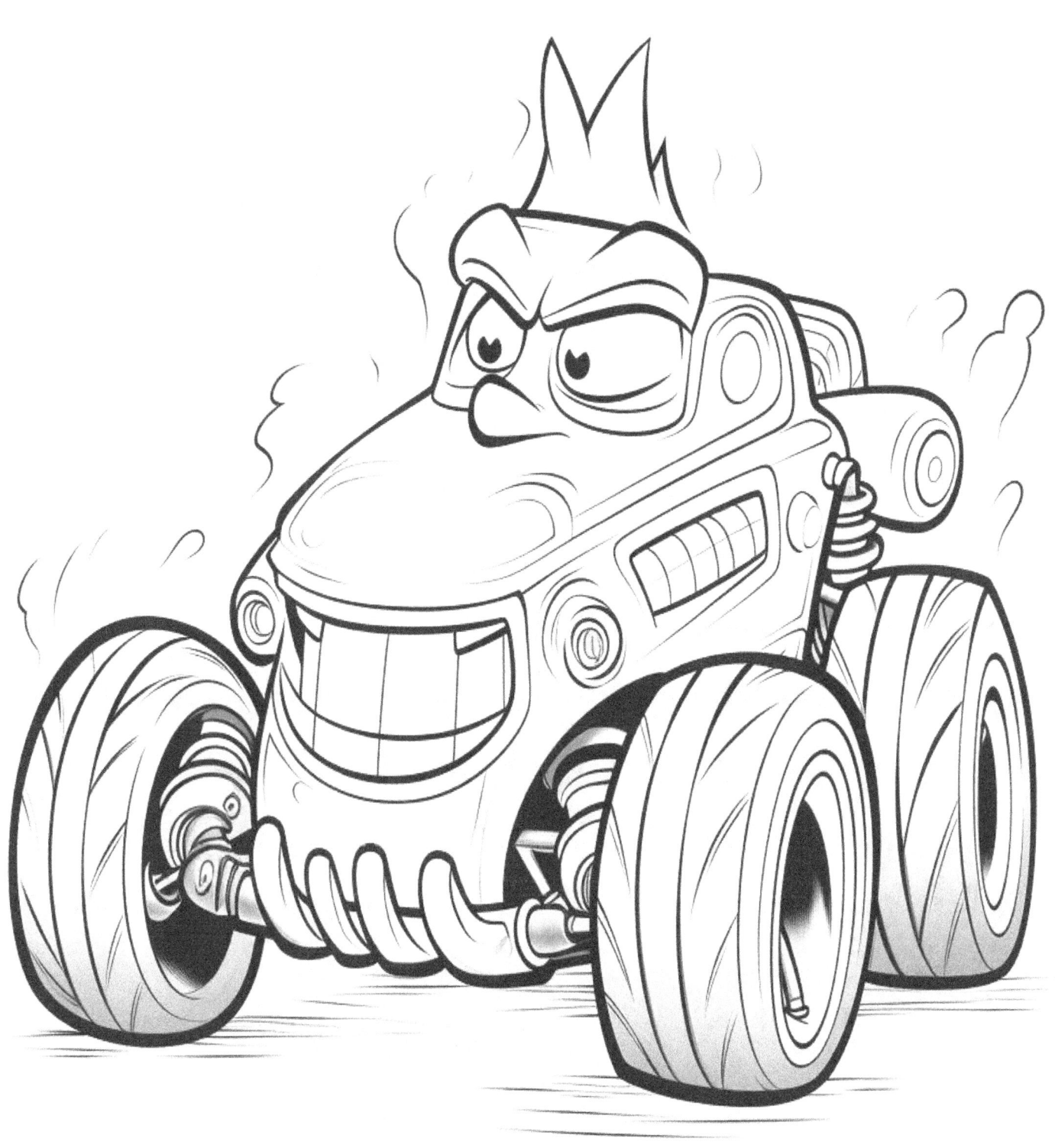

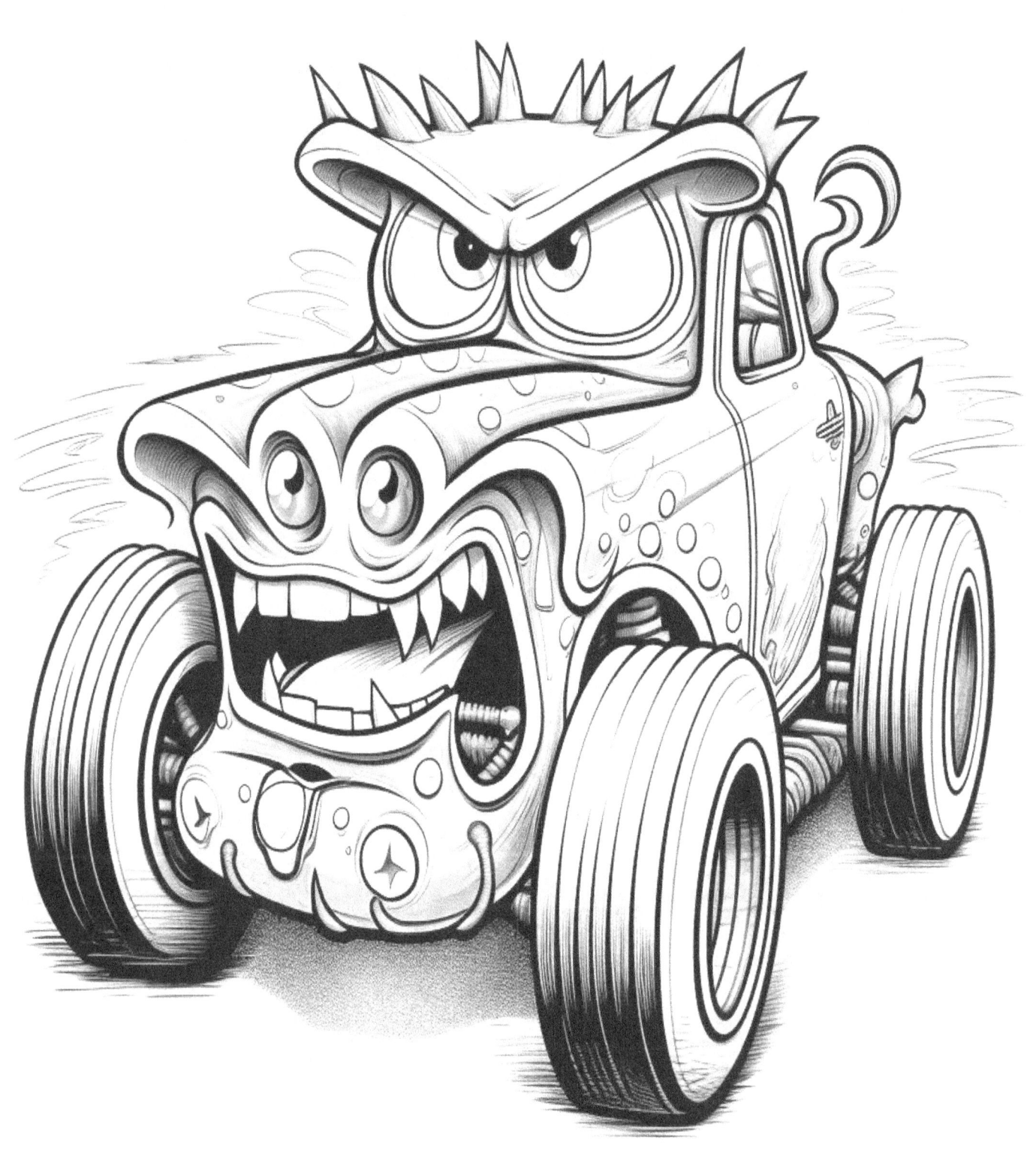

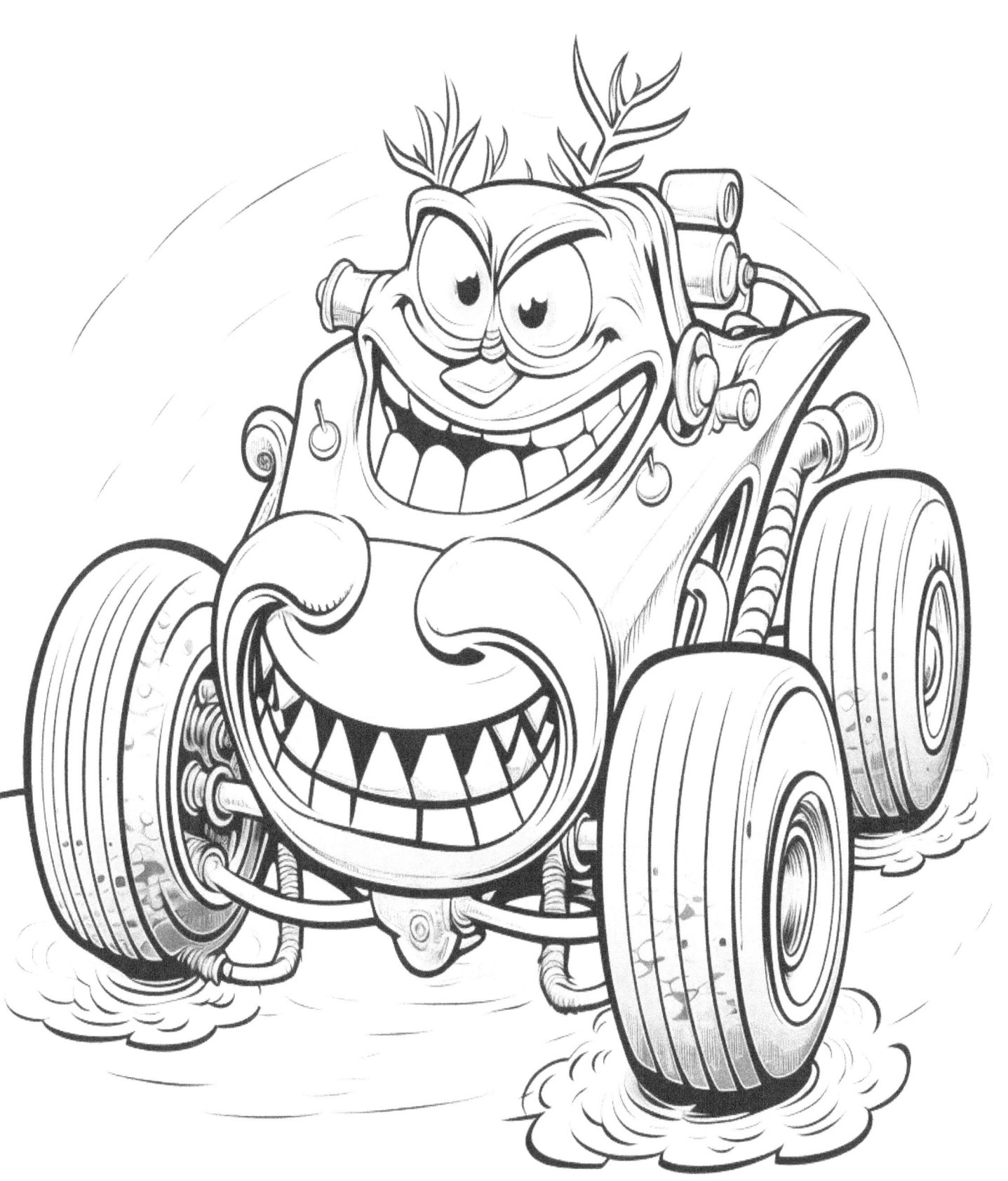

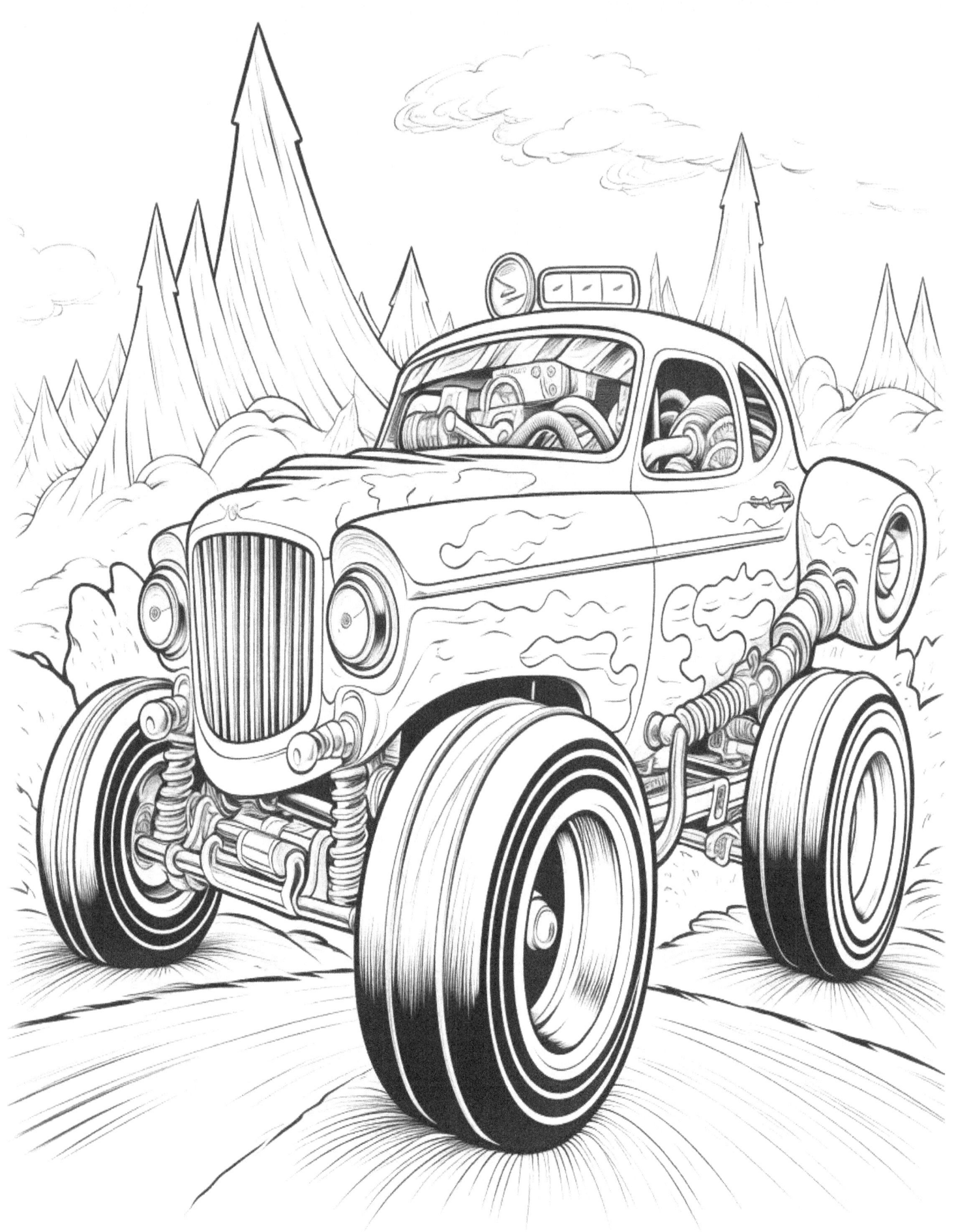

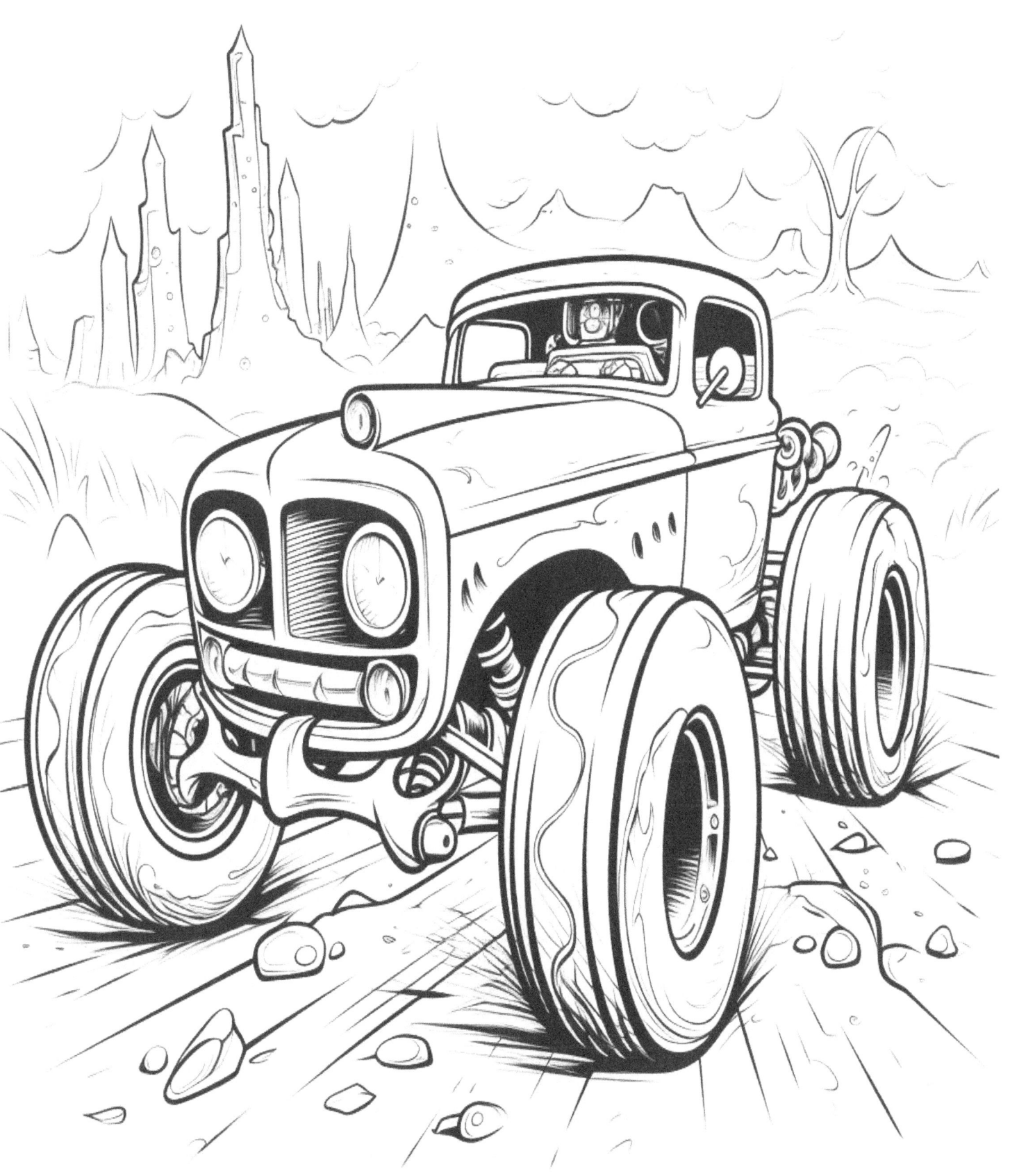

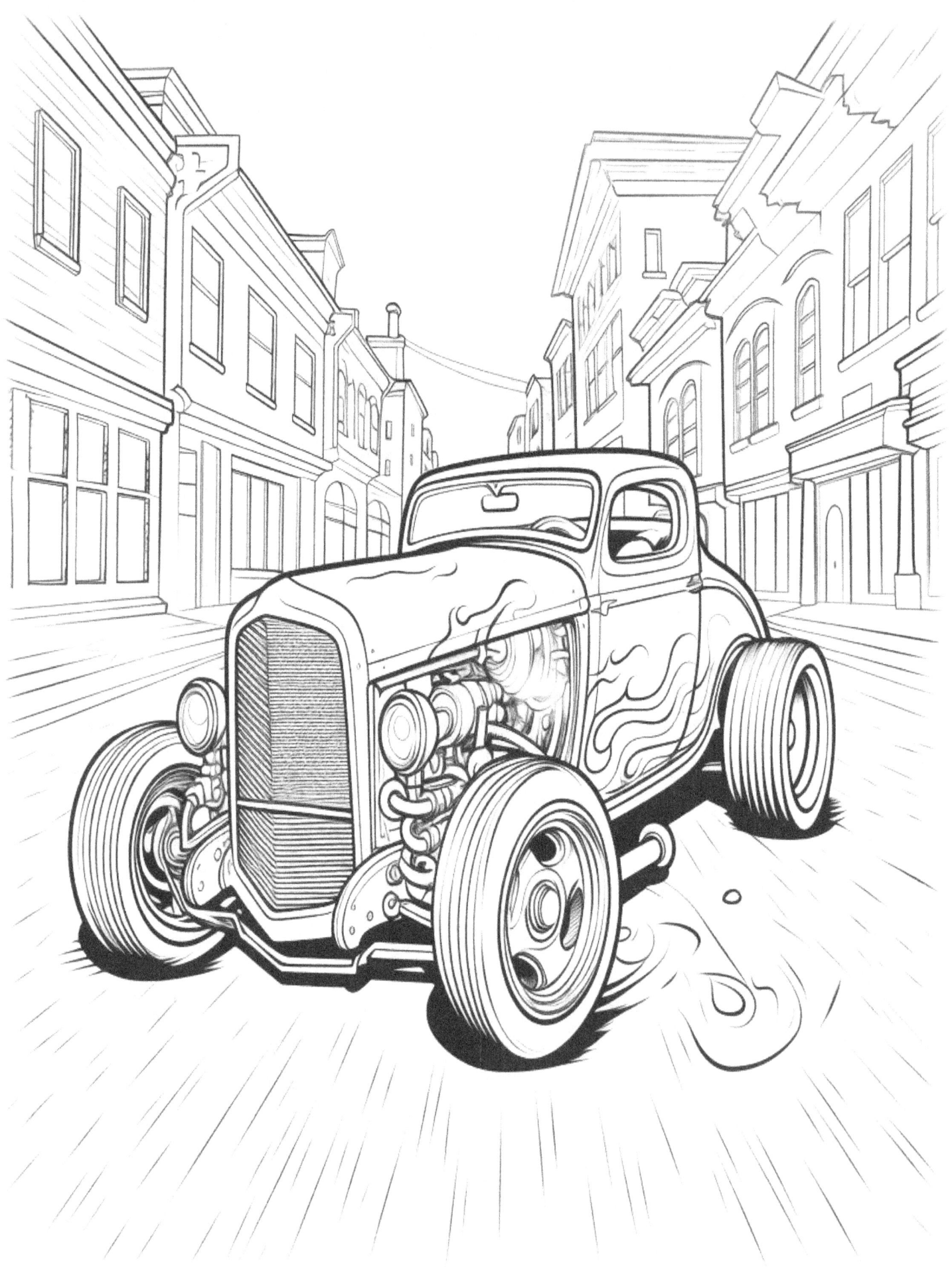

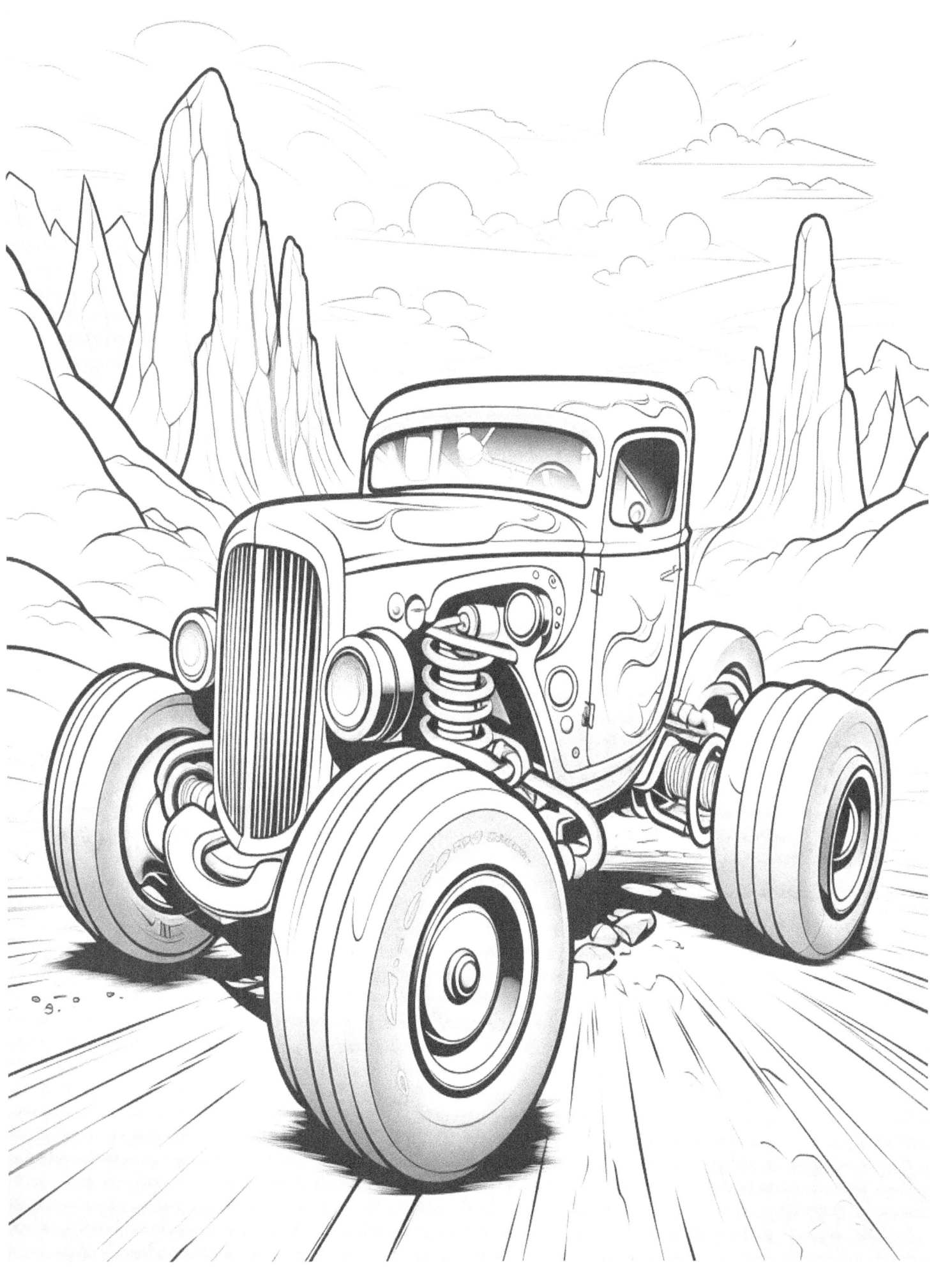

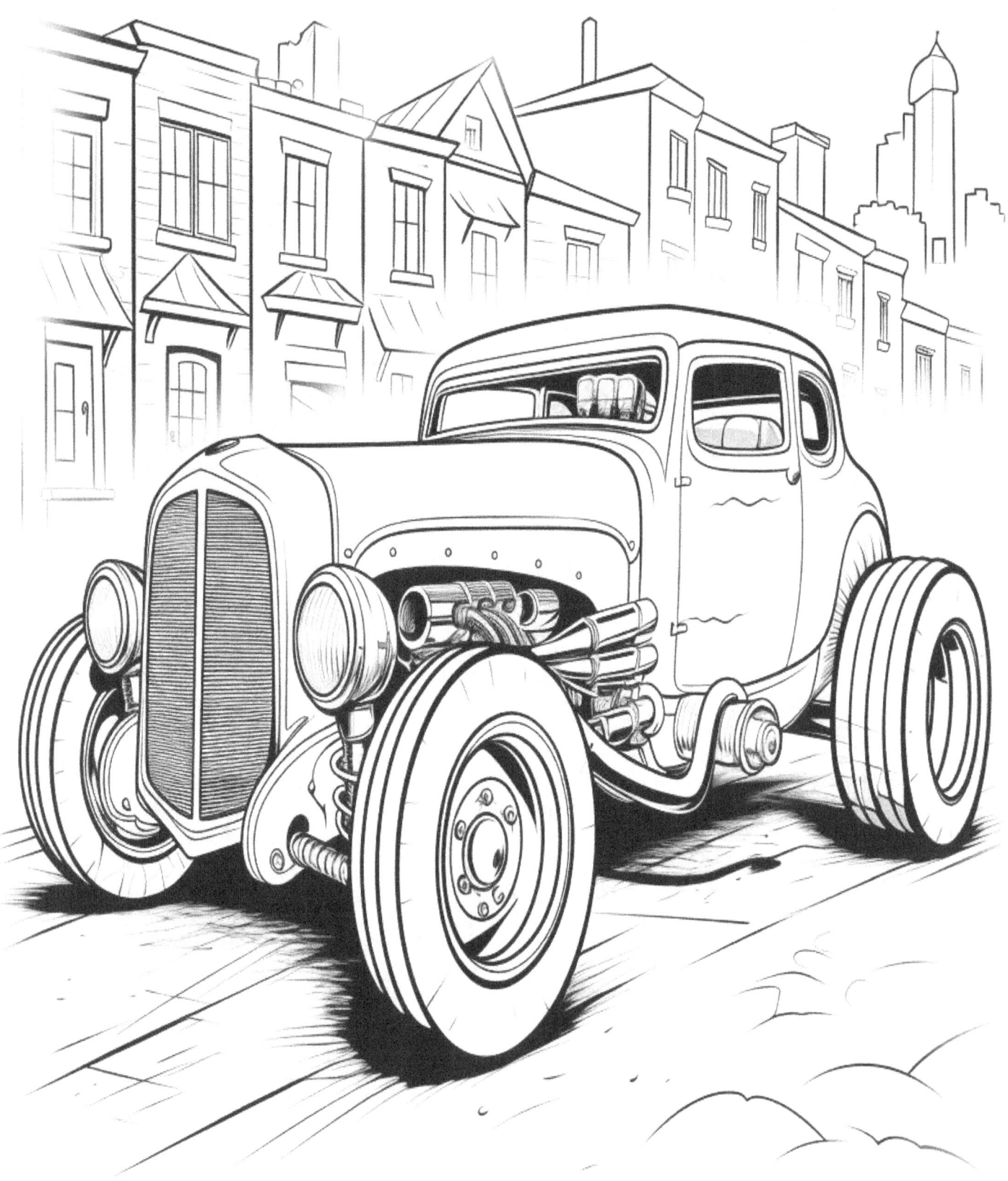

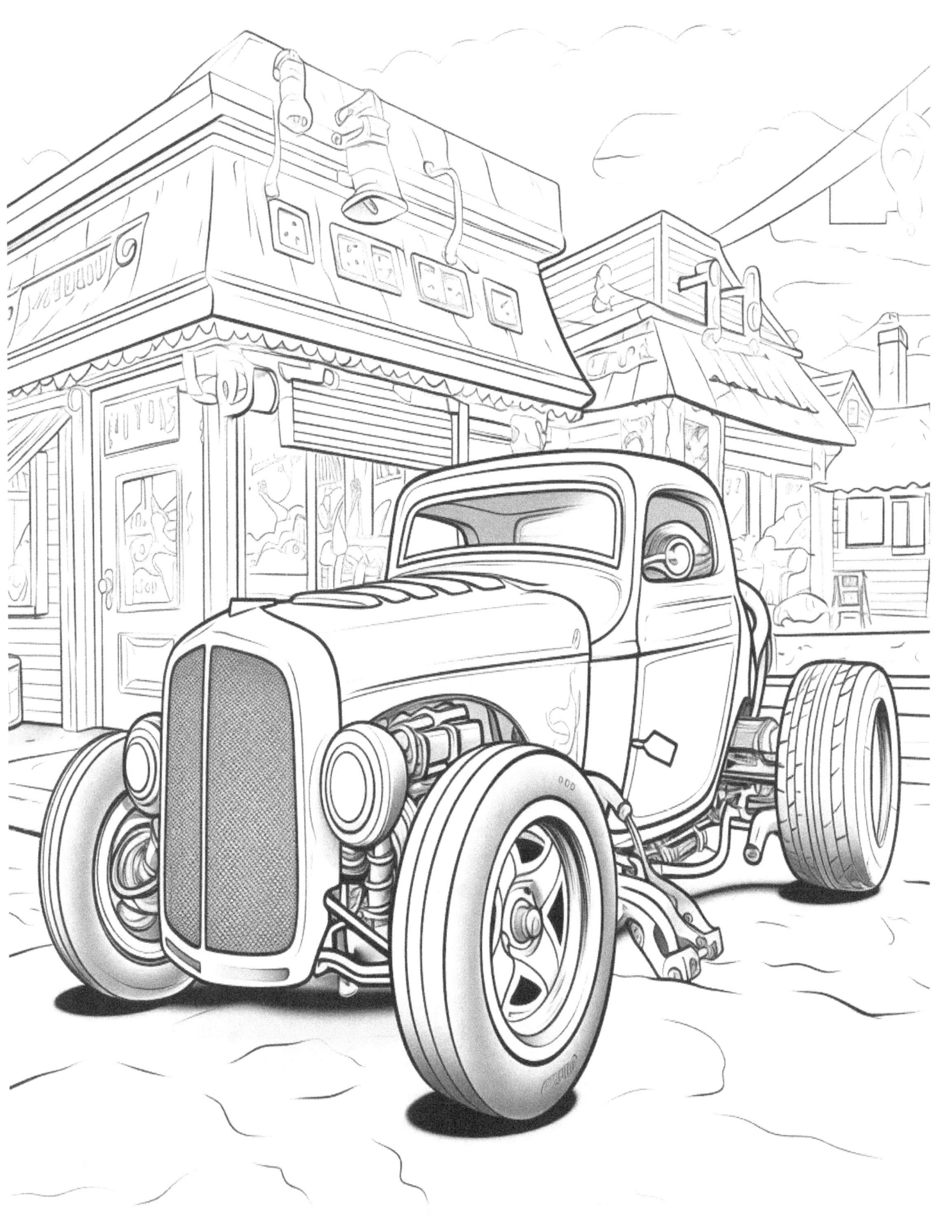

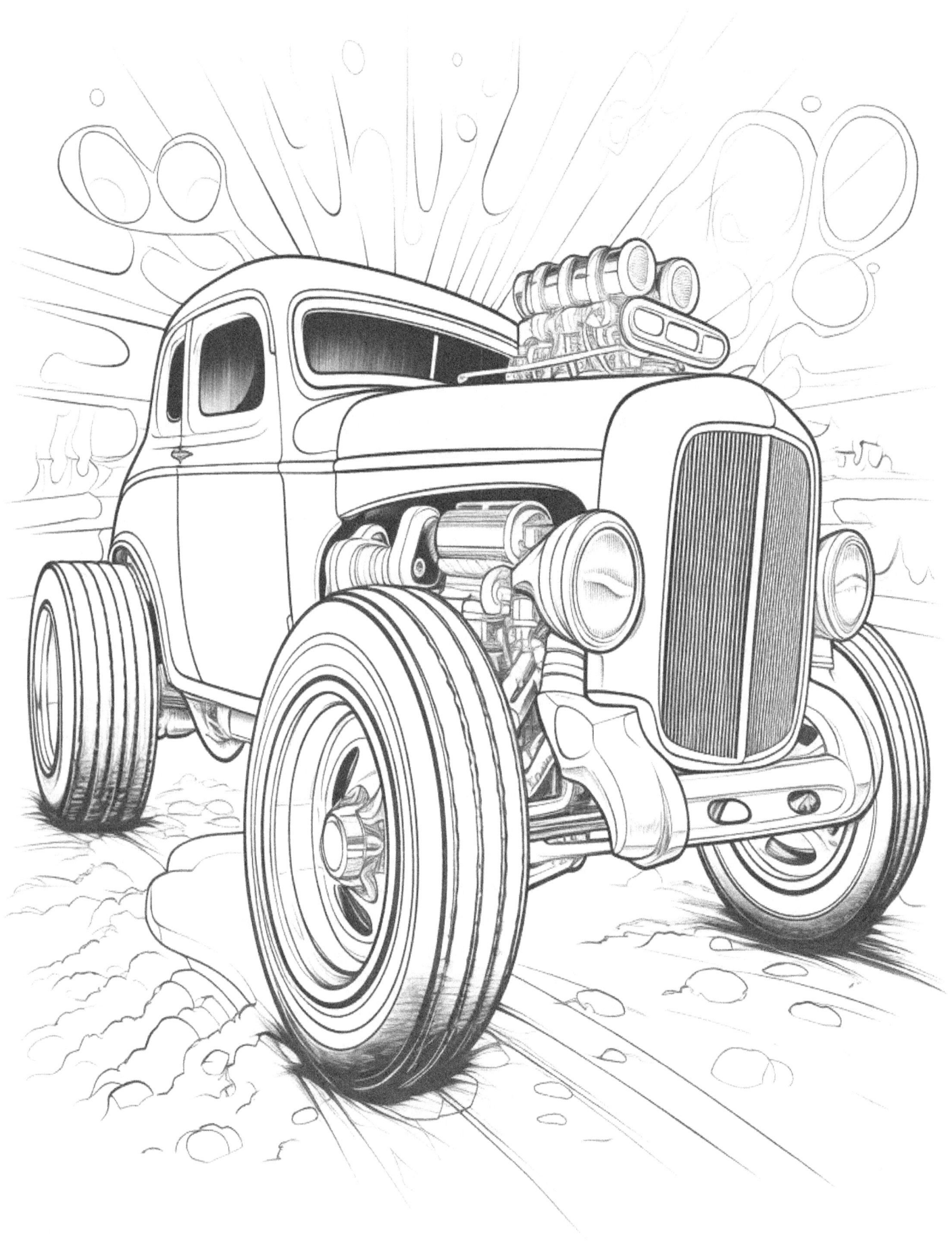

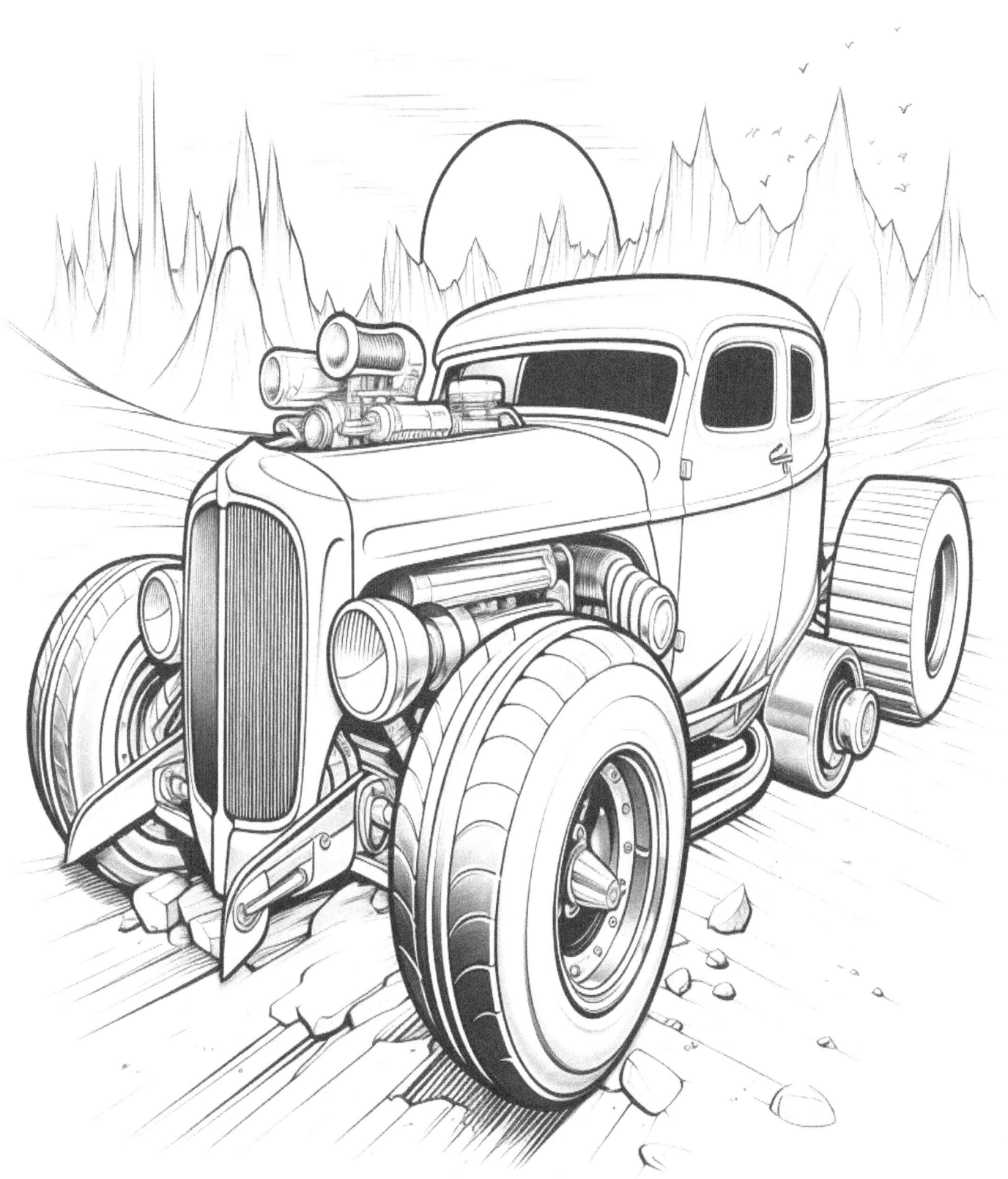

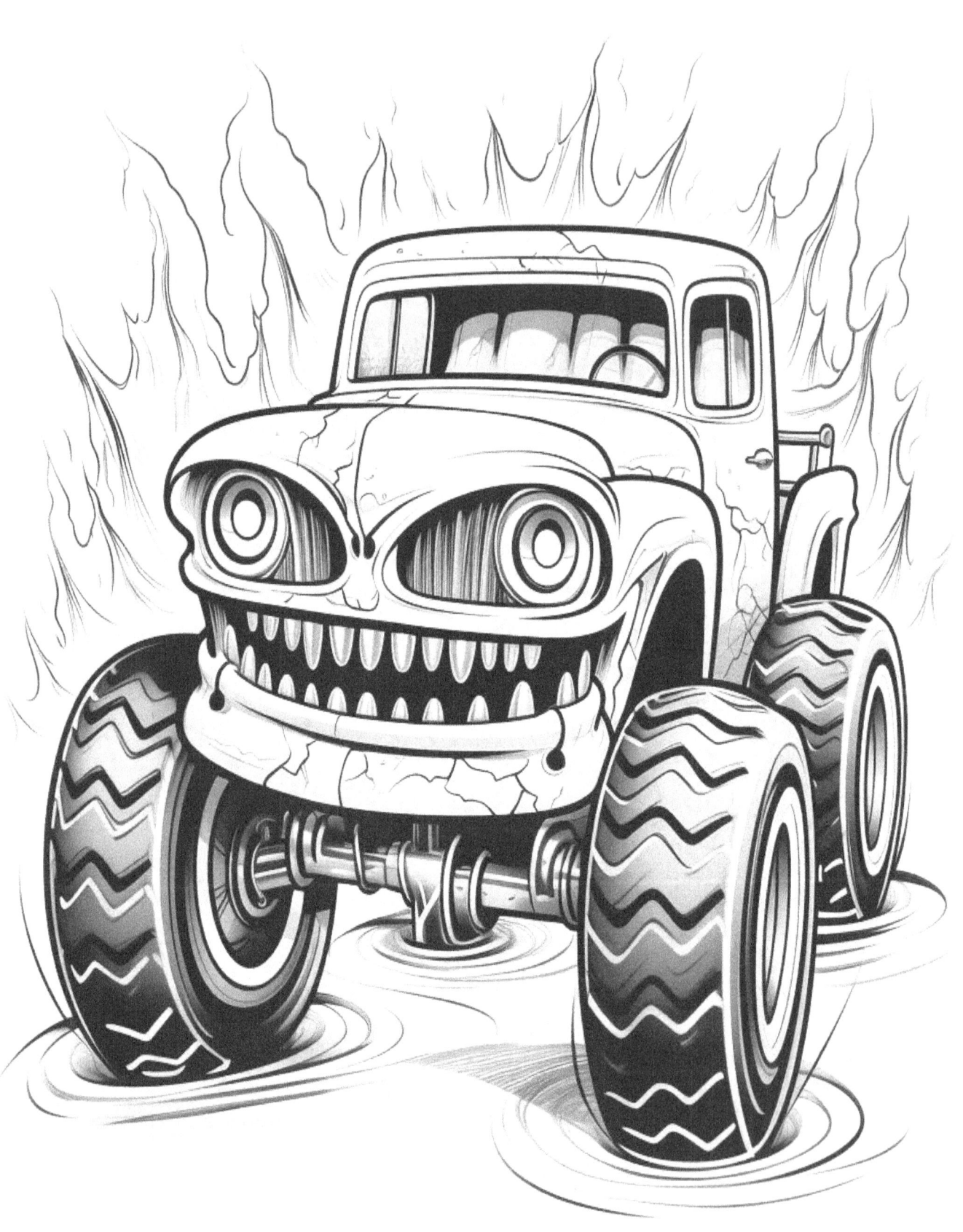

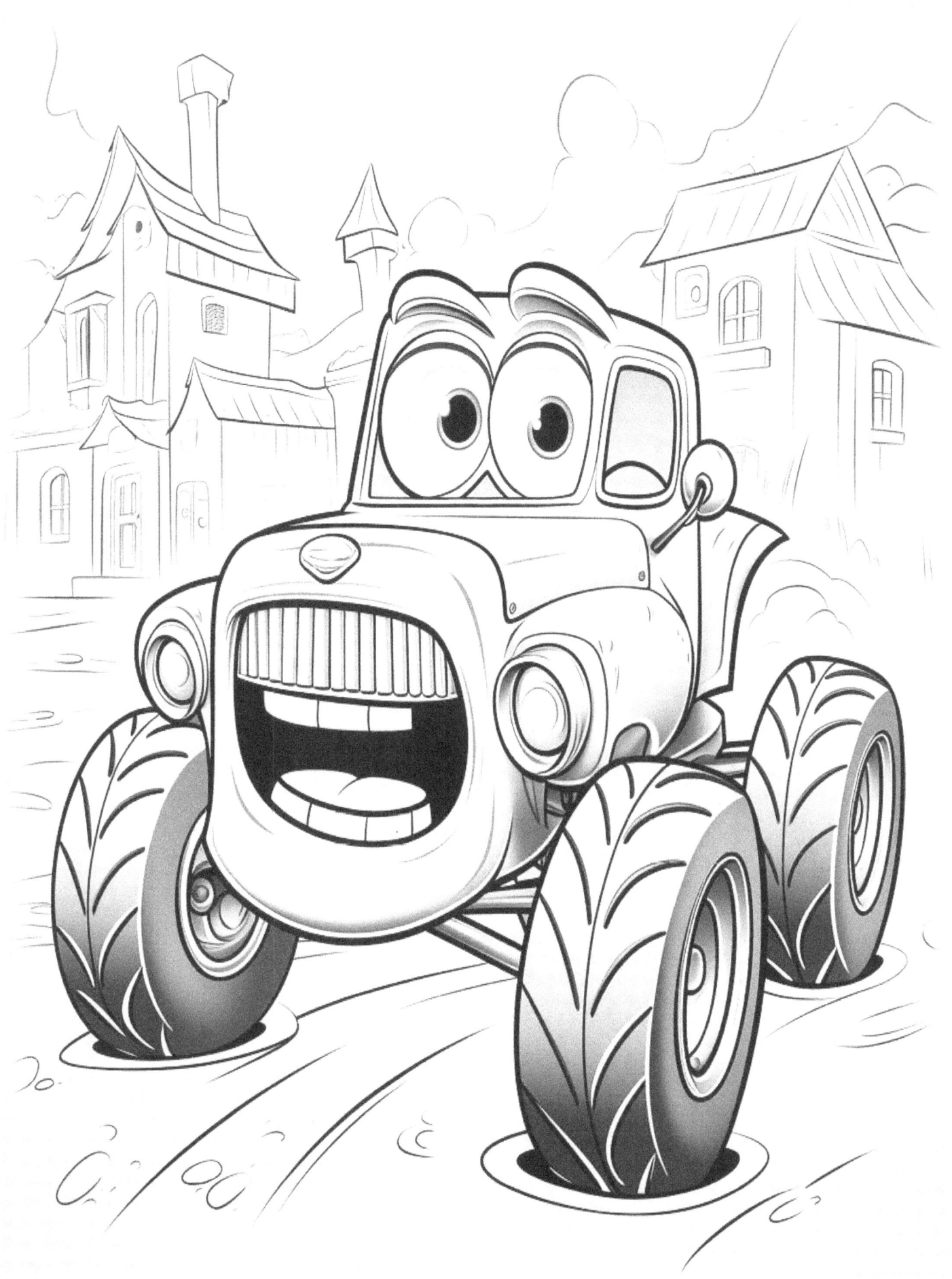

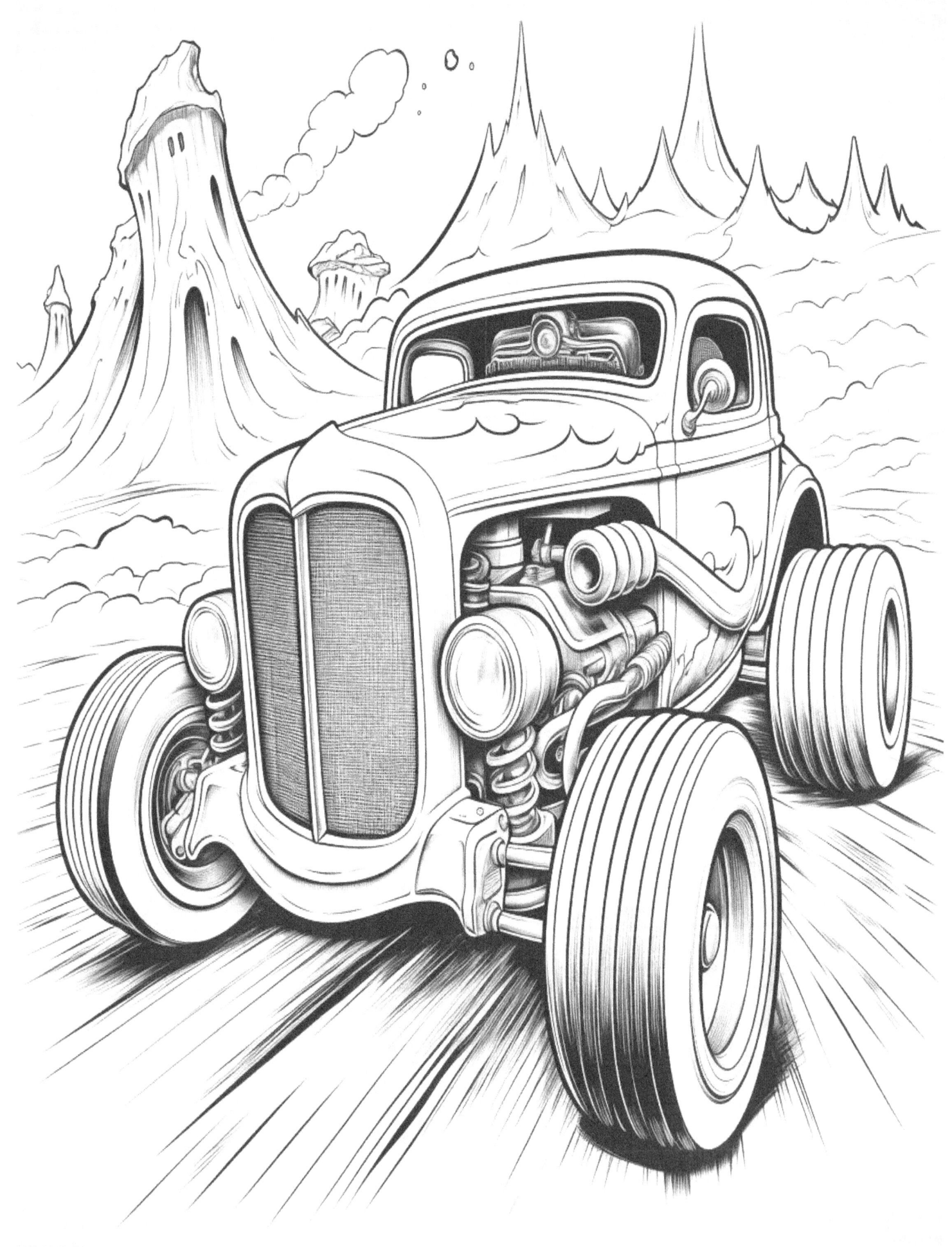

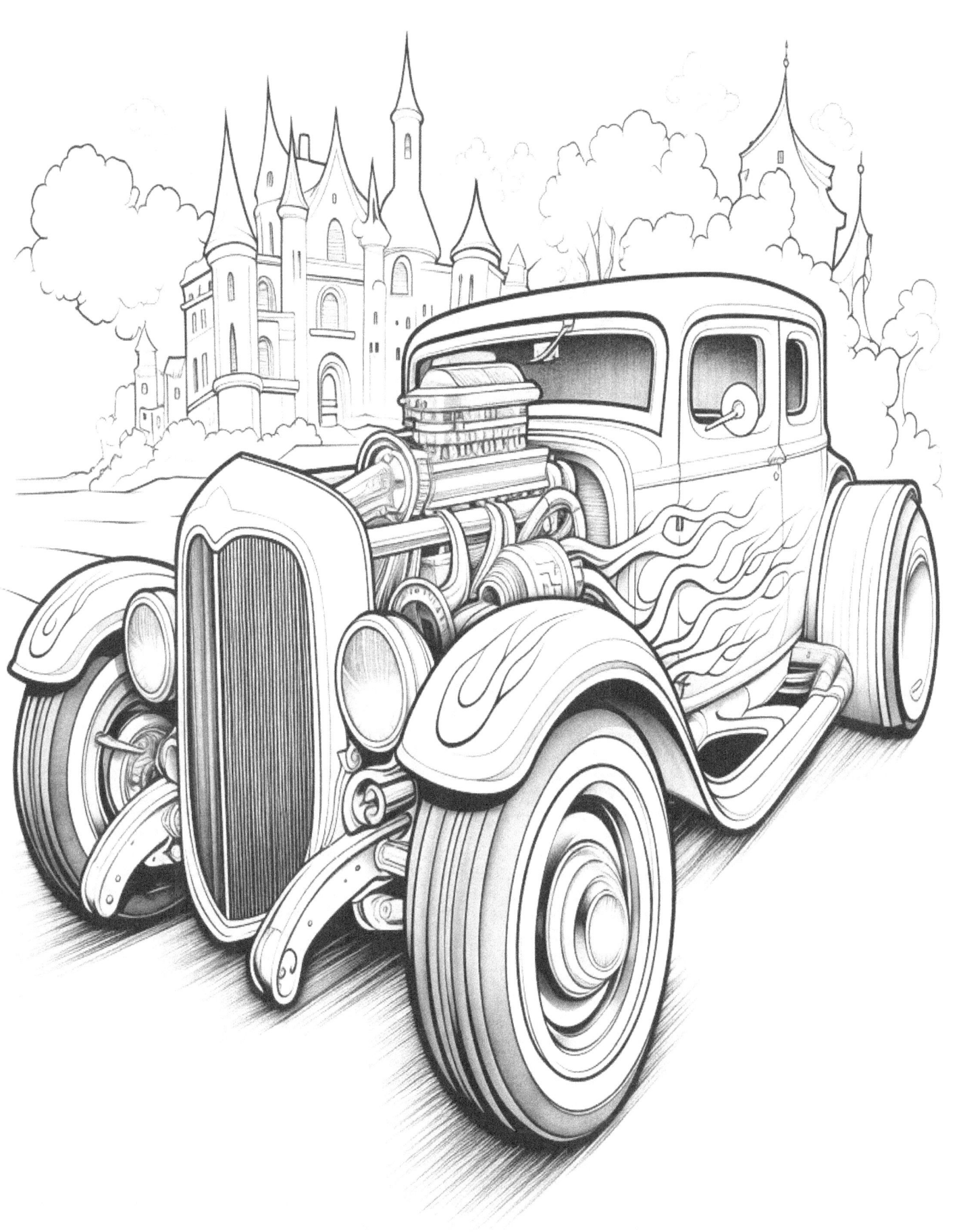

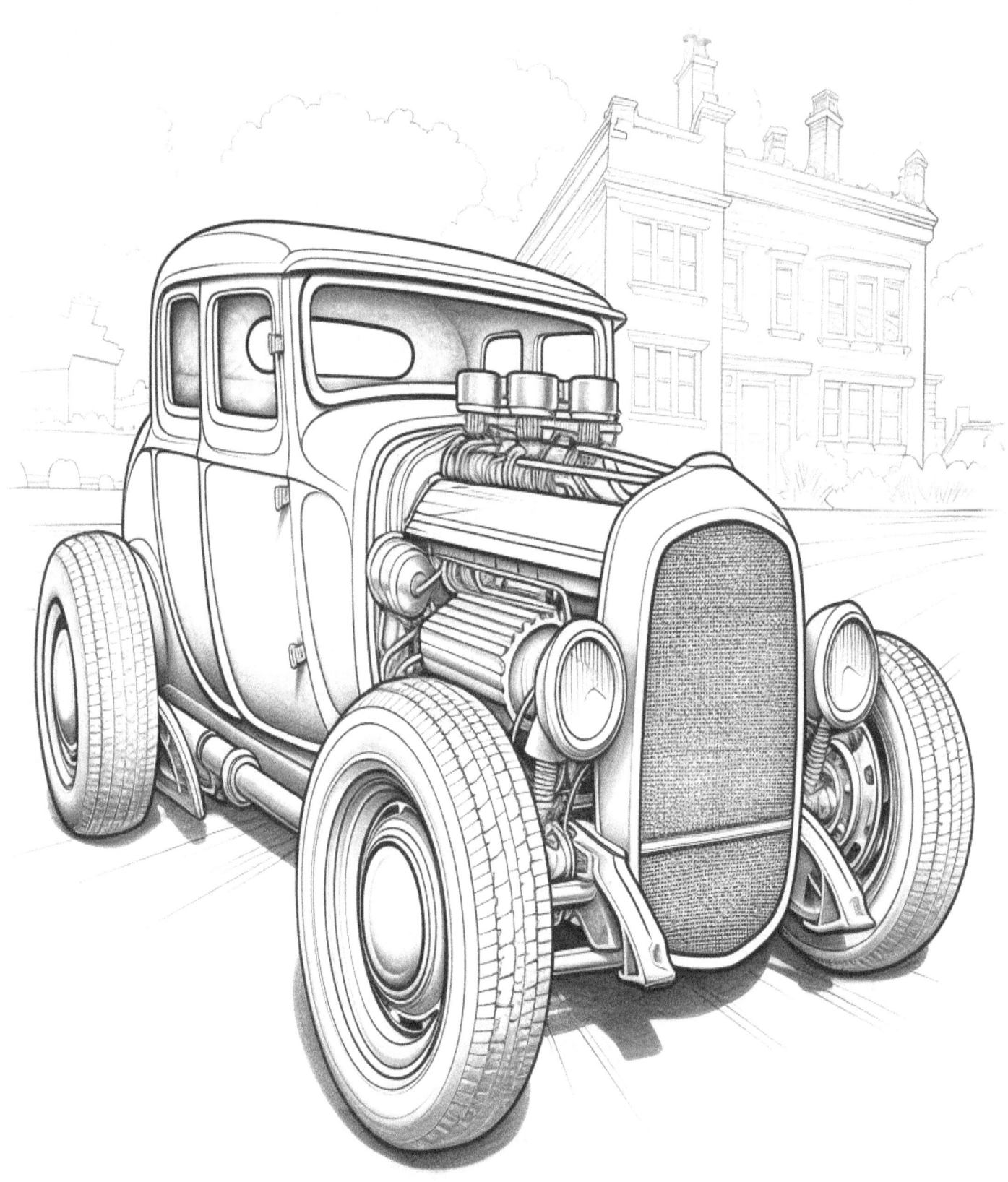

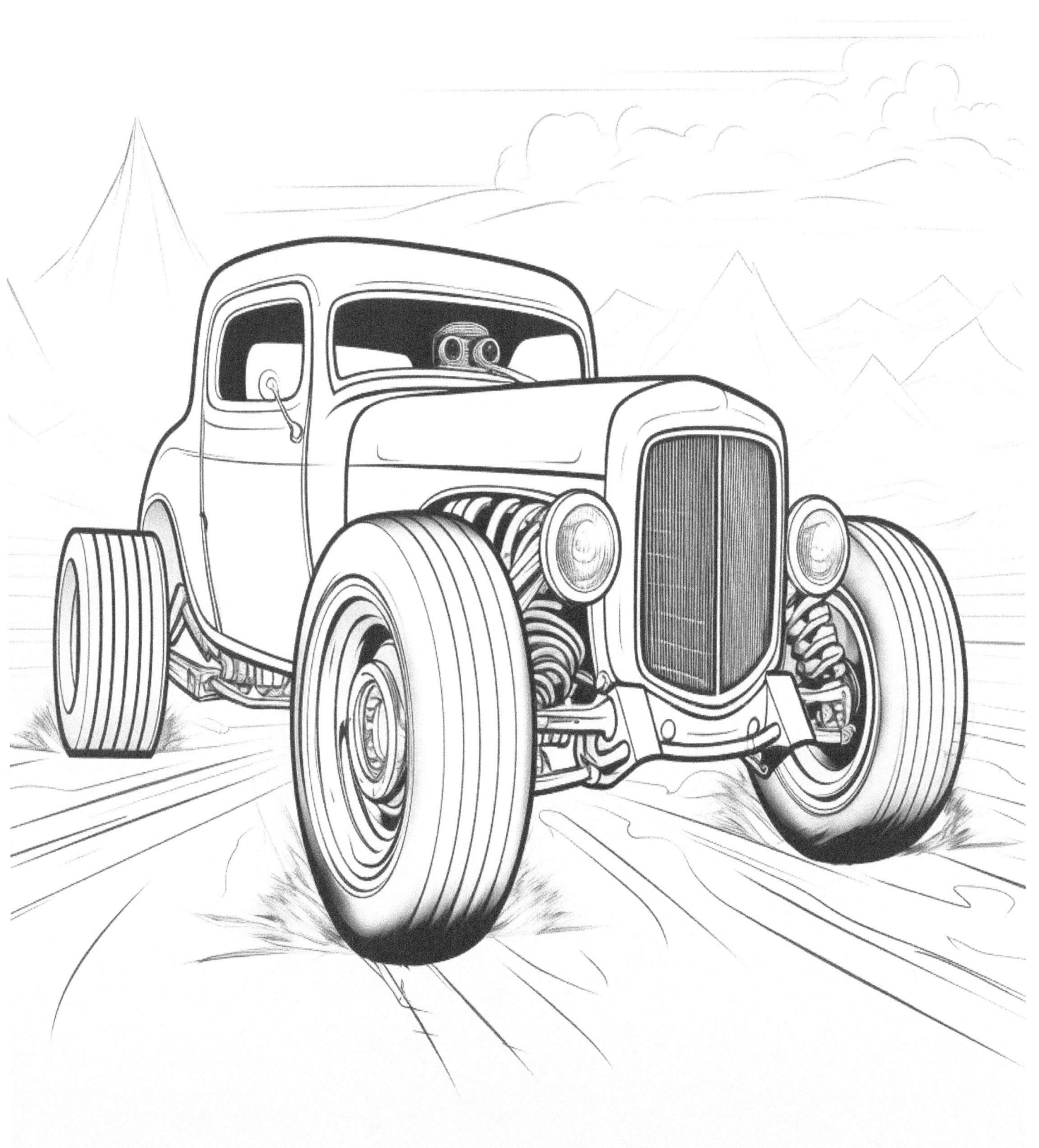

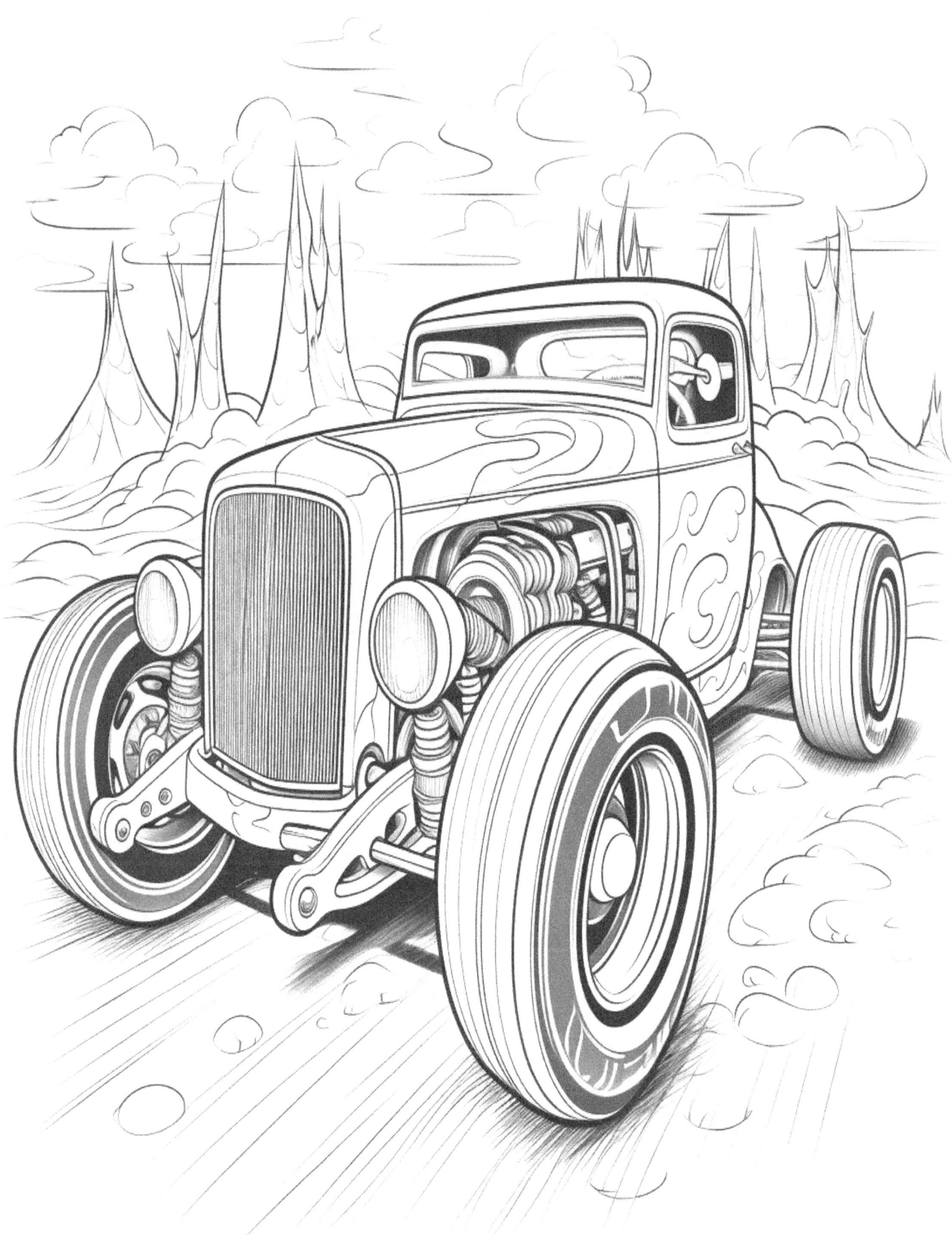

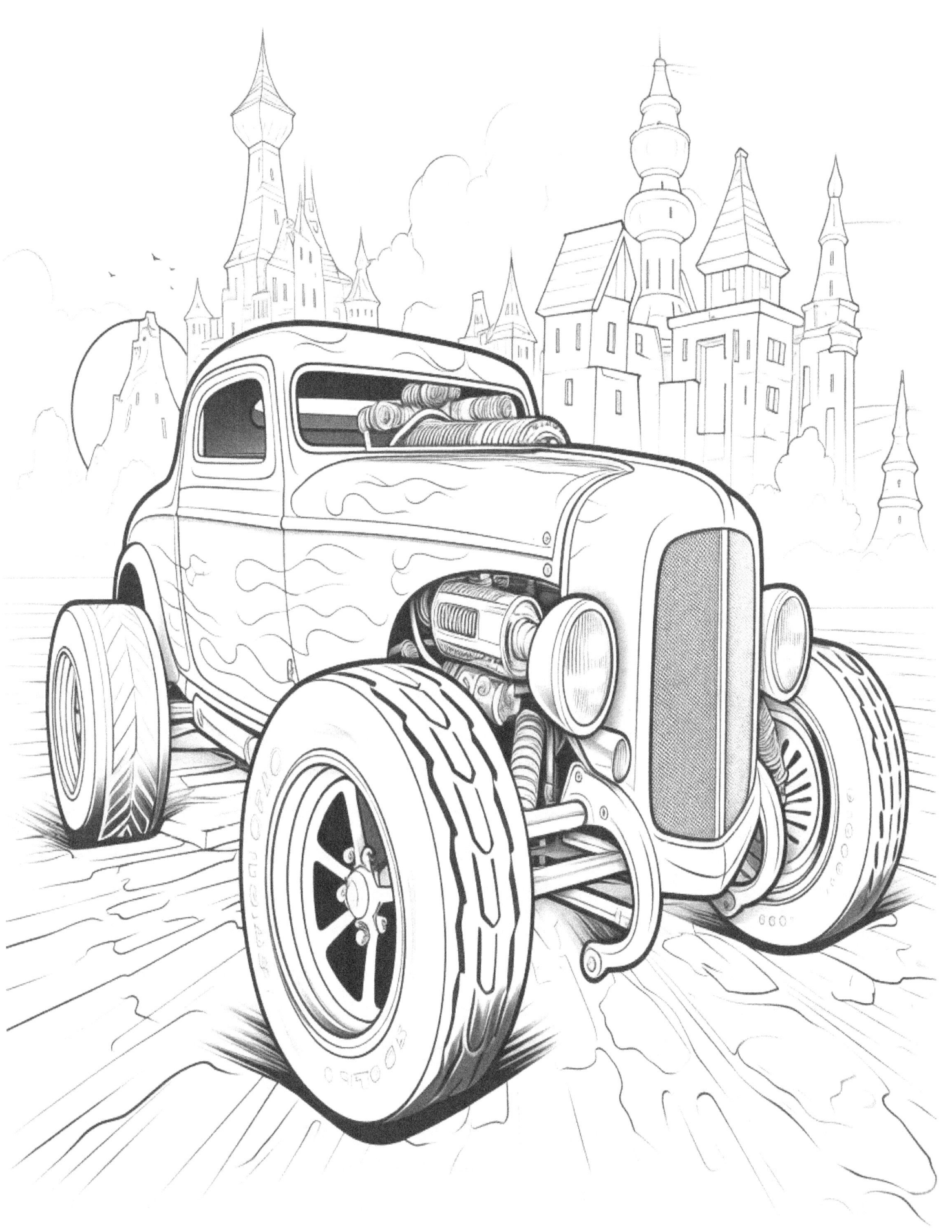

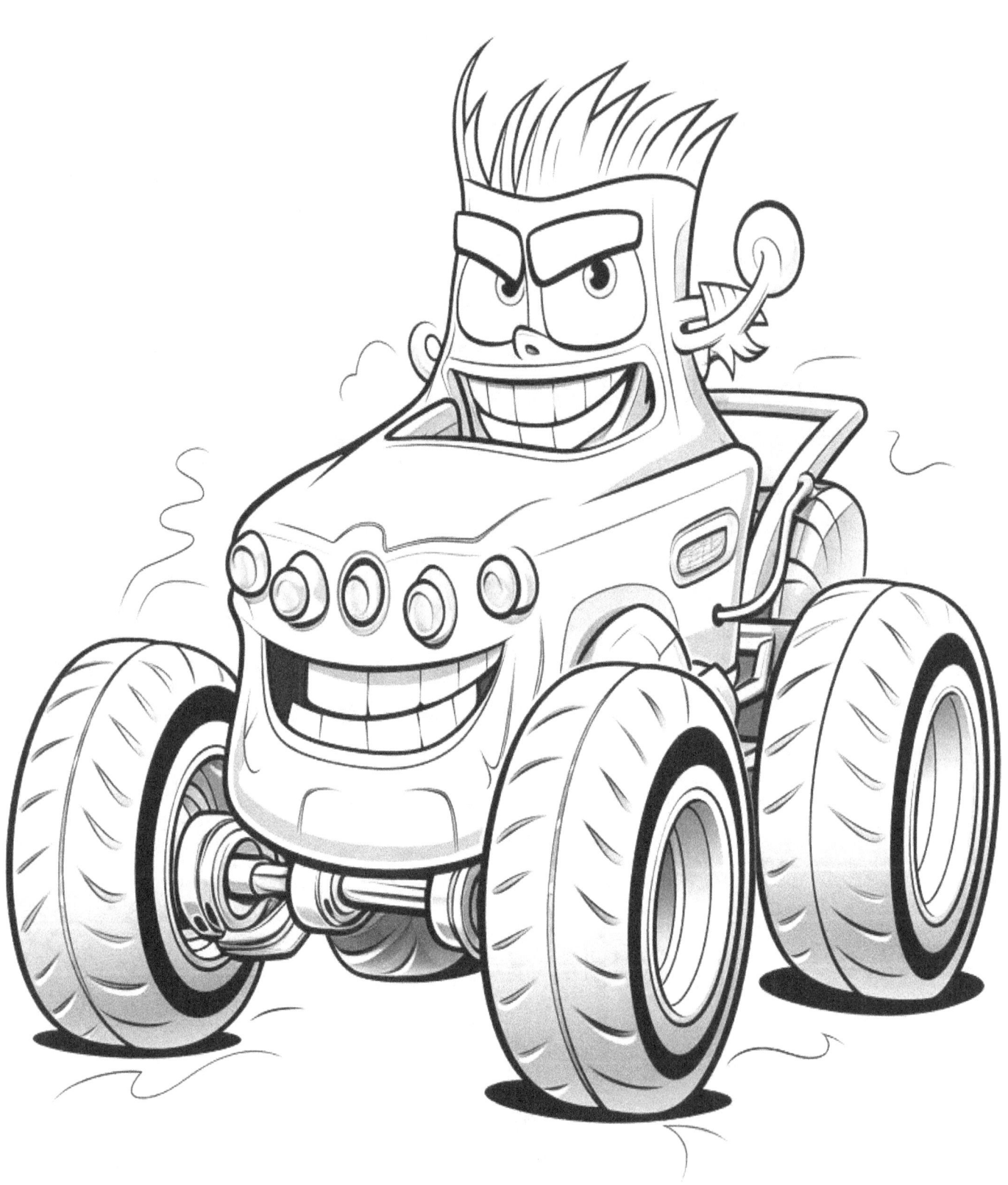

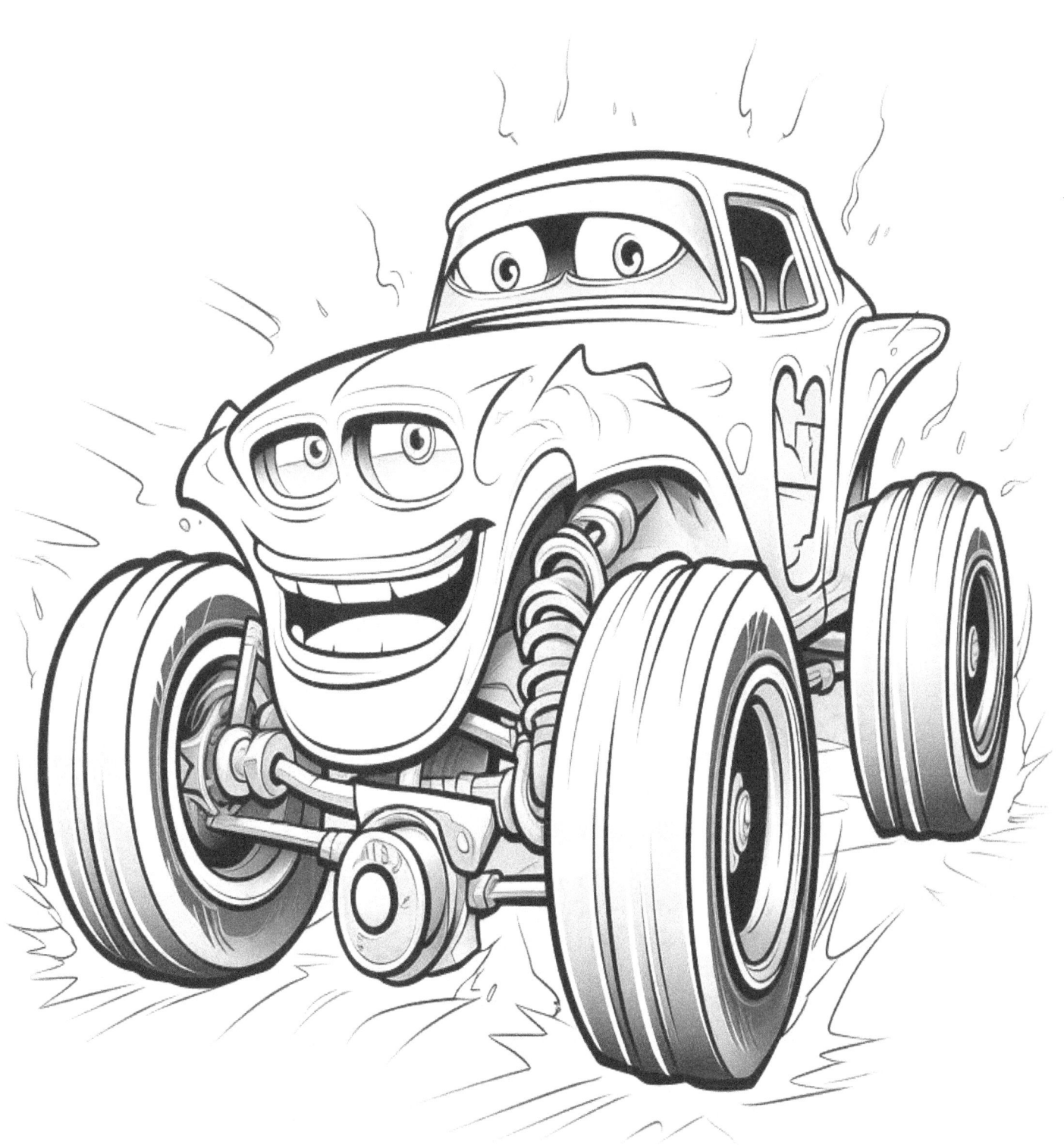

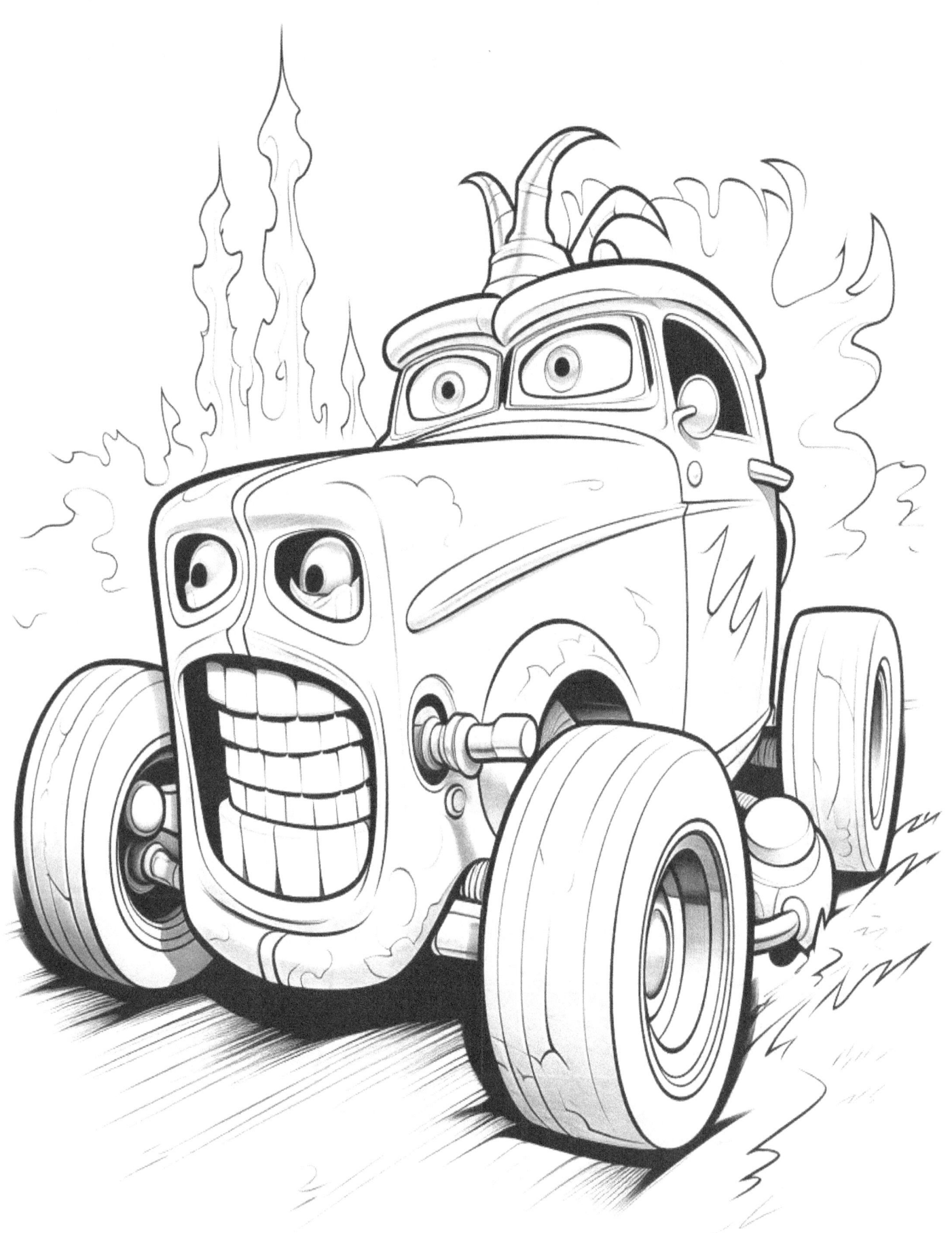

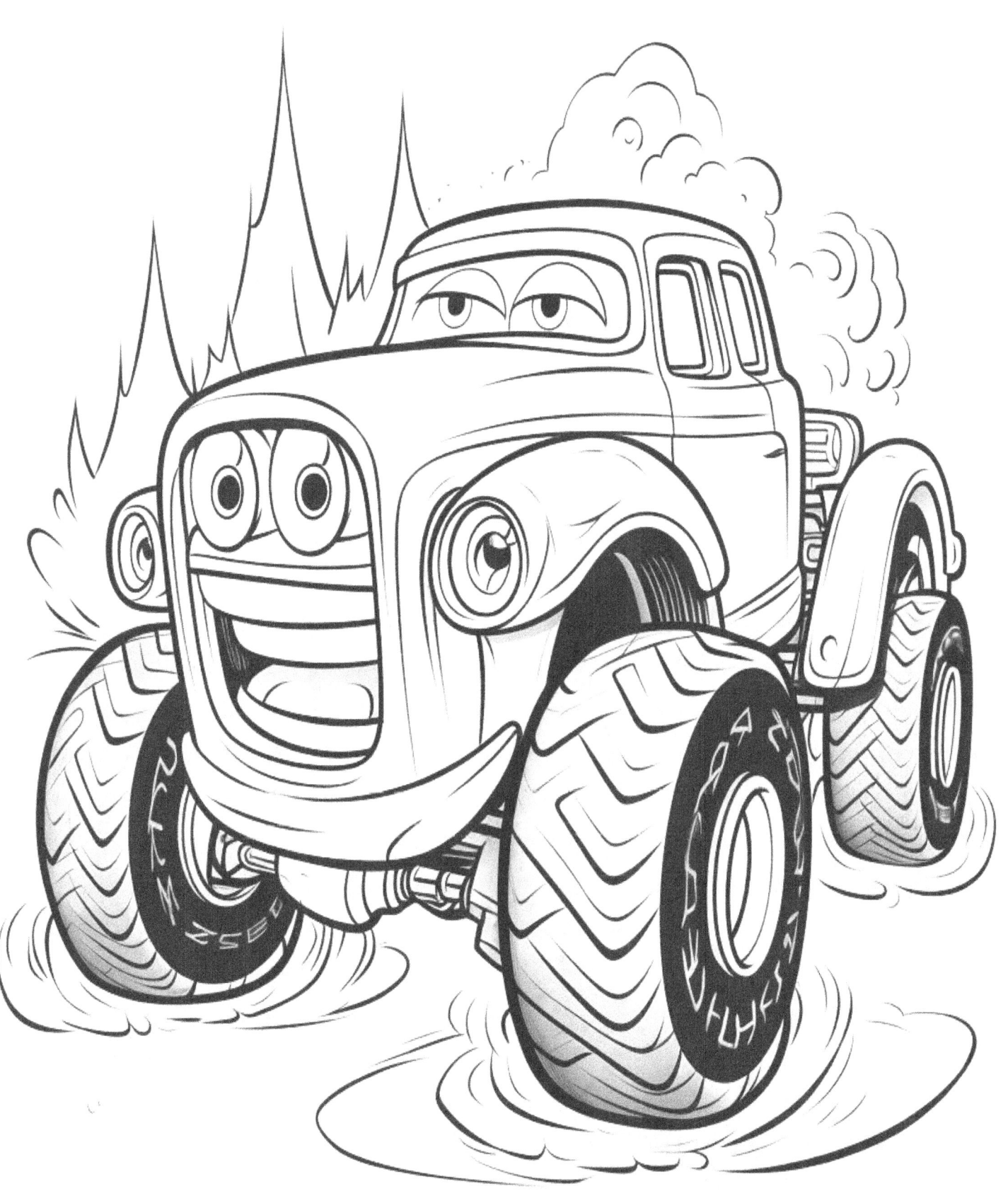

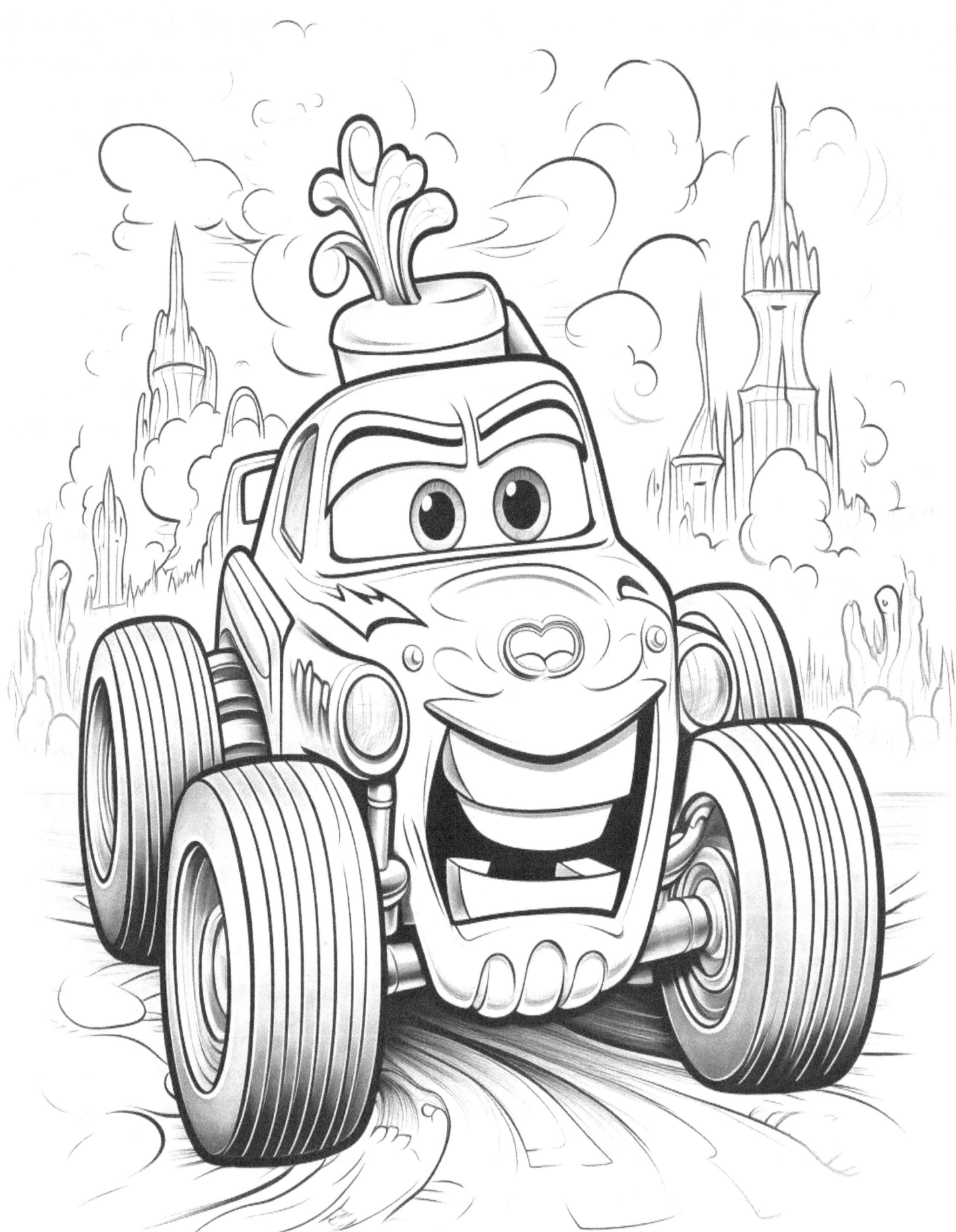

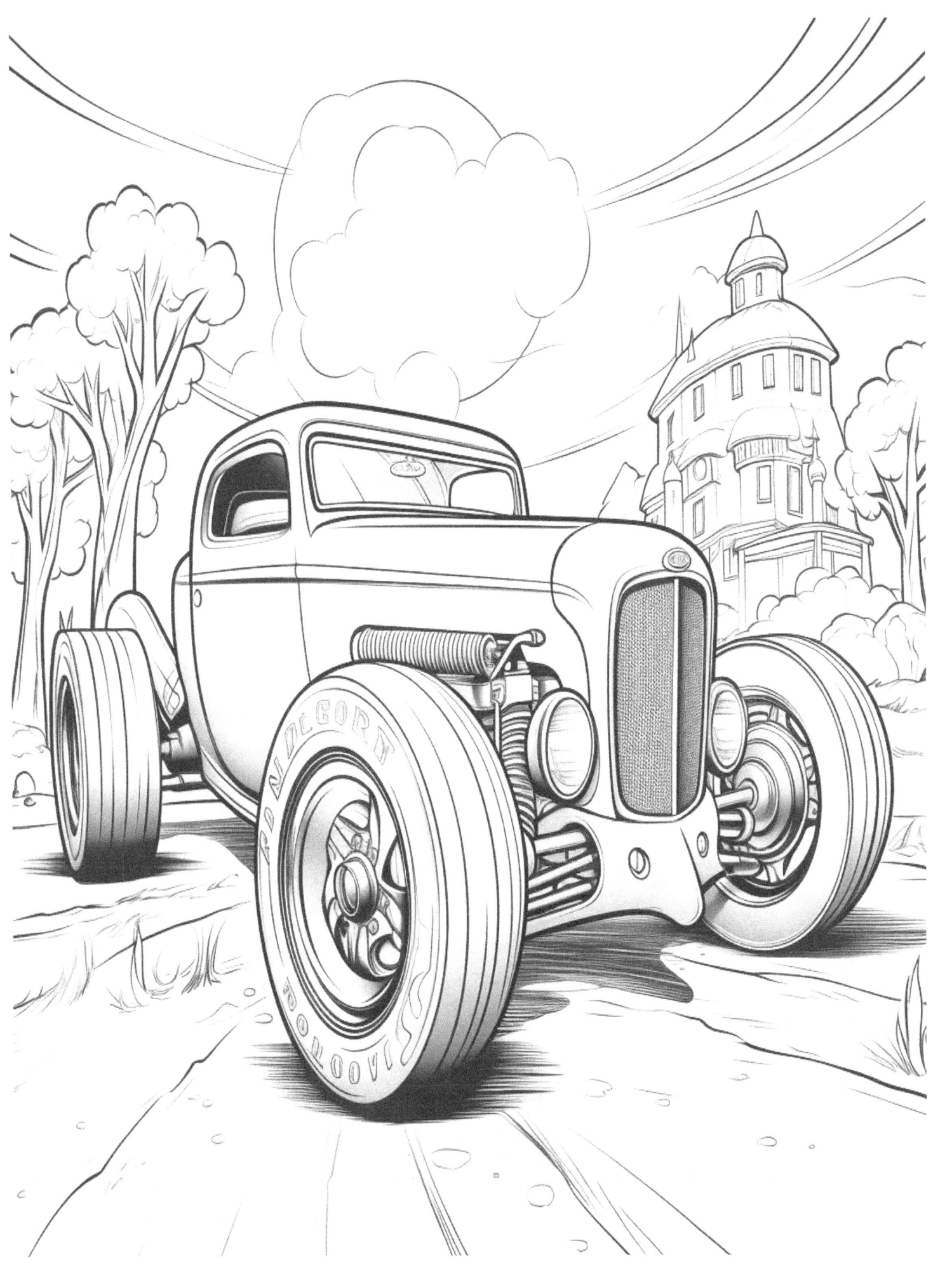

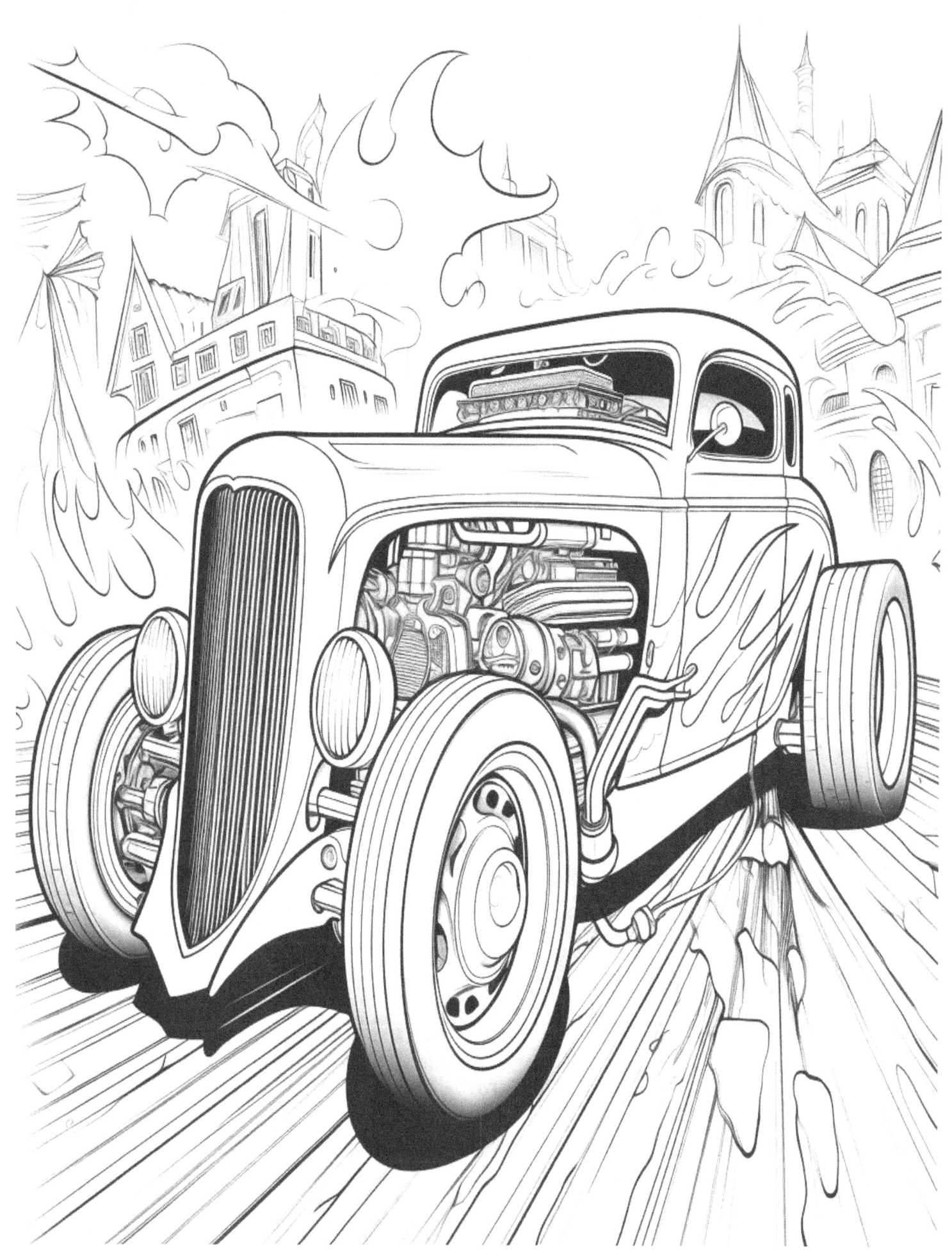

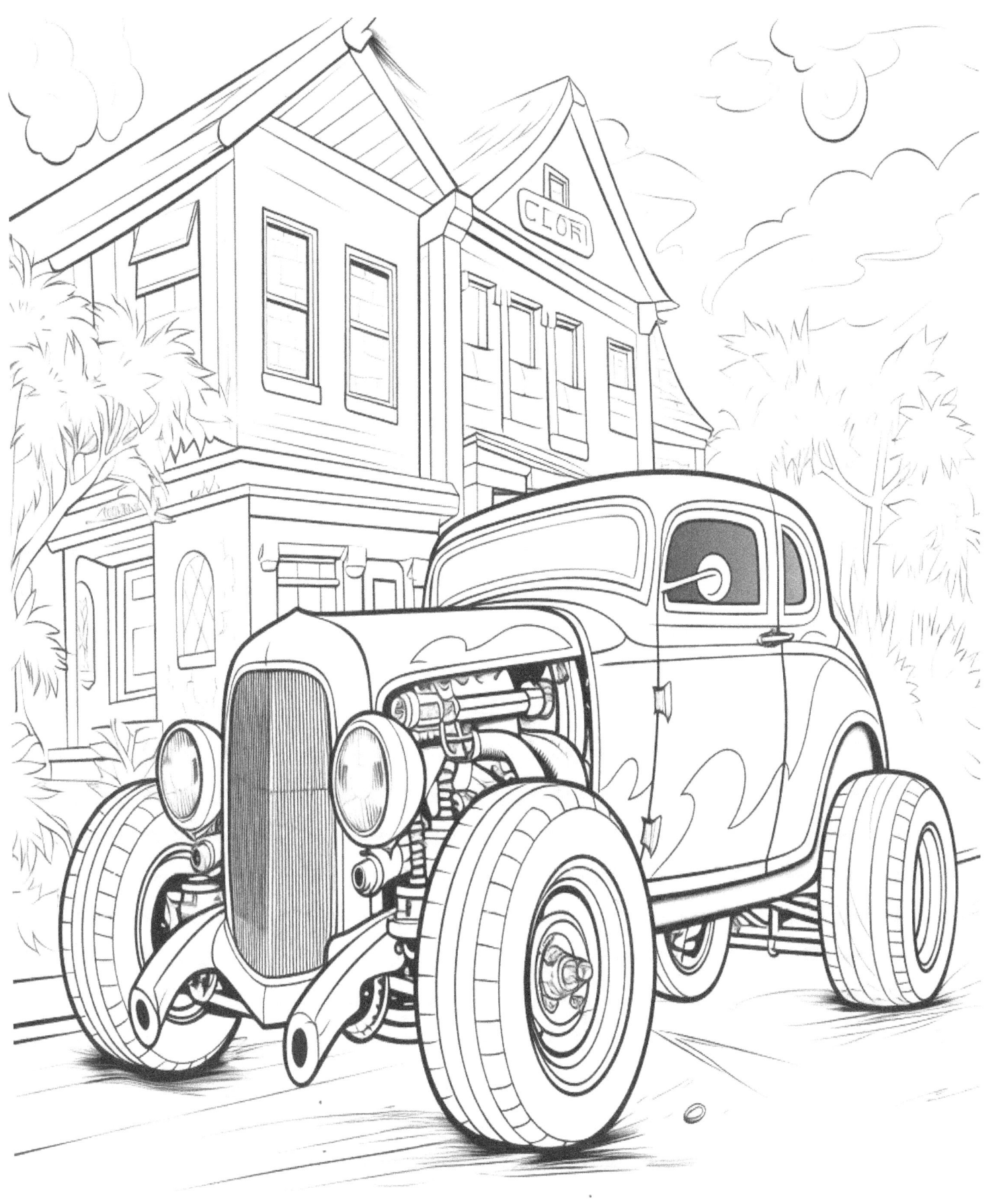

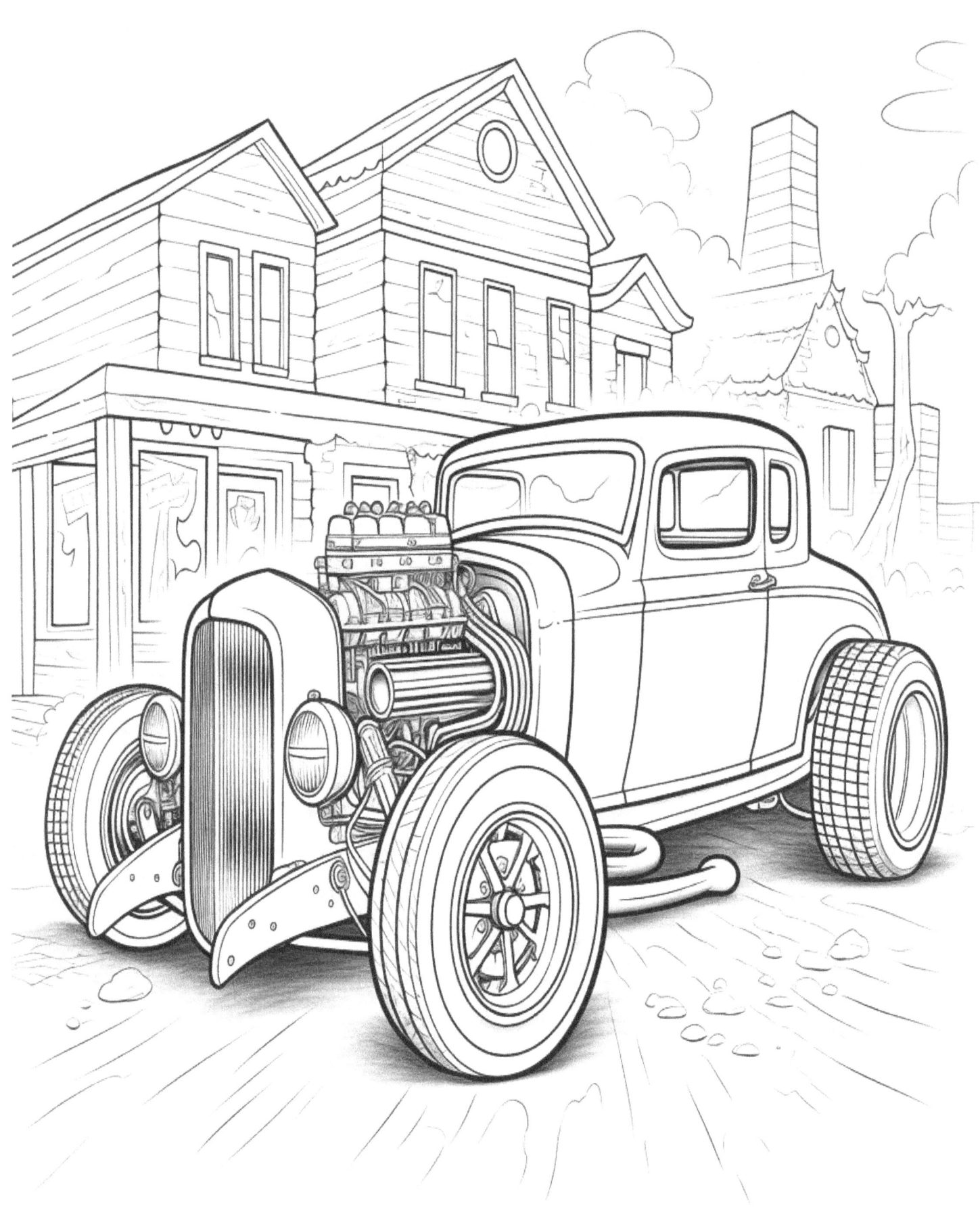

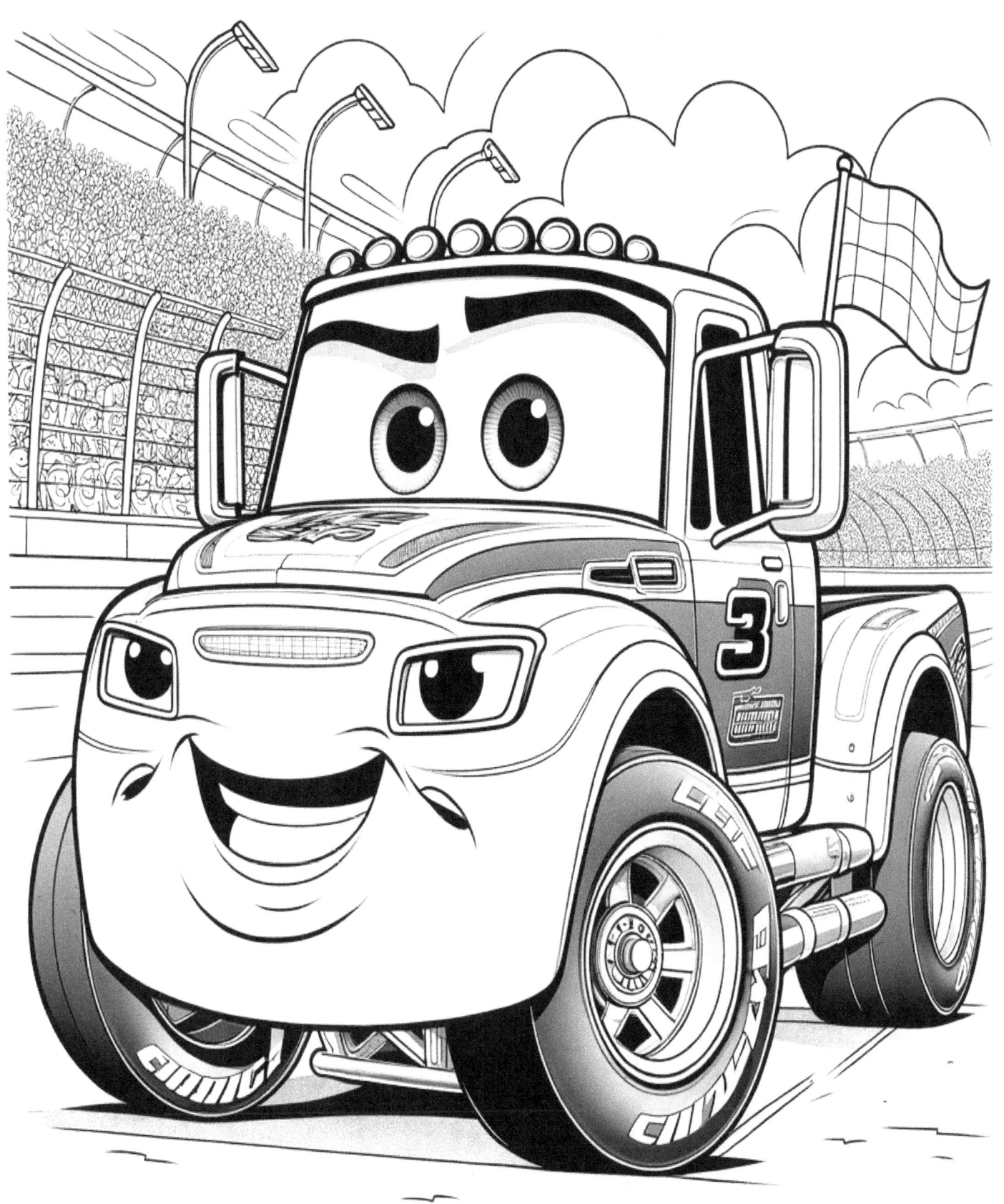

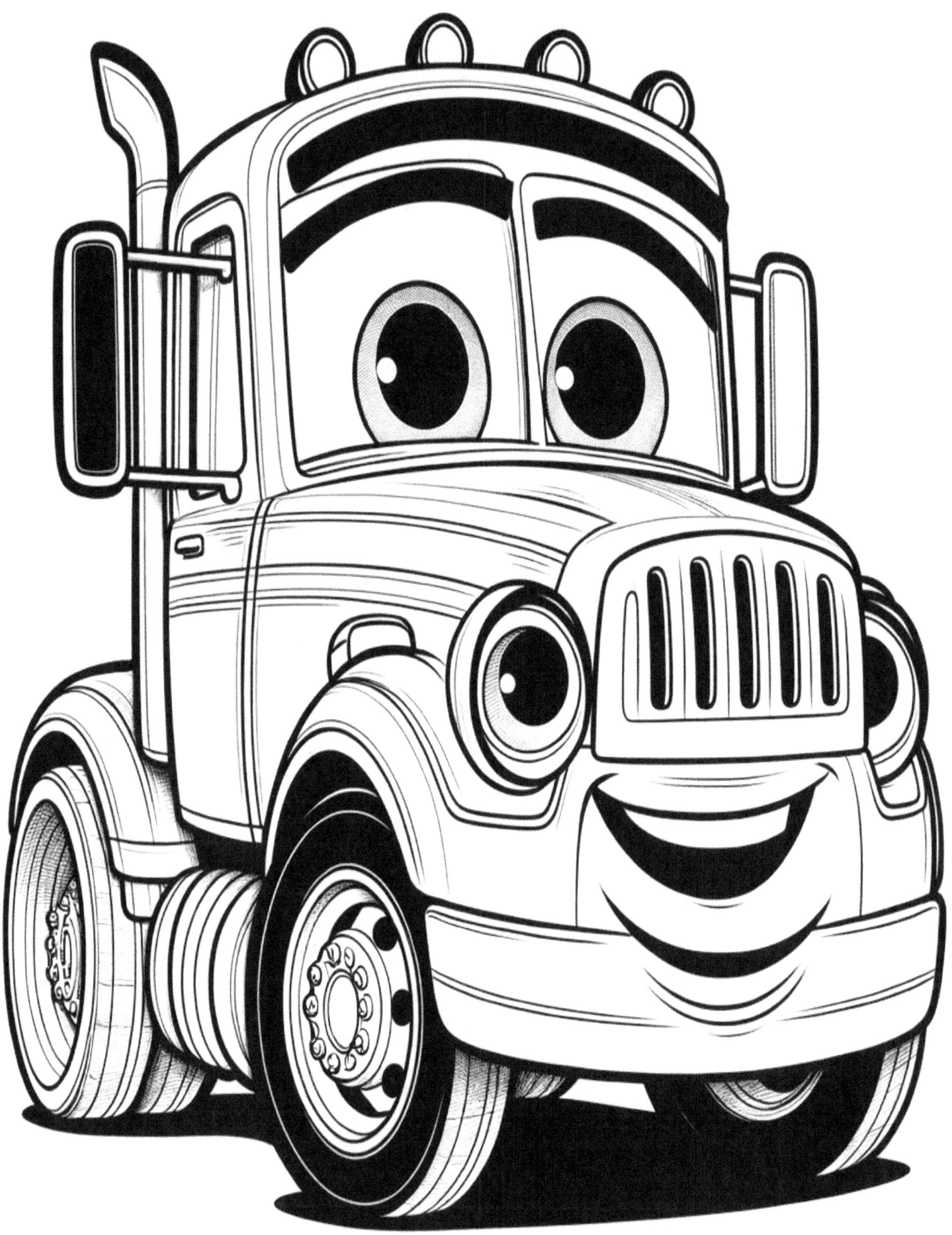

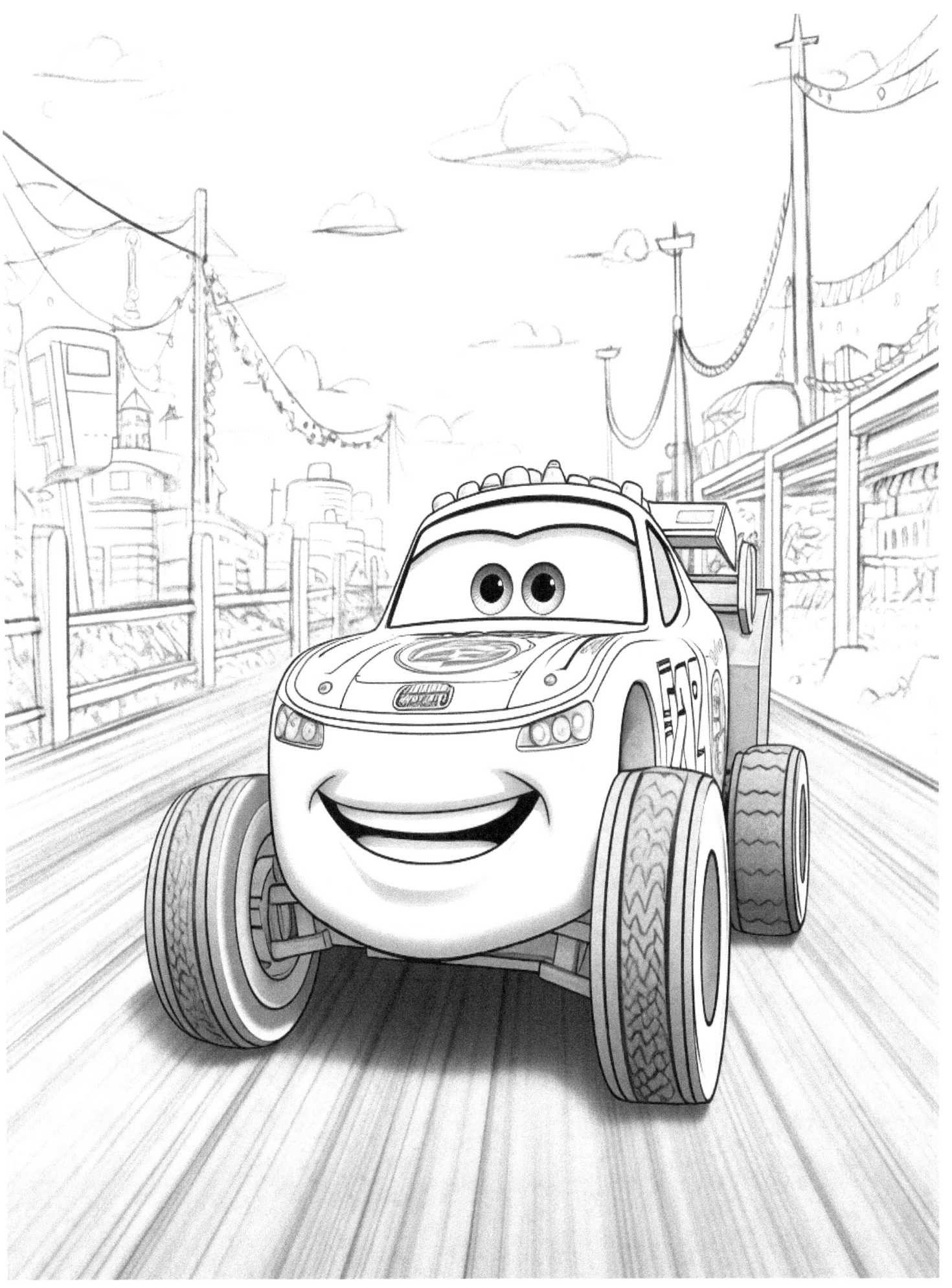

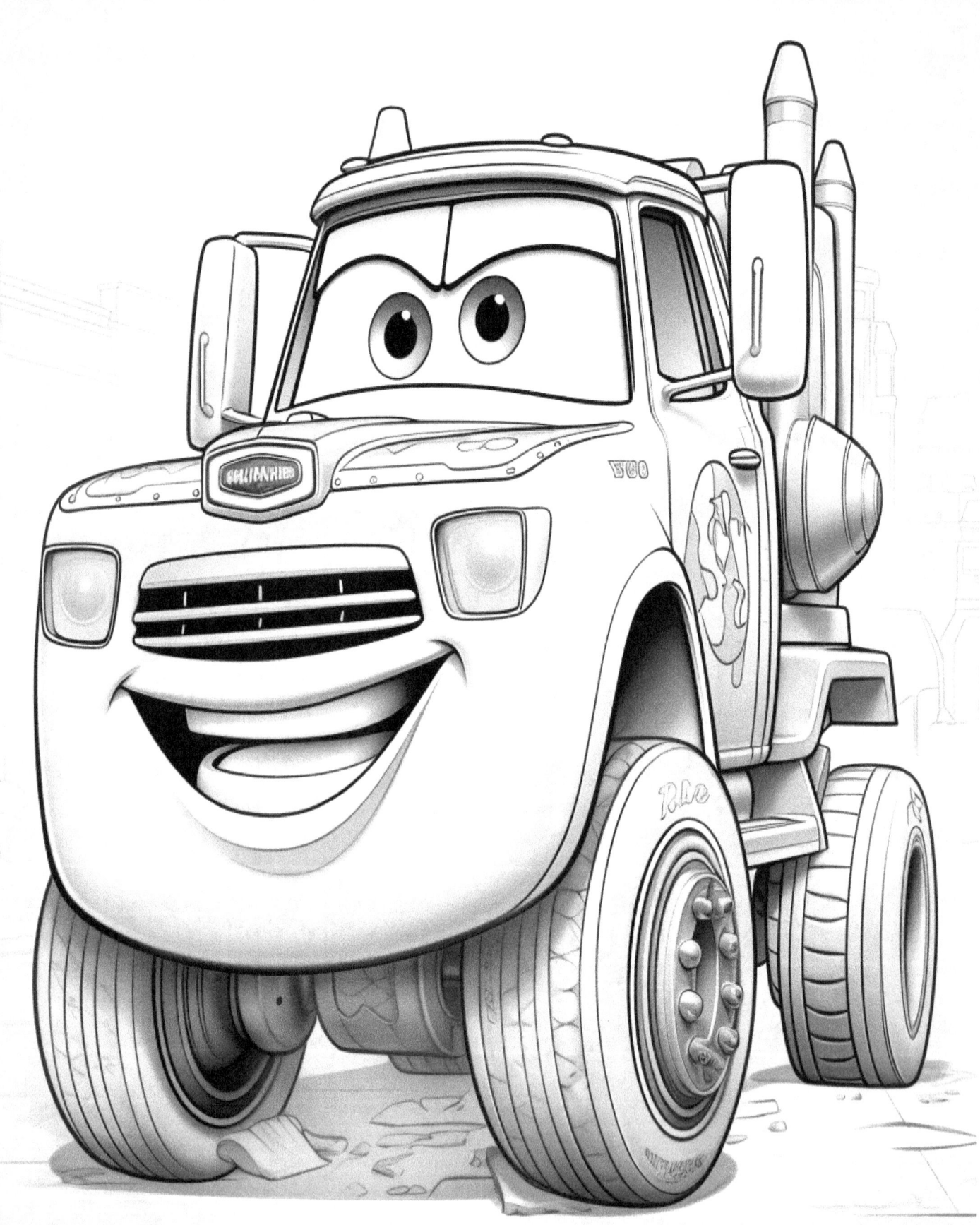

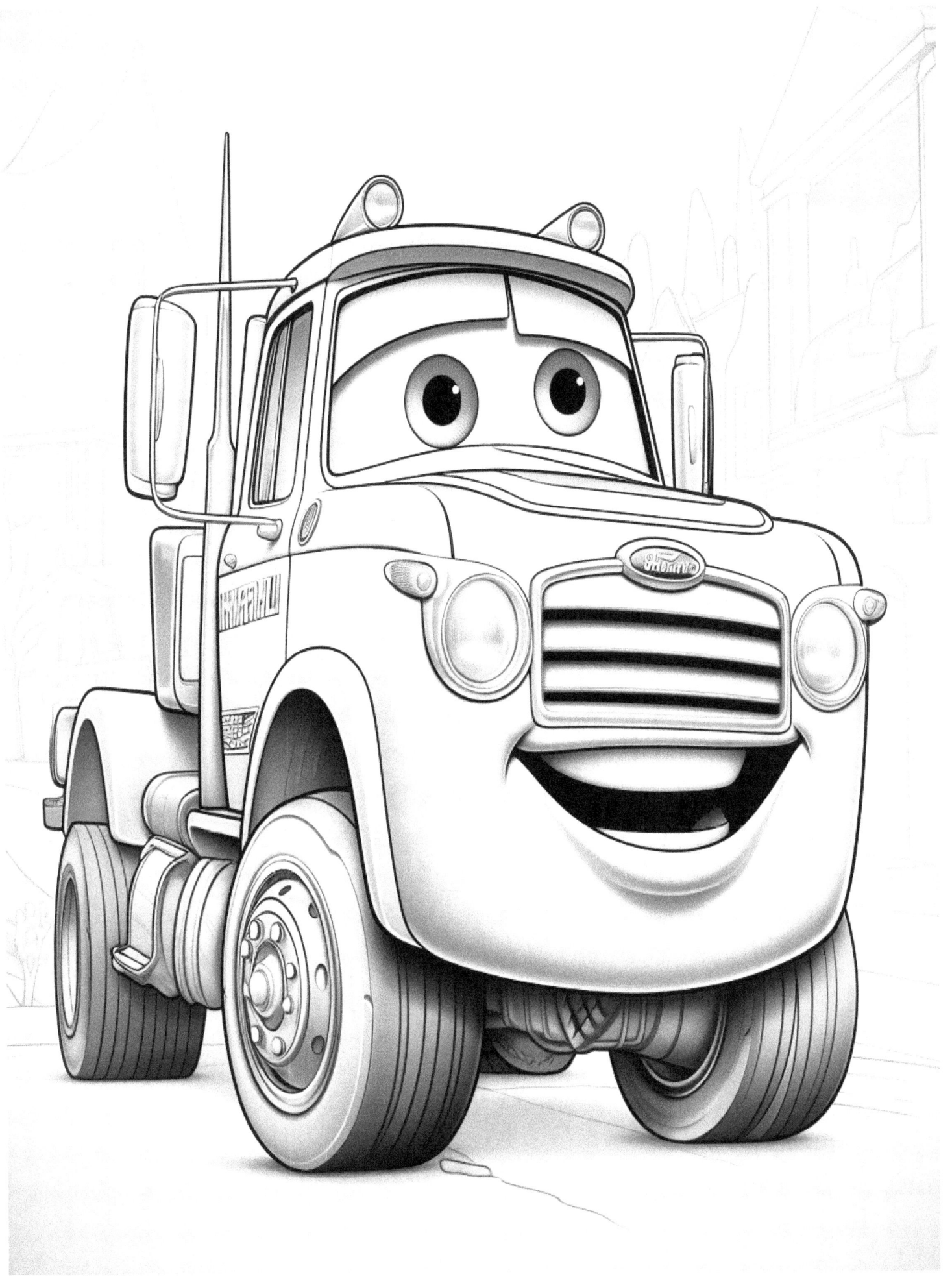

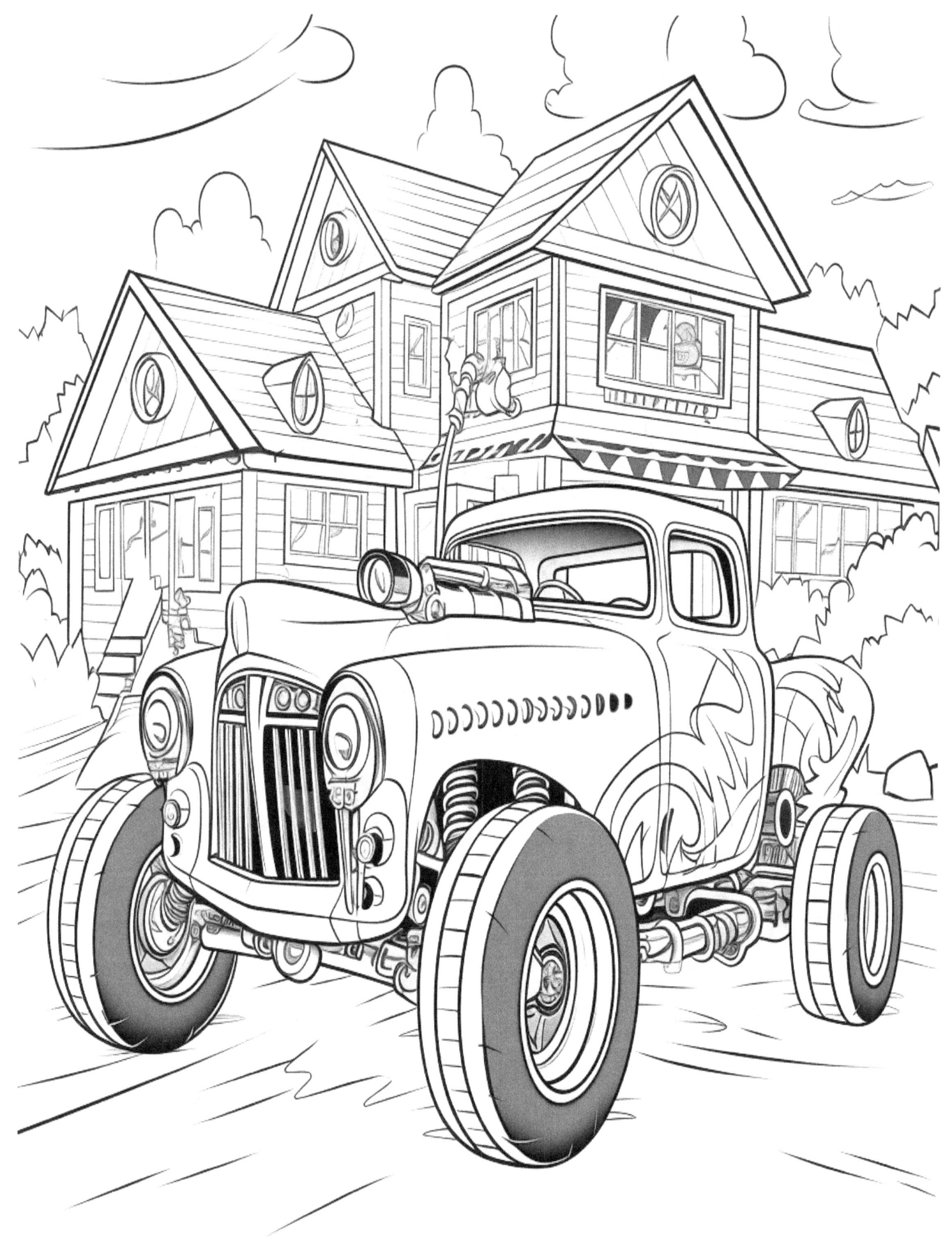

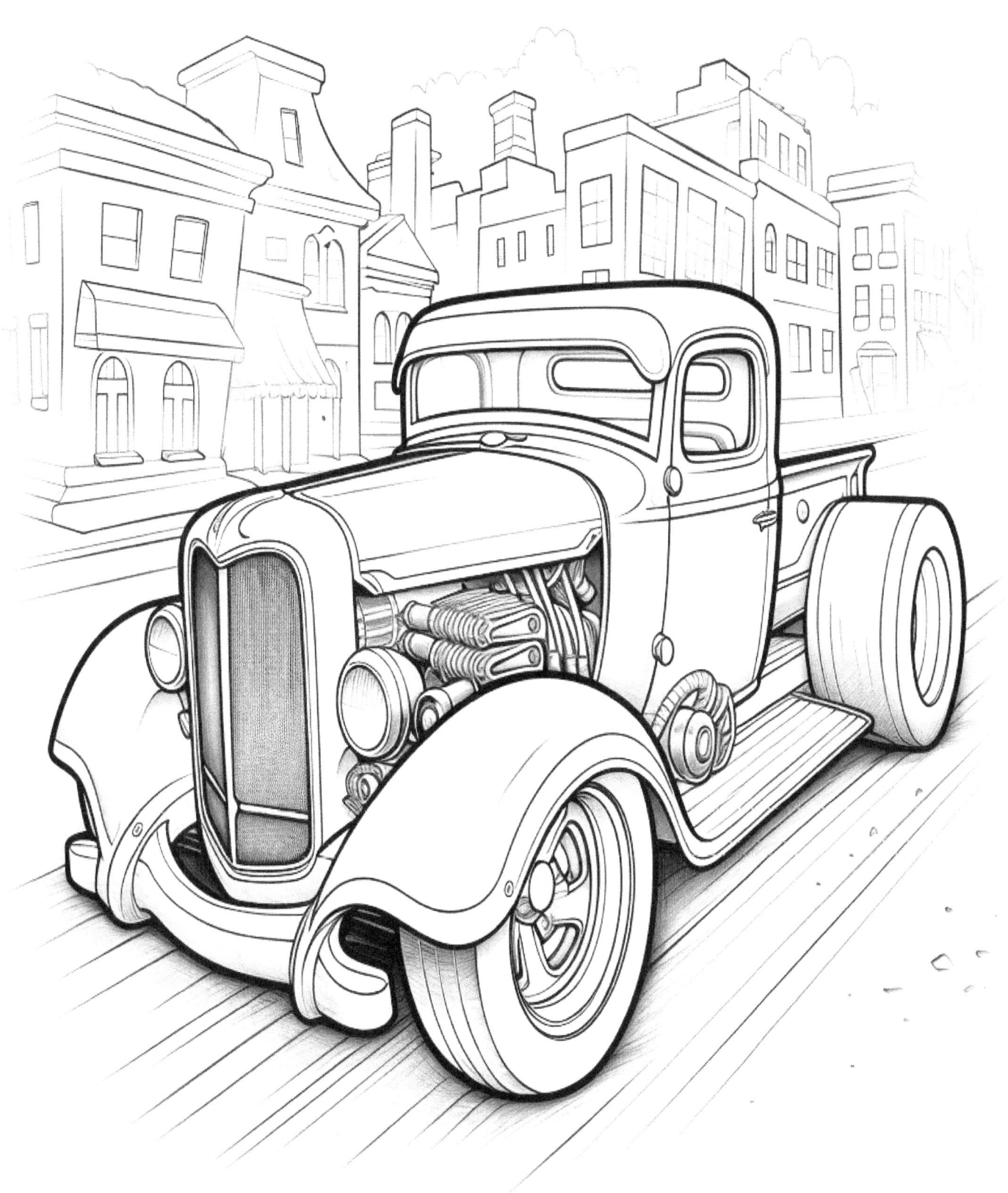

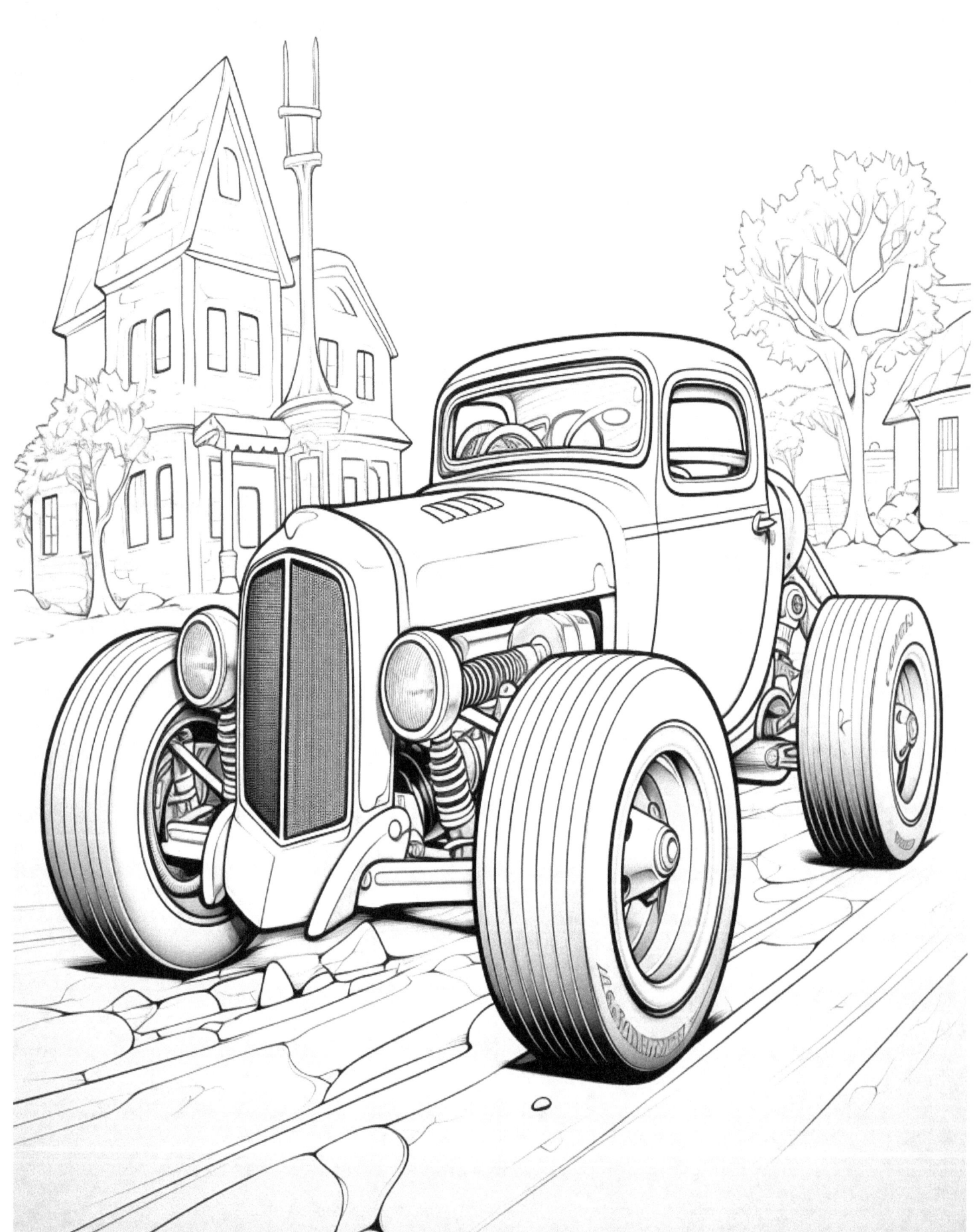

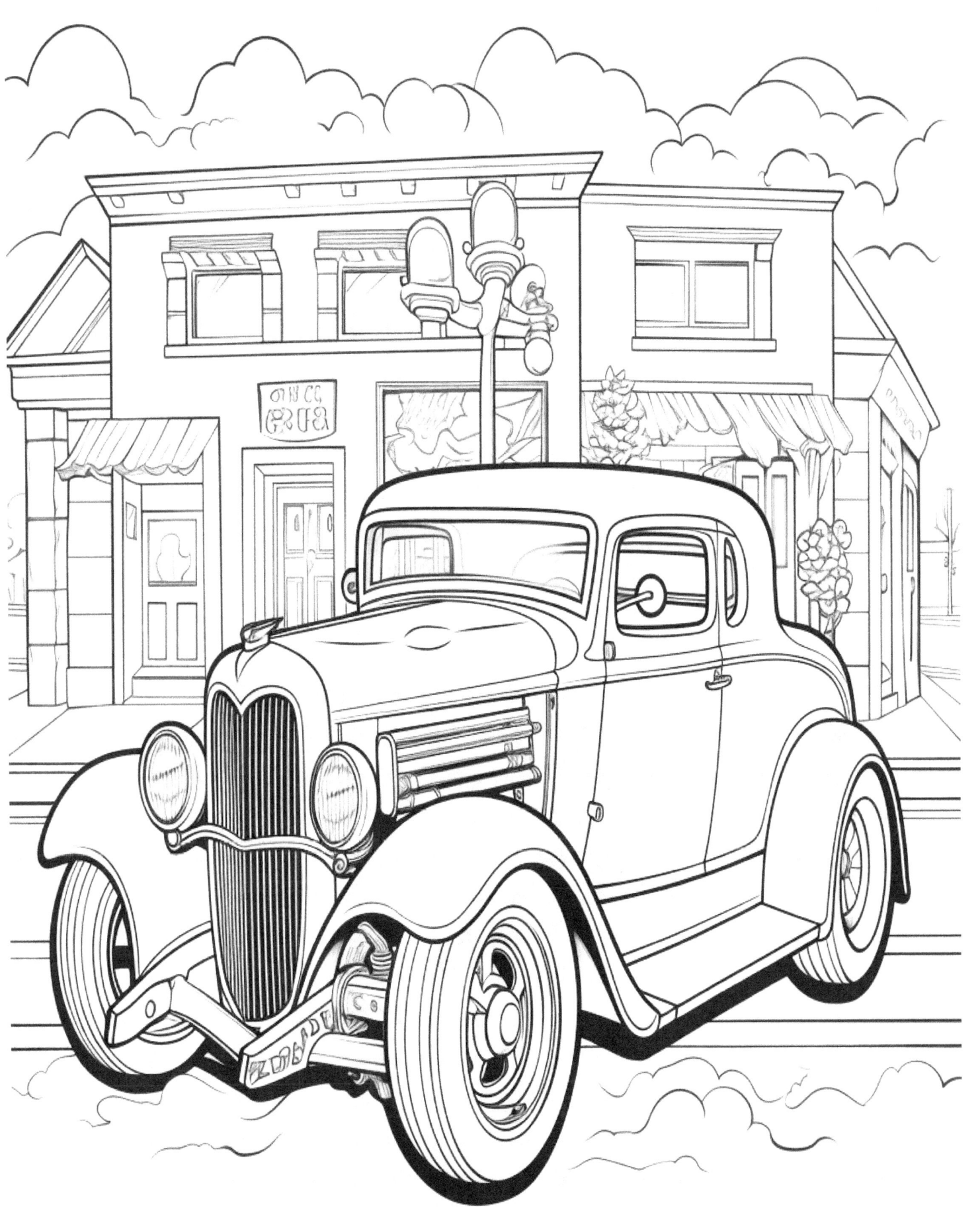

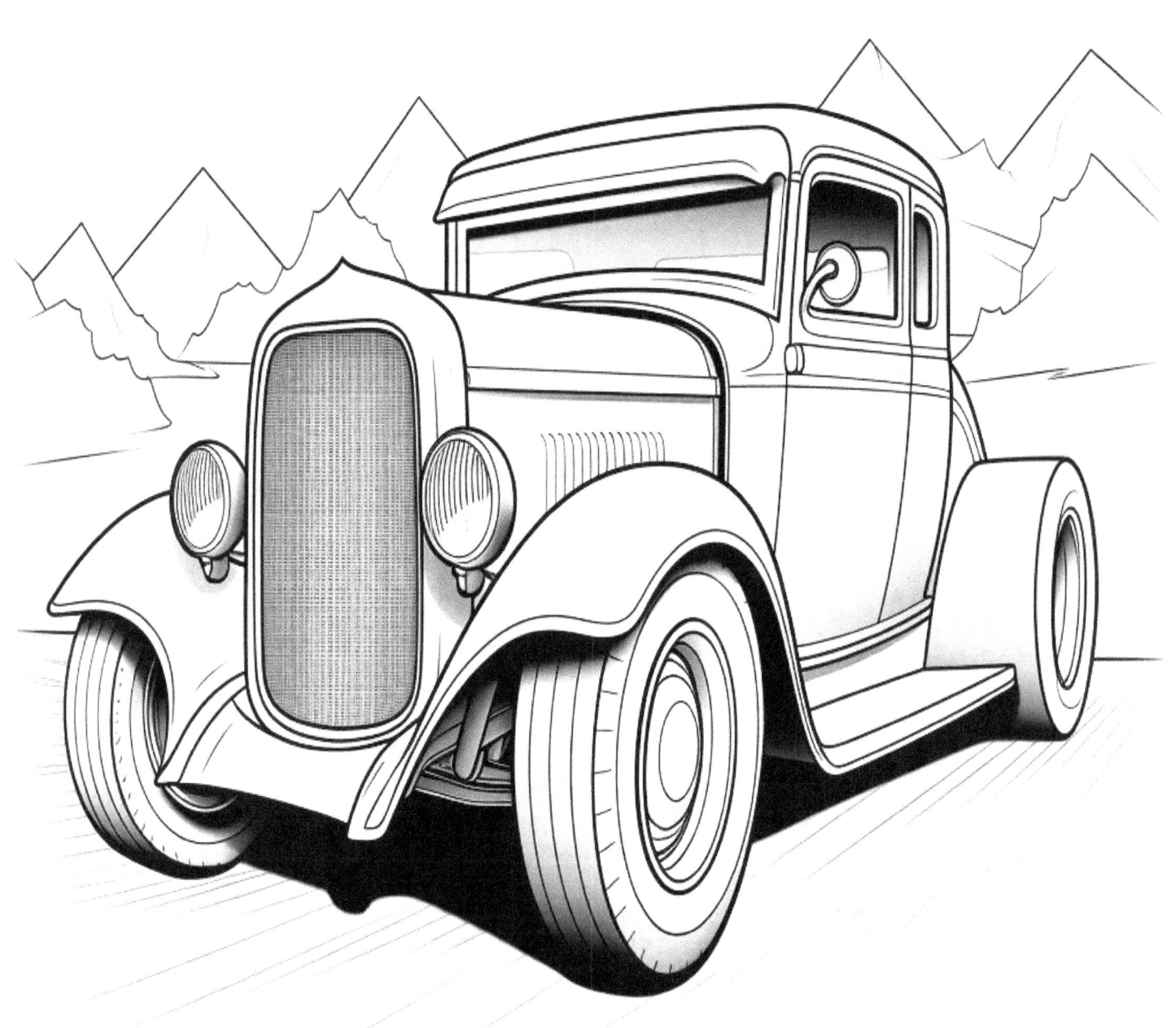

Find Our Books On Amazon

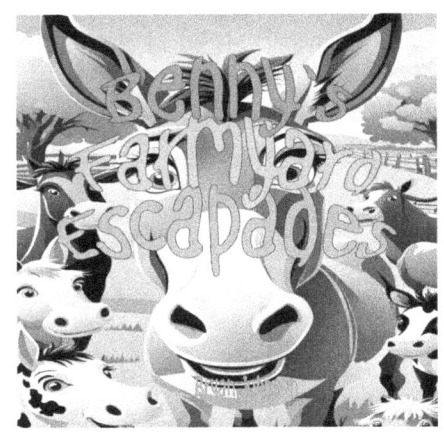

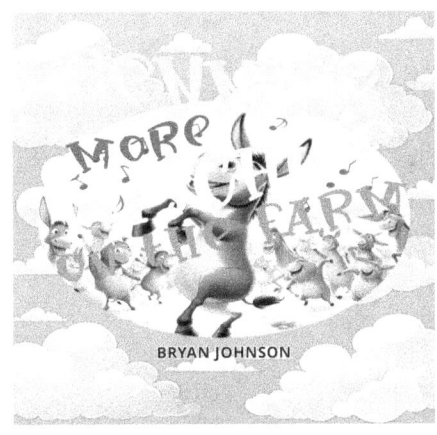

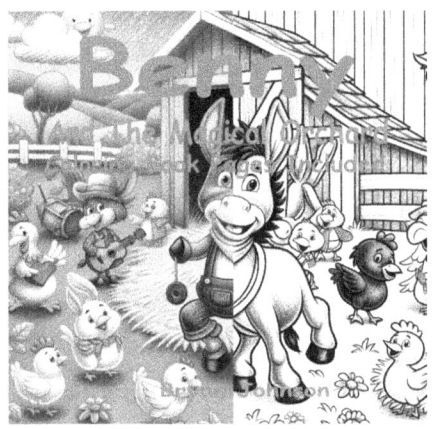

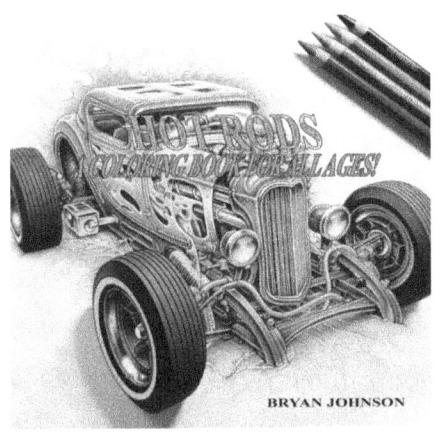

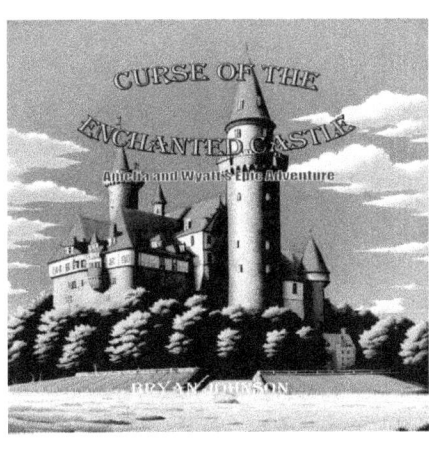